This study is concerned with one, central historical problem: the nature of the changes that transformed the intellectual and spiritual horizons of the Christian world from its establishment in the fourth century to the end of the sixth. Why, for example, were the assumptions, attitudes and traditions of Gregory the Great so markedly different from those of Augustine? *The End of Ancient Christianity* examines how Christians, who had formerly constituted a threatened and beleaguered minority, came to define their identity in a changed context of religious respectability in which their faith had become a source of privilege, prestige and power. Professor Markus reassesses the cult of the martyrs and the creation of schemes of sacred time and sacred space, and analyses the appeal of asceticism and its impact on the Church at large. These changes form part of a fundamental transition, perhaps best described as the shift from 'Ancient' towards 'Medieval' forms of Christianity, from an older and more diverse secular culture towards a religious culture with a firm biblical basis.

THE END OF ANCIENT CHRISTIANITY

THE END OF
ANCIENT
CHRISTIANITY

R. A. Markus

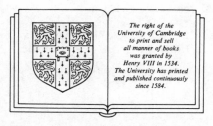

The right of the
University of Cambridge
to print and sell
all manner of books
was granted by
Henry VIII in 1534.
The University has printed
and published continuously
since 1584.

CAMBRIDGE UNIVERSITY PRESS
Cambridge
New York   Port Chester
Melbourne   Sydney

Published by the Press Syndicate of the University of Cambridge
The Pitt Building, Trumpington Street, Cambridge CB2 1RP
40 West 20th Street, New York, NY 10011, USA
10 Stamford Road, Oakleigh, Melbourne 3166, Australia

© Cambridge University Press 1990

First published 1990

Printed in Great Britain by J. W. Arrowsmith Ltd
Winterstoke Road, Bristol BS3 2NT, England

British Library cataloguing in publication data

Markus, R. A.
The end of ancient Christianity.
1. Christianity, history.
I. Title
209

Library of Congress cataloguing in publication data

Markus, R. A. (Robert Austin), 1924–
The end of ancient Christianity / R. A. Markus.
p.   cm.
Includes bibliographical references.
ISBN 0-521-32716-4
1. Church history – Primitive and early church, ca. 30–600.
2. Spiritual – History of doctrines – Early church, ca. 30–600.
3. Theology – Early church, ca. 30–600.   I. Title.
BR219.M37   1990
270.2 – dc20   89-77196 CIP

ISBN 0 521 32716 4 hardback
ISBN 0 521 33949 9 paperback

AS

To Peter Brown

ὡς διδασκαλῷ

Contents

	Preface	*page*	xi
	Abbreviations		xvi
1	Introduction: 'secularity'		1
I	**The crisis of identity**		19
2	'A great multitude no man could number'		21
	Additional note on the holy man and his charisma		25
3	Conversion and uncertainty		27
4	Augustine: a defence of Christian mediocrity		45
5	'Be ye perfect'		63
II	*Kairoi*: **Christian times and the past**		85
6	The last times		87
7	The martyrs and sacred time		97
8	Secular festivals in Christian times?		107
	Additional note on the chronology of Augustine's statements on spectacles		121
9	The christianisation of time		125
III	*Topoi*: **space and community**		137
10	Holy places and holy people		139
11	City or Desert? Two models of community		157
	Additional note on the date of Cassian's thirteenth *Conference*		177
12	Desert and City: a blurring of frontiers		181
13	The ascetic invasion		199
14	Within sight of the end: retrospect and prospect		213
	Sources referred to		229
	Secondary literature referred to		235
	Index		251

Preface

This is not the book I set out to write. My original aim had been to write a study of Gregory the Great (pope 590–604) in his world. Gregory was neither a faithful disciple of Augustine, Ambrose and Cassian: the fathers he liked, above all, to consider his forebears; nor an original, creative thinker such as they had been. His greatness and his creativity lay in another dimension. His own judgement on his work – 'a despicable little trickle' compared with the 'deep torrents and the clear flow of Ambrose and Augustine'[1] – does full justice to it on one level, and is a crude caricature on another. This is the paradox I had wanted to explore. What was it about Gregory's world that so changed the framework of thought, the assumptions about the world, God and man, the shape of discourse, that his questions came to differ so profoundly from those of Augustine and his contemporaries, and that the traditions he inherited from them now furnished material for answers to questions so different? What was the alchemy that so changed the whole configuration of the intelligible world over two centuries?

These were the questions I wanted to consider. It took me longer than it should to realise that this would involve considering the slow change of a whole world of discourse over the two centuries. The theme of my intended book expanded and seemed to threaten to swallow two whole centuries of the cultural, religious and intellectual history of Western Europe. Gregory was receding to a distant horizon, sinking almost below it, remained only just visible in front of the vanishing point of

[1] *Ep.* XII.16a (*Hom. in Hiez. Prol.*).

my widening perspective. But of course the book is no more a cultural, religious and intellectual history of Western Europe between about AD 400 and 600 than it is a study of Gregory I. I have kept ruthlessly to my central question: what was the nature of the changes that transformed the intellectual and the spiritual horizons of the Christian world between around AD 400 and 600?

I have made no attempt in any of my chapters to give anything like a full treatment of its subject, and rarely surveyed the whole range of evidence on any point. The slightness of the attention I have been able to give to the sixth century, and the almost complete absence of Spain from my pages, may be redeemed in the book I still hope to devote to Gregory the Great. Much of my argument rests on the work – often huge in amount – of others. Although some of the chapters will, I hope, be seen to have something new to offer, if the book as a whole has a claim to making any discoveries, it is in the sense defined by Nelson Goodman: 'Discovery often amounts, as when I place a piece in a jigsaw puzzle, not to arrival at a proposition for declaration or defense, but to finding a fit.'[2] I think the way I have put the jigsaw puzzle together is new, and that it fits. My interpretation is more in the nature of an invitation to view the evidence in a new perspective than a claim to affirm some hitherto unrecognised or misinterpreted fact. 'Put crassly, what is called for in such cases is less like arguing than selling.'[3]

Immersion in the literature of the fifth and sixth centuries has slowly eroded any lingering conviction that I may have had at the start that throughout these centuries Christianity stood for a fixed quantity. A Christian believer, or a theologian, may challenge such an assault on the notion of an unchanging 'essence of Christianity'. Did not faith in an Incarnate Lord – however formulated – remain the firm core of the religion? Yes; but the Lord's call, 'Come and follow me', left much of what was involved in following Him unresolved. My enquiry is an attempt to characterise the shift that took place during these centuries in the way Christians understood what was involved

[2] *Ways of worldmaking*, 21.
[3] *Ibid.* 129.

in following their Lord. In my first, introductory, chapter I have tried to clarify some of the conceptual problems which, as it seems to me, need to be faced but have generally been passed over. The stages of this enquiry are enumerated at the end of my introductory chapter.

These two centuries correspond roughly to the timespan of the Christian Roman Empire in the West. The starting point – though I have often found myself driven by necessity to touch on earlier times – is the age of the large-scale christianisation of Roman society at the end of the fourth century and the beginning of the fifth: the age of Theodosius I, of Augustine of Hippo and their contemporaries. The end-point is the time, more or less, of the 'end of the Western Empire', its fragmentation into the barbarian kingdoms of Europe. The study is confined, essentially, to the Western, Latin-speaking provinces. Some of my themes spread across into the Greek world, and even beyond it, to embrace the whole shared world of Christendom. In such cases I have allowed myself the liberty of touching on non-Western evidence; but I have generally confined such excursions either to illustrating what was common to the whole of Late Antique Christianity, or, alternatively, to sharpen some contrast with what was peculiar to its Western versions. In no case have I tried to trace parallel or divergent developments in the Byzantine world. This possibility of isolating a 'Western' Christianity in such a way is itself one feature of the end of an epoch, the epoch I have called 'ancient Christianity'.

In dedicating the book to Peter Brown I have sought to point towards a debt I share with many others: those who have been helped by him to look at the world of Late Antiquity with fresh eyes, and the even greater number of those for whom his work has enlarged the horizons of historical enquiry. To this shared, general, indebtedness I must add the no less immeasurable extent of the help I have personally received over the years from his suggestions, references to literature that would have remained unread, chance remarks that sank into the mind to bubble up again as fresh air through layers of muddy water, and the seminars which, under his guidance, often led their members into unforeseen, surprising places.

Preface

Many friends have helped me to clarify what I wanted to say and to say it more clearly. Among those who have read and commented on parts of the book or early drafts and whom I wish to thank for their labour are Arnold Angenendt, Catherine Delano Smith, Mary Douglas, William Klingshirn, Janet Nelson, Ian Wood. Mary Charles Murray has heroically read the whole. Mountains have laboured; I alone bear the responsibility for the mouse brought forth. Chapter 1, especially, has raised the eyebrows of several of its readers; I cannot have allayed all their anxieties. At a crucial time of my work John McManners invited me to contribute a chapter largely overlapping the theme of this book to the *Oxford illustrated history of Christianity*. Him and the Oxford University Press I wish to thank for providing me with an opportunity to sketch an outline of much of what I wanted to say. I wish to thank Sidney Griffith and my graduate students at the Catholic University of America for giving me the occasion to explore with them the subject matter of chapters 11 and 12 in a series of seminars given there. Invitations from friends to give lectures and seminars at their several universities have furnished many opportunities to clarify thought under their hospitable roofs. For such opportunities I wish to thank Grover Zinn (Oberlin College), Roger Ray (University of Toledo), Elizabeth Clark (Duke University), Robert Wilken (University of Virginia), Ellen Badone (MacMaster University), Alfred Schindler (University of Bern) and Otto Wermelinger (University of Fribourg).

Elizabeth Livingstone has been the most generous of friends, not only to me, but to all those engaged in the study of early Christianity. I wish to place on record my gratitude for her unstinting generosity to me, and my fair share of the gratitude for devoted and fruitful service to all of us, in five continents, whose studies of Christian history and thought her own work has stimulated, assisted and encouraged.

The Leverhulme Trust has given generous support in awarding me an Emeritus Fellowship for two years; and the Institute for Advanced Study at Princeton, in electing me as a member for 1986–7, gave me the benefit of a year with unrivalled facilities and resources to assist my work, in a community of scholars in which the Platonic Idea of an Academic Community has come as near to realisation as anywhere.

References in the footnotes have been given in an abbreviated form. The full details appear in the lists of sources and of secondary literature referred to. Although these are not intended as bibliographies, they are likely to include the greater part of the literature known to me that I have thought relevant and sufficiently important, and not forgotten about.

Abbreviations

AHR	*American Historical Review*
AJP	*American Journal of Philology*
BAR Int. ser.	British Archaeological Reports. International Series
BEFAR	*Bibliothèque des Ecoles Françaises d'Athènes et de Rome*
CC	*Corpus christianorum. Series latina*
CEFR	*Collection de l'Ecole française de Rome*
CIL	*Corpus inscriptionum latinarum*
CJ	*Codex Iustinianaeus*
CRAI	*Comptes rendus des séances de l'Académie des Inscriptions et Belles Lettres*
CSEL	*Corpus scriptorum ecclesiasticorum latinorum*
CTh	*Codex Theodosianus*
DHGE	*Dictionnaire d'histoire et de géographie ecclésiastiques*
DOP	*Dumbarton Oaks Papers*
DSp	*Dictionnaire de spiritualité, ascétique et mystique*
Ep., Epp.	*Epistola, -ae*
GCS	*Griechischen christlichen Schriftsteller*
GRBS	*Greek, Roman and Byzantine Studies*
Hom.	*Homilia, -ae*
HZ	*Historische Zeitschrift*
JAC	*Jahrbuch für Antike und Christentum*
JEH	*Journal of Ecclesiastical History*
JHS	*Journal of Hellenic Studies*
JRS	*Journal of Roman Studies*
JThS	*Journal of Theological Studies*
MAH	*Mélanges d'archéologie et d'histoire de l'Ecole Française de Rome*
MGH	*Monumenta Germaniae historica*
AA	*Auctores antiquissimi*
Epp	*Epistolae*
SRM	*Scriptores rerum merovingicarum*
PG	*Patrologia graeca*

Abbreviations

PL	*Patrologia latina*
PLS	*Patrologiae latinae supplementum*
PO	*Patrologia orientalis*
RAC	*Realenzyklopädie für Antike und Christentum*
RAM	*Revue d'ascétique et de mystique*
RBen	*Revue Bénédictine*
REAug	*Revue des études augustiniennes*
RechAug	*Recherches augustiniennes*
REL	*Revue des études latines*
RevSR	*Revue des sciences religieuses*
RHE	*Revue d'histoire ecclésiastique*
RHR	*Revue de l'histoire des religions*
RTAM	*Revue de théologie ancienne et médiévale*
SC	Sources chrétiennes
SCH	*Studies in Church History*
StPatr	*Studia patristica*
TRE	*Theologische Realenzyklopädie*
TS	*Theological Studies*
TU	Texte und Untersuchungen
VC	*Vigiliae Christianae*
ZKG	*Zeitschrift für Kirchengeschichte*
ZMR	*Zeitschrift für Missionskunde und Religionswissenschaft*

Introduction: 'secularity'

Very early in its history the Christian community was forced to ask itself what it was. Disagreement within the Apostolic community in Jerusalem about the importance of Jewish customs raised the agonising question: was being a Christian a special way of being a Jew – in which case the obligations of Jews would claim obedience from Christians – or was it something else? In the latter case there was a further question: how much, if any, of the Jewish Law was to apply, how much could be dismissed as of no religious importance, ultimately neutral?

How tightly was Christianity bound to particular cultural forms? The question has time and again agitated Christians, clergy, missionaries and their targets; it has furnished a rich theme to novelists and dramatists. What was essential to Christianity, and what was indifferent, merely linked with the particular form of the society in which it was embodied? The question has haunted Christian history. It was felt especially acutely at times of rapid or profound cultural change, or at moments of new encounters with foreign cultures: the transplantation of Christianity from a European into American, Asiatic, or more recently to African, milieus. Consider as an example the perplexities of a remarkable Dominican friar, Diego Durán, working in the later sixteenth century in Spanish America. Driven by the most authentic missionary zeal and fervent ardour to spread his faith, Durán was at the same time exceptional for his desire to understand the culture and the religion of the indigenous Indians. Knowing the tenacity of their ancient beliefs and their attachment to the rituals in which it was expressed, always suspicious that beneath outward conformity with the newly imposed Christian rites ancient beliefs might linger, and aware that rituals and festivals could be ambiguous enough to allow Indians 'to introduce their ancient rites into our [Christian] ceremonies',[1] Durán insisted that 'If any recollection of the ancient religion exists among the natives, it is necessary that it be uprooted' (251, cf. 270, 274). No shred of their old paganism was to be allowed to survive. And yet he had a sense uncommon among missionaries until very modern times that not all that the natives were clinging to need count as religion: much of it, if told, would be 'a story about ancient customs' (269). He knew of many such customs that had once been bound up with the old religion – sweeping the streets at certain times, a practice Durán thought was 'in our time no longer a pagan custom' (237); an ancient ritual dance which in his day had become 'trickery of the feet rather than art of the Devil' (297); the sacred concoction from which images of the gods had in former times been made was now 'eaten as candy' (245). Durán was acutely conscious of a need to distinguish genuine survivals of the old religion – which would need extirpation – and secularised or de-sacralised practices surviving as remnants cut off from their original religious roots – which could be tolerated.

A profoundly and almost anachronistically sharp awareness of a need to distinguish religion from what was not 'religion' – let us provisionally call it 'culture' – underlies Durán's book. How to apply this distinction was a difficult matter, and Durán was often in doubt. His account of an encounter with an old man intent on observing a traditional custom gives a vivid momentary glimpse of the perplexities inseparable from the experience of both convert and missionary: 'He [the old man] accepted [my scolding him for his ancient beliefs and superstitions and for his meagre awe of God] with great humility and swore to me that this practice was not due to ancient belief but was simply their way of doing things, since he already believed in God and the creed of the Holy Mother Roman Church' (277). Durán was sometimes very unsure about where to draw the line between survivals of the Indians' ancient 'idolatry' and 'their way of doing things'. Sometimes he took part, though with

---

[1] *Book of the gods*, 71. In the sequel the figures in parentheses refer to page numbers.

misgivings, in rites he held in suspicion: 'So I pick up my staff and walk along [in a procession originally in honour of Tezcatlipoca], thinking of our gross ignorance, for great evils may be concealed under these customs' (103). Sometimes, even when he thought a custom had lost its religious meaning, he still disapproved (e.g. 251, 169, 171–2, 176–7, 408). It would be surprising if such uncertainties and inconsistencies were absent. What, however, the historian ignores at his peril are the pressures experienced by the missionary, by the convert, and by those who resist proselytism, to make such distinctions.

Modern missionary sensibilities rightly view with anxiety the urge to demand more disturbance than conversion – or 'christianisation' – absolutely demands in the converts' lives and culture. We should not mistake this greater reserve about inflicting brutal change either for no more than fashionable respect for traditional cultures alien to the missionary's, or for diminished seriousness about what being a Christian involves. Its roots reach to layers of theological ambiguity often previously experienced in Christian history. The historian of Christianity must be sensitive to such uncertainty. He should be prepared to consider not only the completeness or otherwise of conversion, but also the extent of unnecessary change inflicted on the convert in the name of Christianity. The historian will recognise that in this context neither 'complete' nor 'unnecessary' possesses any fixed and invariable meaning. The line which separates religion from 'the way of doing things' may be hard to trace, and it will rarely stay still;[2] but to set out to blur or to erase it, to conflate the 'religious' and the 'cultural' change, without first having made the most resolute effort that the evidence permits to keep them distinct, is to preclude the possibility of understanding this whole range of experience. In some way, however they are to be defined and clarified, 'culture' and 'religion', or the 'secular' and the 'sacred', must be distinguished. 'Enculturation' – or 'inculturation', as some theologians like to say – is a problem for historians no less than for missionaries. (I consider the vocabulary below, pp. 13–14.)

---

[2] See Victor Turner on the tendency of 'yesterday's liminal becoming to-day's liminoid': 'Variations on a theme', 43–6.

The distinction is as central to any serious study of the encounter between Christianity and the culture of the Late Roman world as it is to the understanding of its encounter with the Germanic cultures of Western Europe in the early medieval centuries. What is involved in conversion to Christianity? – the question can no more be suppressed by modern historians than it could be by ancient or medieval bishops, clergy or theologians. In discussing the christianisation of the Roman world that great scholar, Arthur Darby Nock, made one of the rare serious attempts to take account of this question. His distinction between mere 'adhesion' and 'conversion' was a way of coming to grips with this problem. 'By conversion', he wrote,[3]

> we mean the reorientation of the soul of an individual, his deliberate turning from indifference or from an earlier form of piety to another, a turning which implies a consciousness that a great change is involved, that the old was wrong and the new is right . . . Judaism and Christianity demanded renunciation and a new start. They demanded not merely acceptance of a rite, but the adhesion of the will to a theology, in a word faith, a new life in a new people.

Two separate problems are raised here. The first is the vocabulary of 'adhesion of the will to a theology' or 'faith'. Twentieth-century scholars, themselves conditioned by the attitudes encouraged by a culture of textuality, like fourth- or fifth-century bishops, have been apt to attach central importance to doctrine and theology in the process of conversion. But Christians were generally more worried about non-Christian cult, what 'pagans' were doing, rather than about what they believed. Thus in a much-cited account of the conversion of some fifth-century Bedouins at the pillar of St Symeon the Stylite, recounted by a Syrian bishop, we are told that

> they came in many thousands, enslaved to the darkness of impiety, were enlightened, by the station upon the pillar . . . They renounced with their shouts their traditional errors; they broke up their venerated idols in the presence of that great light [Saint Symeon]; and they foreswore the ecstatic rites of Aphrodite, the demon whose service they had long accepted. They enjoyed divine religious initiation and

---

[3] Nock, *Conversion*, 7, 14. For bibliographical surveys of more recent work, see Snow and Machalek, 'The sociology of conversion'; Rambo, 'Current research'. See also Parente, 'L'idea di conversione'.

received their law instead spoken by that holy tongue [of Symeon]. Bidding farewell to ancestral customs, they renounced also the diet of the wild ass or the camel. And I myself was witness to these things and heard them, as they renounced their ancestral impiety and submitted to evangelical instruction.[4]

It has been remarked that 'in reading this passage ... we see through Theodoret's eyes and naturally adopt his assumptions. With him, we suppose "that the bedouins have not only discarded their little house-hold ju-jus or icons but have also seized upon a doctrine". And here, with Theodoret, we go wrong.'[5] It may be that the bedouins did patiently listen to the saint's expositions of doctrine; but, if they did, that was not the decisive moment of their conversion, but a sequel. Their conversion was turning their backs on the idols they had worshipped. We shall meet this problem about belief and idolatry again when we consider the conversion of Germanic barbarians, and discuss it further in that connection.

What matters more for our present discussion is the other, and chief, point of Nock's description of what is involved in 'conversion': a 'reorientation of the soul', a 'deliberate turning from indifference or from an earlier form of piety to another, a turning which implies a consciousness that a great change is involved, that the old was wrong and the new is right'. Just how much renunciation of the old does conversion to the new require? Would Theodoret have been content with his Bedouins' conversion had they not, for instance, given up their customary diet of wild ass or camel? Matters of diet, dress and personal ornament have often been seen as bearing a heavy religious charge. Pope Nicholas I (858–67), for example, was asked about such matters by the recently converted Bulgars. Some of their queries received categorical answers: necklaces given to the sick for healing are 'demonic phylacteries', and their users are condemned by 'apostolic anathema'; the death penalty for negligent sentries is contrary to the example – a significant choice! – of Saul's ferocity abjured by St Paul on his conversion; but their

[4] Theodoret, *Hist. rel.* 26 (*PG* 82.147), quoted by MacMullen, *Christianizing the Roman Empire*, 2, and his 'Conversion', 73.
[5] Babcock, 'MacMullen on conversion', 83, quoting MacMullen, 'Conversion', 73.

king's habit of dining alone was 'not against the faith, though it offends good manners'; so in this matter they were offered 'not commands, but persuasion'. But when it came to anxiety as to whether Bulgarian women might wear trousers, not even advice was offered, for this was a matter of indifference (*super-vacuum*): 'for what we desire to change is not your outward clothing but the manners (*mores*) of the inner man'.[6] Here is a spectrum of practices, from what the pope considered as indifferent to what he regarded as supremely relevant.

But is there any criterion to determine relevance? It might be suggested that it is only his previous *religion*, not his manner of life, that the convert would need to renounce. But where does that religion end, and his manner of life, his 'secular' customs or 'culture', begin? What are the boundaries of Christianity, part of its essential substance? What, minimally, will make a convert a 'Christian'? There may be a universally valid and unchanging answer to that question; but a historian can only note the uncertainties, the shifts, doubts and debates concerning it. Assumptions determined by some theological, philosophical or other position may yield certainty: if so, they must at least be openly avowed. From a historical point of view, such certainty must appear as arbitrary dogmatism.

These are fatal uncertainties in discourse about the 'conversion' of individuals and, still more, of groups or nations. The question of just what 'conversion' or 'christianisation' involves cannot be by-passed; but in discussions of the christianisation of the Roman world it is often suppressed. Thus in one of the most recent, most learned and most lively accounts of it we read that

Christianity had not developed its own particular way of doing everything. On many a corner even of religious life it had still to set its mark. Those corners, however, are of concern to us because they help to determine both the point at which a person could count as a convert and the historical impact of conversion. How broad a conformity prescribed by the Church was needed to make one a Christian? And

[6] I take the example from Angenendt, *Kaiserherrschaft*, 70. It is to be found in the pope's *Ep.* 99 (*Responsa ad Bulgarorum consulta, MGH Epp.* 6.568–600), sections 79 (p. 594), 25 (579–80), 42 (583) and 59 (588).

what difference did conversion actually make anyway in the various zones of life?[7]

Crucial questions; but there are hints of a disquieting suggestion that Christianity should somehow have 'set its mark' not only on religious life (and how far does that extend?), but well beyond it, perhaps even 'devised its own way of doing everything'. 'Everything' can presumably be allowed to pass as good rhetoric; but not the more dangerous assumption that we can always recognise a 'corner of religious life' without difficulty; that the boundary between what is 'religion' and what is not is fixed and unambiguous. Matters are only made worse when we are reminded that in the non-Christian world religion touched everything, that the distinction between sacred and secular is essentially a Christian one which we impose on a culture to which it is foreign;[8] the conclusion follows inevitably, that if everything is religion, then everything must be changed in conversion. 'So disturbing and difficult must be conversion, or so incomplete.'[9]

Why must conversion be either disturbing or incomplete – incomplete just to the extent that it has failed to disturb? Here is a large assumption; one about which, for example, pope Nicholas I (see above, p. 5) would have had reservations. The extent to which conversion must be either incomplete or disturbing depends on just where the line is drawn between sacred and secular. That question is crucial, but it contains an important ambiguity to which I will turn in a moment: drawn by whom? But first we should note the readiness – perhaps especially encouraged by the German Protestant tradition[10]– with which it is assumed that almost everything, at any rate most forms of public life and activity, are sufficiently close to the centre of the sacred to make us expect that they should have been objectionable to the Christians and somehow exorcised, abolished, or transformed. Highly questionable assumptions lurk behind remarks such as 'popular manifestations of a genuinely enthusiastic kind [that] should have been intolerable but

---

[7] MacMullen, *Christianizing the Roman Empire*, 74.

[8] *Ibid.* 150, n. 3; see also *Paganism*, 40, 57; and 'What difference did Christianity make?'

[9] MacMullen, *Christianizing the Roman Empire*, 74.

[10] See Harnack, below, ch. 5, n. 17: the conversion of the Roman Empire to Christianity left 'the world in possession all except its gods'.

weren't'; or 'Christian attack had to be broadly directed. So logic prescribed, but necessity prevented.'[11] The question must be asked: whose logic?

It makes no sense to discuss the completeness or otherwise of conversion, or, the converse, its disturbingness, except in relation to preset boundaries for what, looked at from the Christian side, is to count as falling within the sphere of religion or the orbit of the sacred. But how are these boundaries set, and by whom? It is evident that there are two very different answers to this question, and there is an absolute necessity to distinguish them clearly. The boundaries may be drawn by us, twentieth-century historians, anthropologists, theologians; or, alternatively, they may be drawn by fourth-, fifth- or sixth-century bishops, clergy, lay people. This seems an obvious enough distinction; but a long tradition of scholarship seems oblivious to it.[12] If we are to use notions such as 'religion' and 'culture', or 'sacred' and 'secular' and their synonyms in our own sense, well and good; but we must know what we are doing. It is one thing for Late Antique Christians to debate these matters – as they did with passionate intensity in the decades around 400 (see below, chs. 4–5); it is quite another for modern scholars to make judgements about the extent of conversion, to speak of 'half-Christians'[13] and so forth, without defining some conception of a whole Christian or what a genuine conversion would be. The distinction between 'us' and 'them' determines the nature of the task we set ourselves: either we try to describe the processes whereby a society has come to be, or failed to become, 'christianised', in whatever sense *we* define a 'christianised' society; or, alternatively, we set ourselves the task of tracing the shifting boundaries drawn by Late Antique people which determined

[11] MacMullen, *Christianizing the Roman Empire*, 76, 78.

[12] From Guignebert to MacMullen. See further below, ch. 4. A return to sanity is signalled by Gregory, 'The survival of paganism', esp. 230–1. Kahl, 'Die ersten Jahrhunderte', 42–59 is a fine example (dealing with the problem in the early medieval context) of the discrimination required.

[13] Ancient authors rarely use such terms, and their meaning often has little relation to what modern scholars have in mind. See e.g. Augustine, *Enarr. in Ps.*, 64.16 (for bad Christians); the Council of Mâcon (585) c. 8, *seudochristiani* (for people who invade churches' right of asylum). For an interesting use of '*pseudo-Christiani*' (meaning Manichees), retorting to their taunting of catholics with being '*semi-Christiani*', see Augustine, *C. Faust.* 1.3. Augustine generally uses '*semi-Christiani*' to refer to Christians who also practise pagan rites: see Mandonze, *Saint Augustin*, p. 312, n. 6.

how far their society measured up to what *they* saw as a properly christianised society. Both are tasks of supreme interest and worthy of a historian's labours; but they are quite different, and nothing is gained by confusing them.

We encounter the same problem when we consider what historians used to call 'pagan survivals'. Talk about 'pagan survivals' is the obverse of an uncritical use of the notion of 'christianisation': pagan survivals are seen simply as what resists the efforts of Christian clergy to abolish, to transform or to control. What such talk fails to take into account is the sheer vitality of non-religious, secular institutions and traditions and their power to resist change. What is to count as a 'pagan survival'? Obviously, not anything that survives from a pagan past into the life of the person, group or people converted to Christianity, for many ordinary details of daily life are bound to continue unchanged, and so will much of the cultural and institutional framework of that life. What is labelled as 'pagan survival' must again, clearly, depend on how 'pagan' is defined, where the boundaries of what is 'Christian' are drawn and what they allow to be treated as indifferent, or 'secular'. We may not assume that these boundaries are fixed or constant, that churchmen in Northern Gaul in the sixth century drew them in the same place as would have their colleagues in Italy, their lay congregations, or their predecessors in the fourth century; still less where a modern Western scholar might locate them.

To avoid this problem, some historians have taken a minimalist view of what is involved in conversion. In a paper contributed to a symposium on the conversion of the Germanic peoples to Christianity held in 1966, one contributor, Hans Kuhn, writing of the survival (*Fortleben*) of Germanic paganism after 'conversion' to Christianity, warned:[14] 'In order to avoid being led astray into inessentials, one must not include all that is connected with pagan religion and usages related to it. One must keep to the acknowledgement of pagan deities, and to the observances

[14] 'Das Fortleben' (figures in parentheses in the sequel refer to page numbers). The changed perspective between the two symposia, one on the 'conversion' of the Germanic peoples to Christianity held in 1966, the other on their 'christianisation' held in 1982, is remarked on by Raoul Manselli in his introductory discourse to the second, *Settimane*, 28 (1982) 62–5.

and the cult (*Dienst und Kult*) rendered to them' (p. 743). He went on to say that to include morality (*das Ethische*) within religion is misleading, the result of Enlightenment assumptions which have encouraged modern Europeans, especially in the Protestant traditions, to see religion within an ethical perspective (p. 744). On these lines he concluded that 'all that belongs to the lower (*niederen* – "popular"?) religions in a broad sense has little significance for our problem. It certainly had a more tenacious life than the cults of the greater gods, but hardly stood in the way of christianisation and was hardly touched by it' (p. 746).

This has the merit of clarity. Behind it lies the attitude, shared by much of modern missiological thinking, which is inclined to frown upon missionary strategies which tend to disturb the delicately balanced ecology of a culture by insensitive proselytising. The implicit assumption on which it is based minimises what is included in the scope of conversion: baptism, certainly, renunciation of overt idol-worship, and very little else. On this assumption, whatever it is that is taken to be necessary to make a Christian, once the line which marks him off from a pagan is crossed, it will make no sense to ask whether 'paganism' survives in the convert.[15] To be sure, questions may be raised about the quality of the convert's Christianity, whether he is a good or a bad Christian; but there is no immediately obvious criterion which would allow us to decide how much of his previously habitual conduct, beliefs, customs and attitudes are relevant to determining the answer to that question.

A minimalist answer such as we have just considered must seem no less arbitrary than the expectation that Christianity should develop 'its own way of doing everything' (see above, p. 7, n. 7). To avoid this kind of arbitrariness, without falling into the trap of the light-hearted pragmatism so deeply ingrained in much historical work, especially in the tradition of scholarship prevalent in the English-speaking world, an alternative approach to the whole question has found favour, notably among an influential group of French historians. This approach does away with the need for a preliminary clarification of the meaning of

[15] See Schmitt, "'Religion populaire'": 'rien n'est "survécu" dans une culture, tout est vécu ou n'est pas' (p. 946).

terms such as 'religious' and 'non-religious', 'sacred' and 'secular'. The necessity for such a dichotomy is altogether side-stepped. Also avoided is the assumption that verbal symbols such as creeds are uniquely privileged expressions of religious beliefs. Ritual behaviour can count as no less effective an expression of commitment. The urge to adopt such an approach has been particularly strong among scholars engaged in the study of historical periods of profound religious and cultural change at the same time, such as took place in early medieval and early modern Europe, or in the Spanish conquest of Latin America. Its appeal is, no doubt, at least in part, a consequence of the growing interest in the vast areas of belief, custom and ritual that escaped or resisted the control of clerical elites, the life that went on outside the walls of churches and monasteries, outside schools and councils, courts – papal, royal or episcopal.

This alternative approach conjures the problem of distinguishing sacred from secular effectively out of existence, and thereby avoids the difficulties raised by the approaches we have considered. It does this by transposing discussion of 'christianisation' from the language of religion into that of culture, or, to use the vocabulary of one of its most distinguished practitioners, Jacques Le Goff, of two 'levels of culture': the learned, ecclesiastical and more or less cosmopolitan culture common to the clerical classes of Latin Europe, and the 'folklorique'.[16] Le Goff has sketched some of the ways in which each has adapted itself to the other, and, notably, the ways in which they have resisted adaptation; for, in his view, the chief feature of their co-existence throughout the Middle Ages remained their mutual impermeability.[17] In this manner Le Goff and others have strengthened the revolt against the idealised image of a 'Christian Middle Ages' popularised by the Romantic movement and by the Catholic neo-Scholastic revival. Scepticism about the myth made Le Goff go so far as to represent medieval Europe as missionary territory as late as the end of the fifteenth century. Other historians have been happy to take views akin to Le Goff's.[18]

To take this last step is, patently, to breach the logic of his

---

[16] Le Goff, 'Culture cléricale'.
[17] 'le refus de cette culture folklorique par la culture ecclésiastique': *ibid.*, 786.
[18] For a survey, see Van Enghen, 'The Christian Middle Ages'.

own approach. For, having first transposed the problem from a religious into a cultural register and concluded that mutual acculturation failed to take place in the medieval West, Le Goff then simply re-translates the conclusion – legitimate as it may be in its own terms – into religious terms, as if failure of acculturation between clerical and folklorique could be equated, without any questions asked, with failure of christianisation. The latter, however, has been excluded from the discourse at the outset by the adoption of a language which has suppressed talk about it. To draw any conclusions about religion from a description of cultural change we must enter the deep and muddy waters in which we found ourselves drowning (above, pp. 6–7), which Le Goff is – understandably – reluctant to enter. If we wish to answer questions such as 'how Christian (or pagan) was medieval Europe?', or, for that matter, Late Roman society, what we need to know more about is not only the life-styles, beliefs and ritual practices of medieval peasants and the gulf that separated them from those of clerical and literate elites, but the meaning of the question we are asking. What shall count as 'Christian'? What kind of society, or culture, shall qualify? What we need to guard against above all is deceiving ourselves that we have answered this question when we have observed the failure of two levels of culture to interpenetrate.

Shorn of the false implications drawn from it, however, such a procedure has much to recommend it. By-passing the need for distinguishing 'religion' from 'culture', or 'sacred' from 'secular', it avoids the difficulties and ambiguities of defining these terms and tracing the borders of the territories they are applied to. The substitution of 'clerical' and 'folklorique' as the categories in which the discussion is conducted brings an obvious gain in clarity: comparatively definite, unproblematic notions, they designate identifiable social groups or classes as the culture-carriers. This vocabulary is, admittedly, more easily applied in the early medieval than in a Late Roman context. Notoriously, if one can speak of a 'Christian culture' in the Late Roman world, it is one shared in great measure with its non-Christian counterpart. At best, it is a sub-culture of a Late Antique *koine*. There just is not a different culture to distinguish Christians from their pagan peers, only their religion; and any attempt to invent one reveals itself as a disguise for what is simply a difference of religion. Of the model of an elite religion contrasting with a popular religion which one might (following Le Goff's example) try to use to circumvent the distinction between 'pagan' and 'Christian', Arnaldo Momigliano's devastating critique has once and for all delivered us.[19] This ill-fit apart, the vocabulary of 'levels of culture' has the decisive advantage that it falls readily into line with a now fairly general reluctance, especially among cultural anthropologists, to allow a dichotomy between 'religion' and 'culture'.

So far I have allowed myself the liberty of using 'sacred' and 'secular' somewhat informally, and more or less as synonymous with the conceptual doublet, equally problematic, of 'religion' and 'culture'. It is not a historian's business to sow confusion where generations of anthropologists have laboured to achieve clarity, and rather than attempt to define these terms formally, I merely indicate the kind of contrast I wish to convey in using them. For most anthropologists it would, of course, seem odd to use the terms as mutually exclusive. In E. B. Tylor's usage 'culture' or 'civilisation' in their wide sense included knowledge, belief, art, morals, law, custom and so forth; more recently, 'religion' has been defined as a 'cultural system'.[20] In such a view religion will be one among a number of constituents which, taken together, constitute a 'culture': 'an historically transmitted pattern of meanings embodied in symbols, a system of inherited conceptions expressed in symbolic forms by which men communicate, perpetuate, and develop their knowledge about and attitude towards life.'[21] It will suffice for our purpose to note that, given a precise enough definition of religion as a cultural system,[22] a religion can still be distinguished from other constituents of a culture. To avoid offence to anthropological ears, therefore, I shall prefer to distinguish 'sacred' from 'secular' within a 'culture', rather than distinguishing 'religion' from

[19] 'Popular religious beliefs'; see also Brown, *The cult*, 12–22, which should be read in the light of Murray, 'Peter Brown'.
[20] Geertz, 'Religion as a cultural system'. On the distinction between culture and social system, see Geertz, 'Ritual and social change', 144–5. Niebuhr, *Christ and culture*, 32ff., seems to be groping after a definition akin to this.
[21] Geertz, 'Religion as a cultural system', 89 (cf. 250).
[22] Such as Geertz gives *ibid.*, 90. (Its details do not concern us here.)

'culture'. My aim, however, in using both vocabularies, is to distinguish within our discourse one sector from the rest, its 'non-religious' components. It goes without saying that I do not intend thereby to give it, or any other cultural system, a privileged part in relation to others. I merely wish to render the general sense of a distinction which would have been made by reflective Christians in the period here under discussion.

Despite all its problems and disadvantages, I need therefore to keep a vocabulary which distinguishes these two spheres. I shall be less concerned to trace the progress of 'christianisation' in extent or depth, or its obverse: the 'vast mass of cultural forms passed on from paganism to Christianity',[23] or with 'pagan survivals', than with the attitudes taken to such survivals. We shall need to discriminate within a spectrum of possibilities. Many practices inherited from a pagan past were simply carried on, unquestioned by bishops or clergy, accepted as matters of indifference, with a good conscience. Others were attacked, legislated and preached against as sinful indulgence or sacrilege, or tolerated with reluctance as unavoidable evils, to be prohibited when practicable. But lay and clerical perspectives did not always coincide. Among practices disapproved by clergy we need to allow for a distinction between those which their congregations regarded as harmless customs without religious significance – as, for example, many claimed the observances of the New Year celebrations to be – and customs they thought properly carried over from pagan into Christian cult: could a martyr, for instance, be more suitably honoured than by getting drunk on his feast day? Lay and clerical forms of spirituality could be in conflict on such matters, and lay resistance to clerical demands sometimes played an important part in shaping the forms of Christian spirituality; a part which is misunderstood or concealed in discourse cast in terms either of 'pagan survivals' or of 'folklorique culture'.

In other words, what I shall be primarily concerned with is the manner in which Late Roman Christians, lay and clerical, drew the line which distinguished what they would have seen as their 'religion' from the rest of their activity and experience,

[23] Geffcken, *The last days*, 325.

their 'secular' lives and its setting (which I sometimes also refer to as their 'culture'). My investigation will be concerned, essentially, with Late Roman Christians' conception of Christianity itself: how far did they think its boundaries reached? What was included within its essence, what was left in a penumbra of contingent accidentals, indifferent or inessential to the core of their religion? I do not believe that the limits of clerical tolerance were entirely capricious, and I shall try to spot some of the pressures which modified them and brought about shifts in the line that bishops and clergy wished to separate acceptable customs from 'idolatry' in the lives of their people: a line they often found hard to draw for themselves, or insisted on drawing differently from the way their clergy may have wished.

The two centuries with which this book deals are the period in which much of the secular government, the provincial and local administration, and secular education and culture were running down in the Western Roman provinces. In this sense it could be said that Western Europe was being drained of the 'secular'. The shifts in the social structure and the administrative functions, the growing prominence of military and clerical at the expense of the civil powers, and the eclipse of secular education and learning, at the expense of literacy and to the profit of a more clerically orientated and a more scriptural culture, have all been much studied. I shall not go over ground here that has been well covered by others. Rather, my purpose will be to explore the forms in which men responded intellectually and imaginatively to these shifts.[24]

Nobody seriously doubts that in ways such as these Western Europe was being drained of the 'secular' in these centuries. The 'secular' can be defined as that sector of life which is not considered to be of direct religious significance. What, within a given culture, it includes will therefore be determined not only by the institutions and the patterns of living within it; it will also depend on the manner in which these are interpreted. I shall suggest that it is not only the world that changed in these two centuries – a matter generally agreed – but also the framework of thought, imagination and discourse within which it could be

[24] See Markus, 'The sacred and the secular'.

interpreted – a subject much less explored. For this purpose we shall need to distinguish more carefully than has usually been done this process of drainage from the intellectual and spiritual shift which accompanied it.

My enquiry is, therefore, a piece of intellectual history, albeit one conceived in a somewhat broader sense than the phrase is usually made to bear. Henri-Irénée Marrou, that greatest of historians of Late Antiquity, has spoken of the Church animating a society 'wholly sacral' (*toute sacrale*) after the end of Antiquity. He had in mind the loss of a set of institutions and of a culture which had in Late Antiquity, even in its christianised form, kept its 'autonomy'.[25] Sociologists of religion have familiarised us with the process of 'secularisation': a process wherein areas of life, thought, activity and institutions are withdrawn from religious or ecclesiastical domination or influence. The process I shall try to describe is the reverse, something like the process Marrou had in mind when he spoke of the loss of 'autonomy'. I shall call it 'de-secularisation'. This is not simply the gradual collapse of 'secular' culture and institutions; nor is it, as it is often made to appear, the progressively wider and deeper 'christianisation' of Roman society and culture. Accompanying these there was something else, a change in the nature of Christianity itself: a contraction in the scope that Christianity, or, more precisely, its educated clerical representatives and officials, allowed to the 'secular'. We shall have to persist in asking the question what is meant by 'christianisation' and by 'pagan survivals', and to exercise extreme caution in the use of these concepts. For one of the forms in which this change in the nature of Christianity manifested itself was in the tendency to absorb what had previously been 'secular', indifferent from a religious point of view, into the realm of the 'sacred'; to force the sphere of the 'secular' to contract, turning it either into 'Christian', or dismissing it as 'pagan' or 'idolatrous'. As we shall find, the spread of an ascetic mentality through Christian society had much to do with this re-drawing of the boundaries.

Part I sketches the uncertainties that the Constantinian revolution brought to the Christian community's self-understanding,

---

[25] 'La place du Haut Moyen Age', especially 608, 609.

especially with the large-scale christianisation of Roman society from the end of the fourth century. This was the situation in which its own Christian past, and the proper form of life in the new conditions of the present, became problems that had to be faced. Part II explores some of the pressures that led to the eclipse of the 'secular' dimension in Christians' consciousness. Part III considers the final outcome, the absorption of the 'secular' in the 'sacred' as ascetic norms came to penetrate wide sections of Christian society and to colour aspirations far beyond the walls of the cloister. That ascetic take-over signals the end of ancient Christianity.

I

THE CRISIS OF IDENTITY

Quid sit christianum esse? – what is it to be a Christian? Early in the fifth century an unknown follower of Pelagius set out to answer the question in a letter to a young man.[1] The question was not far below the surface amid the many anxieties at the end of the fourth and the beginning of the fifth centuries. This was the age of Ambrose and Chrysostom, of Jerome and Augustine, as well as of Pelagius and Cassian. In the religious history of Europe, especially of Western Europe, the half century from about 380 to about 430 marks a watershed. On the surface lie the great debates: the debates between pagans and Christians as well as those within the Christian group. In one way or another the debates of these decades all revolved around the question: what is it to be a Christian? What gave the question urgency was the rapid and far-reaching process of christianisation of Roman society which was reaching a climax at this time of dramatic change.

[1] *Ep. ad adolescentem* (Caspari), *PLS* 1.1377

2

'A great multitude which no man could number'

'Can any of the faithful doubt that at the hour of the [eucharistic] sacrifice the heavens open at the priest's calling, that in this mystery of Jesus Christ the choirs of angels are present, the heights joined to the depths, earth linked with heaven, the visible united with the invisible?'[1] In this rhetorical question Gregory the Great summed up the Christians' conviction that their group was part of a vast community. The congregation in the church was an outlying colony, its prayer a faint imitation of the perfect praise unceasingly offered to God by the angels and the saints in heaven. The Church on earth lived in the constant company of a larger community. To that community it was made present in its worship, especially in the celebration of the eucharist. Doubt, variety and development long continued to accompany the Church's attitude towards its dead members: were they to be pitied or envied? Did they need the intercession of the living, or the living theirs? Such doubts took a long time to resolve. Theological reflection and popular piety often found themselves in uneasy relationship where the cult of the dead was concerned. Clerical control was fragile and old custom tenacious.[2] But about the fellowship of the dead and the living in the community of the faithful there was never any doubt.

From the start, this belief was close to the bedrock of Christians' faith. It had far-reaching implications for their attitude to death and burial, and it helped to shape the cult of their dead.

---

[1] *Dial.* IV.60.3. On this theme see Erich Peterson's pioneering work, *Das Buch von den Engeln*, and in general Emery, *L'unité des croyants*.
[2] See Kötting, 'Der frühchristliche Reliquienkult', 8–9 and Février, 'La tombe chrétienne'. See further below, ch. 10.

These matters will be further explored in a later chapter. For the present, we must note that it was one of the principal constituents of their sense of their own group-identity. To be a Christian meant being a member of a group that extended across the gulf which divided heaven and earth. Augustine was echoing faithfully this universal conviction when he said that 'this Church which is now travelling on its journey, is joined to that heavenly Church where we have the angels as our fellow-citizens', for 'we are all members of one Body, whether we are here or anywhere else on earth, now or at any other time from Abel the just to the end of the world'.[3] When it celebrated the eucharist, the Christian group celebrated, and at the same time made actual, its own presence in the heavenly community. Angels hovered around the eucharistic altar and carried the congregation's self-offering to the throne of God, bringing back his blessing. Monastic choirs were particularly apt to become points of intersection of heaven and earth, places where, for an hour, their boundaries could cross. Gregory of Tours tells a moving story about the premature death of a young monk, and his inconsolable mother: her grief was turned into joy on hearing her son's voice in the singing of matins. So close were the angels at the community's prayer that monks were told to turn aside if they needed to spit, lest they spit upon the angels gathered in front of them.[4] Choirs of angels could on occasion be seen present not only in church, but even at ordinary meals.[5] The eucharist was the privileged moment at which the Church's inner being was made fully real; but the group lived in perpetual proximity, even intimacy, with the larger community of which it felt itself to be a part. The saints were God's friends, but they also remained men's kin. Together with them, the whole community was in God's presence.

Most Late Antique people lived, like the Christians, in a universe which included an unseen world as large and as varied as the visible. The invisible world was taken for granted as readily

---

[3] *Sermo* 341.9.11; see below, ch. 7, n. 2.

[4] Gregory of Tours, *Glor. mart.* 75; *Reg. Mag.* 48.6–9. See also 47.6, 21–4. Angels are ubiquitous in this (probably Gallic) *Rule*: e.g. 10.13, 39; 34.9 – they provide the monks' continual surveillance; 20.14 – they are their communication-media; 95.19 – monks outside their monasteries apparently risked being mistaken for angels!

[5] As at the great episcopal banquet in Gaza in 407: Mark the Deacon, *Vita Porphyrii* 92. I still accept, despite the difficulties, some kernel of authenticity in or behind this work.

as the visible, and could be, indeed, had to be, treated with a cool sobriety to discriminate between the saint and the sorcerer. If it is true that 'the easy-going unity of heaven and earth . . . which had passed on to them [Late Antique pagans] such a richness of well-tried means of access to another world' could no longer be taken for granted, it is also true that the Christian community was an exception in this 'crisis in the relations of heaven and earth'.[6] In its 'communion of saints', and perhaps only there, could men still find the daily experience of a 'city common to gods and men'.[7]

If we wish to escape from entanglement in the prejudices about early Christianity encouraged by the Reformation we shall do well to start with this neglected piece of the Christian creed. It expresses the fact that in the Church's early centuries, the holy was not a distant, remote world which had to be made accessible through the agency of intermediaries. Rather, it formed the permanent context of life, always and everywhere present, animating a community larger than the little group gathered around the altar, ready at any moment to manifest blessing or power. The divine was always *there*, like a huge electric charge waiting to break through the cloud, to be earthed by the Church's lightning-conductors – worship and the means provided for carrying it on: the altar, the church building, the community, or one or other of its members. Access to the holy was by means of the ordinary routines of worship in the gathered community, and through the ministrations of its properly authorised members. To understand the special place and the function of holy men in the Christian community, we have to see them as representative persons acting for the community rather than as individuals with privileged access to a reality they had to mediate to their fellows, a reality not accessible to the ordinary run of Christians.[8]

Thanks to Peter Brown's *The cult of the saints*, it can no longer be said that 'the full implications of what it meant to contemporaries to join Heaven and Earth at the grave of a dead human

---

[6] Quotations from Brown, *The making*, 99.
[7] *civitas communis deorum atque hominum*: Cicero, *De leg.* I.23; *De fin.* 3.64.
[8] It will be evident that I wish here to shift the emphasis on the 'holy man' or the 'friend of God' to be found in some of Peter Brown's writings. See Additional note to this chapter on the holy man and his charisma, below.

being has not been explored as fully as it deserves'.[9] His own book has done just that, and done it with the deep imaginative sympathy which allows the past to retrieve its own meaning from our trivialising prejudices. There is, however, one dimension of the Christian cult of the saint, his tomb and his relics, which is not caught in this net. This is the peculiarly close link between the Christian saint and his Church, especially the Church in its historically extended existence through time.

To understand the change in the nature of Christians' sense of their identity, it is necessary to come to grips with their sense of what it was that constituted them a group, and, in particular, a group enduring through time. If the saint's tomb is the place where Heaven and Earth meet, it is also the place where the Church's past and its present meet. For the prototype of the Christian saint was the martyr; and, as in due course holy men and women who had not died for Christ came to take their place alongside the martyrs, the figure of the martyr still remained the paradigm of the saint (see below, chs. 5 and 7). The cult of the saints, widely though it was to extend its range, had its undisputed origins in the cult of the martyrs. Christian enthusiasm for the cult and its phenomenal growth in the fourth century can only be understood when it is firmly anchored in the historical consciousness of post-Constantinian Christians. That there was a real caesura between the recent past and the present in their minds is not open to doubt; but it is hard to know how rapidly an awareness of it faded as the Great Persecution became an ever more remote memory, as they began to take for granted the recognition which their Church came to enjoy. It is certainly easy to underestimate their alienation from their own past, and the consequent need they felt to make that past, once more, their own. For them the age of the martyrs retained something of the flavour of a heroic age; but it was growing daily harder to recognise it as the heroic age of their own Church, increasingly wealthy, prestigious and privileged. Somehow they needed to reassure themselves that their Church was the heir of the persecuted Church of the martyrs. In this 'annexation of the past' the cult of the martyrs, as I shall show, played a crucial part.

[9] *The cult*, 1 (sic).

For the Roman Empire Constantine may have brought a reformation;[10] but to the Christians it was a revolution. (On all this see below, chs. 6–7.) Much of this book will be concerned with exploring some of the many ways in which Christians adjusted – sometimes over centuries – their view of themselves and of the world to this revolution. To take the measure of the cataclysmic change which the 'Constantinian revolution' meant for the Christian Church it is perhaps necessary to have experienced something of the guilt and the shame for the Christian Church's willingness to accept, to enjoy and to exploit it and to carry the burden of its 'establishment' throughout so much of the history of Europe.

Our exploration must begin with trying to understand the uncertainties that coming to terms with the Constantinian revolution inflicted on Christians of the late fourth century.

ADDITIONAL NOTE ON THE HOLY MAN AND HIS CHARISMA

The shift referred to in note 8 above is intended to be from the holy man's charisma understood primarily in terms of his power as an intermediary, towards charisma understood as representative. It should be noticed, however, that Brown seems himself to have initiated such a shift in the remarkable retrospect on his earlier work in his 'The saint as exemplar'. He invokes a conception of charisma which owes more to Edward Shils than to Max Weber: 'Charisma is seen less in terms of the extraordinary, set aside from society, so much as the convincing concentration in an event, in an institution, in a discipline or in a person of lingering senses of order and higher purpose' (p. 9). Compare Shils, who writes:

In principle, a belief recommended by a concentratedly and intensely charismatic individual has no past. Its authority depends on its immediately present contact with the source of its authority or validity. Its persuasiveness rests on the immediacy of the link to the source of the charisma which reception provides. This is what Max Weber meant when he spoke of charisma as being revolutionary and antitraditional. (*Centre and periphery*, 188)

For such a model of charisma Shils substitutes another, which need not be revolutionary and could be intensely traditionalist:

[10] See Barnes, 'The Constantinian reformation'.

25

the quality which is imputed to persons, actions, roles, institutions, symbols and material objects because of their presumed connection with 'ultimate', 'fundamental', 'vital', order-determining powers. This presumed connection with the ultimately 'serious' elements in the universe and in human life is seen as a quality or a state of being, manifested in the bearing or the demeanour and in the actions of individual persons; it is also seen as inhering in certain roles and collectivities. It can be perceived as existing in intense and concentrated form in particular institutions, roles and individuals – or strata of individuals. It can also be perceived as existing in attenuated or dispersed form. (*Ibid.* 127; cf. 256–7)

It is important, however, not to exaggerate the opposition between the two conceptions of charisma. Even in Max Weber's terms they can sometimes be found to overlap, as in the 'charisma of office'. Ascribed status may confer power which can appear as that of an intermediary. All I wish to assert is that Christian communities in Late Antiquity did not feel conscious of a need for individuals who could mediate privileged access to the divine to them. (It may, however, be the case that such a need appeared with the gradual 'magicisation' of much of the Church's sacramental and devotional life in the early Middle Ages; and that the role of the holy man underwent a corresponding change.)

For similar reasons I think that the antinomies enumerated by Jonathan Z. Smith (see especially his essay, 'The temple and the magician', pp. 187–9, but also underlying several other essays in the volume *Map is not territory*), miss some essential features of Christianity in the period here considered.

3

Conversion and uncertainty

The 'drift into a respectable Christianity'[1] which followed the
last great conflict between aristocratic pagan Romans and the
Christian régime of Theodosius I in the 390s had been preceded
by a long preparation. The attitude among Christians towards
pagan secular culture was by no means uniform, and had had
a chequered history. From the later second century Christians
had been moving fast – and not only in Alexandria – towards
an assimilation of secular culture. Even in the West, hostility
towards it is easily exaggerated. Tertullian's rhetorical flourish
must not be misunderstood: *quid Athenae Hierosolymis?* ('what
has Athens to do with Jerusalem?')[2] is evidence not so much of
a tip of a submerged iceberg of hostility to secular culture as of
a need felt to strengthen Christians' sense of their separate
identity at a time of rapid assimilation which seemed to pose a
threat to it. Since that time Christians had moved even further
towards accepting the values and the culture of their pagan
contemporaries.[3] In the later third century they were beginning
to penetrate every level of Roman society and to assimilate the
culture, life-styles and education of Roman townsmen. The
conversion of Constantine and the ensuing flow of imperial
favour did nothing to reverse this, but brought growing respectability, prestige and wealth. Around 350 very little separated a
Christian from his pagan counterpart in Roman society. Danc-
ing, rowdy celebrations, especially those connected with

[1] The phrase is Peter Brown's: see his 'Aspects of the christianisation', a pioneering
study to which I owe much. See also Plinval, *Pélage*, 391–2.
[2] *Praescr.* 7. See Markus, 'The problem of self-definition', 5–7.
[3] The following summary is based very largely on my discussion in 'Paganism'; see
also Markus, *Christianity*, 123–40.

cemeteries, the theatre, games, resorting to baths, a variety of magical practices and the like, often aroused suspicion and provoked denunciation by bishops; but they were part of that vast 'shared territory' which Christians inherited from the pagan past.[4] This accommodation to a received culture was not confined to 'popular religion'. Christianity was no longer a low-class religion. The conversion of the upper classes had begun; the growth in social mobility and the vast expansion of the civil service brought the conditions for the advancement of many Christians; pagan men of learning were showing increasing interest in Christianity. Long before his conversion to Christianity in 355 the pagan rhetorician Marius Victorinus was said to have assured the Milanese priest Simplicianus that he, too, was a Christian; when the priest refused to accept the claim until he saw him in his congregation Victorinus replied: 'do walls then make a Christian?'.[5]

Victorinus' mocking retort allows us to see how little divided the outlook of a cultivated, philosophical pagan around the middle of the fourth century from that of his Christian counterpart. The image of a society neatly divided into 'Christian' and 'pagan' is the creation of late fourth-century Christians, and has been too readily taken at its face value by modern historians. Unlike Christianity, with its growing world-wide cohesiveness, 'paganism' was a varied group of cults and observances. It never constituted a single coherent religious movement analogous to either Christianity or Judaism. It existed only in the minds, and, increasingly, the speech-habits, of Christians. In so far as a particular section of Roman paganism acquired some sort of homogeneous identity – as did that of some groups of Roman aristocrats in the last decades of the fourth century – it was a response to the growing self-confidence and assertiveness of a Christian establishment, whose threat to their traditions they were beginning to appreciate. The so-called 'pagan revival' of the fourth century is nothing more than the vague sense of apprehension in the minds of pagan aristocrats congealing, suddenly, into the discovery that Christianity was on the way to

[4] See MacMullen, *Christianizing the Roman Empire*, 74–85. I return to this theme in another context. For fuller discussion see below, ch. 8.
[5] Augustine, *Conf.* VIII.2.3–5. On Victorinus' conversion, see Hadot, *Marius Victorinus*, 52–8; 235–52, and Markus, 'Paganism', 7.

becoming more than a religious movement which had been favoured by a number of recent emperors; that it was becoming a threat to much of what their class had long stood for. A generation after Victorinus' conversion the position had changed. It now made sense to speak of 'paganism' and 'Christianity' as a division running through at least one section of Roman society.

This profound shift obtrudes in the manner Augustine tells the story of Marius Victorinus' conversion. More than forty years had passed. Victorinus' passage from neo-Platonism to Christianity had been a smooth progress along the route of a fourth-century intellectual. But Augustine, re-telling it, was unable to comprehend the ease with which the pagan rhetor had passed into the ranks of the Christians. His incomprehension made him represent Victorinus' paganism, anachronistically, in militantly anti-Christian terms, and his conversion to Christianity as a dramatic renunciation of his pagan past and a painful break with the circle of his aristocratic friends. This picture turns the realities of the 350s into a fiction which reflects the realities of the 390s. Another symptom of the novelty of the situation around 390 is Augustine's change of view about one of the most cultivated men of the following generation, Mallius Theodorus. It is the obverse of his report on Victorinus. In 386, as a freshly converted Christian of pronounced philosophical bent, Augustine had praised Theodorus in the most glowing of terms in one of the earliest of his surviving works, *On the blessed life*, dedicated to him. Theodorus was one of the circle of intellectuals at Milan through whom Augustine had come to know neo-Platonic writings. Like Augustine, he had retired from a distinguished public career into a 'dignified leisure' to pursue his intellectual activity. In 397, when Augustine was settling down to the writing of his *Confessions*, he had just returned to high office. In his *Confessions* Augustine's admiration had cooled: Theodorus was now a 'man inflated with monstrous pride'; and at the end of his life Augustine will blame himself for having praised him, forty years before, in terms that had been 'too extravagant, though written to a man both learned and Christian'.[6] His return to public life can

---

[6] *Retract.* I.2; *De beata vita* 1; and *Conf.* VII.9.13. On Mallius Theodorus, Courcelle, *Recherches*, 154–6.

hardly account for Augustine's disfavour, and – unlike some modern commentators – Augustine never thought Theodorus had compromised his Christian religion. Theodorus was Augustine's foil to Victorinus: whereas Victorinus had been (in Augustine's view) the sign of contradiction, Theodorus was the philosopher who failed to appreciate the need to take sides in the world which had come into being around both of them.

When Augustine was writing, nearly half a century after Victorinus' conversion, Christian and pagan were more sharply polarised in Western society. The conflicts of the age of Julian, and in the West in the 380s and 390s between the pagan aristo-cratic reaction and the Christian court, had put a question mark against the easy symbiosis of Christianity and pagan culture. The traditional literary culture of educated Romans had come to be inextricably linked with their traditional religion, and came to be drawn into the conflict. If this created the conditions for a literary and artistic revival which it is not absurd to call a 'Theodosian renaissance', it also made it harder for Christians to appropriate the culture which came to be seen as the preserve of pagan religion. The easy-going view that could be taken in the 350s of pagan society and secular culture was becoming questionable to the generation of Jerome and Augustine. Their misgivings about the 'fables of the poets, the polished and inflated lies of the orators and the garrulous hair-splitting of the philosophers'[7] made them resist the tide which was sweeping Christians towards a wholesale assimilation of the secular culture of their society.

Their hesitation, however, proved no lasting obstacle, and may, in any case, have been very largely confined to the Latin West. As far as we can judge, Julian's reign had made very little impact on the intellectual life of Eastern Christians. Even among Westerners, however, the rift that opened in the last quarter of the fourth century between pagans and Christians closed very quickly. If Jerome and Augustine belonged to the generation for which the conflicts of the 380s and the 390s were a recent memory, their successors could see them in a distant haze of romantic sentiment. About the time of Jerome's death in 420

[7] Augustine, *Ep.* 101.2; cf. Jerome *Ep.* 21.13.4

and Augustine's ten years later, the confrontations of the late
fourth century between Christians and pagans were receding
into the mists. In reality, the struggle was over, the battle lines
breaking up. Paganism was dying out fast in the senatorial
families, and the Church's view of mixed marriages was soften-
ing. From the 430s the popes were making common cause with
Roman aristocrats in a revival of classical architectural traditions,
and the Christian descendants of Symmachus and Nicomachus
Flavianus were carrying on their ancestors' literary activities,
securing the continuity of their secular interests. Mass-christianisation of Roman society from the highest level down was depriv-
ing Christians of a clearly felt and easily discernible identity in
their society.

The Christian literature of the period testifies to a loss of
confidence over the central problems: what was special about
the calling of a Christian; what was the nature of Christian
perfection? These anxieties were not confined to Western Christians, but it is among them that they were most widespread and
most acutely felt. Why this should be so would require a fuller
investigation of these questions as they affected the Greek-
speaking world than is possible here. Among the things that we
would have to take into account if we were to try to explain this
divergence would undoubtedly be the very much later and less
thorough christianisation of the Latin West. Western Christians
could not look back on a long period of cultural assimilation.
They were more isolated among their intellectual equals and
lacked confidence in their ability to absorb the culture of their
peers without the self-questioning which is so marked a feature
of Latin Christianity in the later fourth century. Moreover, in
the East the social conditions were lacking for the polarisation
of pagan and Christian public opinion around an old pagan
aristocracy faced with a Christian court and a growing body of
new families risen through service and patronage, and, increasingly, Christian in their allegiance. Whatever the reasons, the
comparative lack of confidence among the Christian elite in the
West – very much smaller and more isolated than in the East –
is plain to see. At a time when Greek Christians could condemn
Julian's pagan revival as a misguided attempt to introduce 'novel-
ties' against the established order, Western Christians were still

31

stigmatised as 'the foolish' (*stulti*) who reject the venerable traditions of the Roman past.[8] As a consequence, when the large-scale
christianisation of Roman society gathered pace in the later
fourth century, Western Christians were not well prepared
theologically or spiritually for the experience.

As early as in the time of Constantine we hear complaints
about people who conformed to the emperor's religion from
no profounder motives than opportunism. Did such Christians,
who had 'crept into the Church from sheer hypocrisy',[9] deserve
to be called 'Christians'? As the respectability of Christianity and
the advantages to be derived from adhering to it went on growing
through the fourth century, the problem of what constituted
real Christianity became more acute. It became truly pressing
in the generation which grew up at the end of the fourth century,
the first for which paganism had ceased to be a force still to be
reckoned with, and at a loss to discern its identity in a society
which was undergoing rapid mass-christianisation. The question
of what it was that defined a Christian had never been easy to
answer; but it had become especially troubling in an age when
Christianity seemed to have become so easy. How much of the
old life could be carried over into the new? To this question
there was no clear answer, or there were too many. In the last
years of his reign Constantine allowed the inhabitants of an
Umbrian town to honour him and his dynasty with celebrations
of theatrical spectacles and games and the dedication of a temple
in his honour 'so long as it would not be polluted by the lies of
any contagious superstition'.[10] The emperor thought, and his
successors continued to think, that a clear line could be drawn
to separate the traditional celebrations, the temple with the priest
attached to it, from the pagan religion with which such observances had traditionally been associated. The celebrations could
be disinfected, their significance secularised. But not all Christians were equally confident. Many thought – as did Augustine
– that it was harder to banish pagan idols from people's minds

---

[8] Julian's introduction of *ta nea*, against *ta palaia*: Gregory Nazianzen, *Or.* 5 (*PG*
35.713). *Stulti*: Ambrosiaster, *Q. vet. and novi test.* 7 (*CSEL* 50.306, 307); 15(*ibid.*, 310)
etc.; *Instituta maiorum, usus antiquior, mores parentum*: Symmachus, *Rel.* 3, *passim*.
[9] Eusebius, *Vita Const.* IV.54.
[10] *CIL* XI.5265. See below, ch. 8, pp. 109–10, esp. n. 7.

than from the temples.[11] The churches were filled with people who had come to them 'in their bodies' (*corporaliter*) and needed admonishing to abandon their former ways.[12] Similar worries brought John Chrysostom into collision with the court at Constantinople. Conformity with the fashions of high society was not easy to distinguish from idolatry.

There was a wide no-man's land between explicit pagan worship and uncompromising Christian rejection of all its trappings and associations. It left ample room for uncertainty. This uncertainty has led many modern students into the trap of imposing a clarity of outline on fourth-century Christianity which was alien to it. Thus the distinction sometimes made between 'Christians' and 'semi-' or 'paganised' Christians[13] pre-empts an answer to the question which worried many of Augustine's contemporaries, and short-circuits the effort to understand their worries. To speak of a poet such as Ausonius as a 'semi-Christian' is to apply a yard-stick to their religious commitment which might have seemed inappropriate to them or their contemporaries and is based on the historian's assumptions about what sort of a culture or life-style is to count as 'Christian'. Such assumptions have bedeviled much of the discussion of the religion of the Late Roman educated elites.[14] The same uncertainties spread all the way through the lower strata of Roman society. Augustine's pious mother, Monica, found her African devotional practices frowned on in Italy, as 'resembling the

---

[11] Augustine, *Ep.* 232.1. Cf. *Enarr. in Ps.* 98.2.

[12] Augustine, *De cat. rud.* 7.11.

[13] The classic discussion is Guignebert, 'Les demi-chrétiens', who is, however, careful to distinguish his 'demi-chrétiens' (identified as those 'indécis' who could not free themselves from 'l'hypnose du passé' (74)) from other half-christianised pagans; he appears to have in mind, principally, those who continued to participate in pagan religious rites (e.g. 90). Daut, 'Die "halben Christen"', deals with the educated classes. Most recently, Bonner, 'The extinction of paganism'. O'Donnell, 'The demise', defining 'paganism' more carefully, can write, without contradiction, that 'Paganism – the worship of false gods – was fast departing from the Roman scene; but paganism – a tolerant, even careless attitude toward worship in general – was a more tenacious institution' (p. 65).

[14] Helen Waddell, for instance, in the course of a splendid characterisation of Ausonius, remarked that 'for his religion, Christian or pagan are words too absolute: he will write of Easter or a Vigil of Venus with the same temperate pleasure' (*The wandering scholars*, 36). Cameron is more judicious on Claudian, whose case is certainly less clear: see *Poetry and propaganda*, 189–227. For a discussion of Rutilius Namatianus' religion, see Doblehoeffer, *R. Cl. Namatianus*, I.27–33.

superstitions of the heathen', and one of her son's first efforts as a newly ordained bishop was to try – with less than complete success – to purge the African Church of the baroque exuberance of its traditional celebration of the martyrs.[15] There was no clear line to be drawn between acceptable convention and sinful or even sacrilegious licence, and the boundaries were constantly shifting from place to place and year to year. The crucial uncertainty was precisely over this question. Is a man's religion to be determined by reference to his style of living, the manner in which he honours his dead relatives, his literary culture or even the kind of artistic decoration he has on his lamps or wedding presents? What is to count as the decisive criterion? There were no clear answers to these questions in the period we are considering, and we should not rashly assume an answer. There were many thoughtful and cultivated people whom these questions did not disturb; they worried others all the more for that.

One instinctive response was to turn to the ancient ascetic tradition embedded in their religion and to draw on its resources to help them define their identity in the emerging Romano-Christian culture. Ausonius is a good example of a poet whose Christianity the prejudices of modern readers have made questionable; but it is not likely that either he or his friends would have entertained any doubts about it. As a man of letters and a teacher of distinguished pupils in Gaul in the 360s and 370s, he had not been exposed to the malaise about secular culture which was to afflict so many of his younger contemporaries. The conventions of his literary art are apt to conceal rather than to display his inner convictions. We must not be misled by the ambivalence of his mode of expression: tolerant, easy-going, averse to all forms of fanaticism, his urbane, aristocratic culture is permeated with pagan motifs. But nowhere in his writings can the slightest opposition be discovered between the two components of his mind: his Christian beliefs and his classical culture, heavy with the weight of pagan imagery as it was.[16] He would

[15] See *Conf.* VI.2.2 and *Ep.* 22.3–4, and 29 on a moment of crisis in Hippo consequent on an attempt to prohibit rowdy banqueting in church, in line with what Ambrose had done at Milan, while Augustine was still a priest; and Saxer, *Morts, martyrs, reliques.*

[16] For a sane characterisation of Ausonius' religion – for all that it is conducted in the language of 'semi-Christianity' and 'syncretism' – see Riggi, 'Il cristianesimo'. See also Bowersock, 'Symmachus and Ausonius'.

have been baffled by Jerome's view that the conversion of a
Roman senator demanded a revolution – such as Jerome's friend
Pammachius had wrought – in his life-style and the conversion
of a man of letters in his style of writing.[17]

If no such thought disturbed Ausonius, it did disturb his
pupil, the Christian poet Paulinus, who thought it his duty to
make the Word of God the 'culture of his mind'[18] and could
speak of the discontinuity of the orators' and philosophers'
worlds, of the rich and the powerful, and that of the Christian,
in terms that would have satisfied even Jerome.[19] Ausonius and
Paulinus shared a literary culture, a way of life based on landed
wealth, and high status in Roman provincial society. They also
shared their religion, and a form of Christian spirituality in
which images of the Gospel blended with an ancient Latin
tradition reaching back to Virgil and beyond. They both saw
the life of the great senatorial estate in terms of a withdrawal
from the busy distractions of town life, as a *secessus in villam*,
the life of recollection and return to rural simplicity, close to
the soil and the rhythms of God's nature.[20] 'Your wilderness',
Paulinus once wrote to a correspondent, 'is not a desert, but a
place set apart [*non deserta sed secreta*], untouched by the world's
darkness and avoided by the waiting demons'.[21] In the seclusion
of domestic tranquillity Paulinus found a refuge from the turmoil of public life in 'rural repose' (*ruris otium*).[22] This
'spirituality of the great landowners' is a distinct undercurrent
in the ascetic literature of the fifth century.

Religion, culture and spirituality linked Ausonius and his
equally distinguished and even richer pupil Paulinus. What came
to divide the two friends was Paulinus' renunciation of his, and
his wife's, enormous wealth, and their joint decision to retire to
Nola in Italy to devote themselves there to the service of Saint
Felix at his rural shrine. The old Ausonius was baffled, wounded

[17] See Duval, 'Saint Cyprien et le roi de Ninivé'.
[18] *Ep.* 23.7. Walsh, *Letters*, vol. 2, 303 n. 51, suggests that the phrase may be a deliberate
christianisation of Cicero, *Tusc.* 2.13.
[19] *Ep.* 50. Walsh, 'Paulinus of Nola', however, rightly observes (p. 569) that Paulinus
does so 'consciously adapting the genre [here, that of the Epithalamion] to a Christian
message'.
[20] See Fontaine, 'Valeurs antiques'. Traces of such ideas are also to be found in Ambrose.
[21] *Ep.* 26.1.
[22] *Ep.* 5.4. See Frend, 'Paulinus of Nola'.

by what seemed to him friendship betrayed. In his affectionate and respectful defence of his decision – 'an agony of love and compassion'[23] – Paulinus seems to assume the Christianity of his beloved teacher and friend; but he sees it now across a deep gulf which has opened up between them. What divided them was the ascetic renunciation which so impressed men such as Ambrose, and Sulpicius Severus, writing of Paulinus only a year or two after his action.[24]

The step from Christianity to renunciation of wealth, prestige and the enjoyment of material goods, which seemed such a long one to Ausonius, was a short one for Paulinus. Like many other ascetics – Salvian (ch. 11, below) is a good example a generation later; his letter of explanation to his parents-in-law provides many parallels to Paulinus' apologia to Ausonius – Paulinus felt the need to withdraw from the comfortable Christianity which his place in society offered him. Asceticism was coming to be the mark of authentic Christianity in a society in which to be a Christian no longer needed to make any very visible difference in a man's life. In Paulinus' mind conversion to Christianity and to a life of monastic withdrawal were divided by only a hair's breadth. 'We must seek to resist', he wrote to a friend, Jovius, 'the Siren's seductive song, to avoid the lotus-eater's oblivion: for attachment to the outward loveliness of temporal things [*omnes rerum temporalium species*] makes men forget their common fatherland. Tossed on the sea of life, we must strip ourselves of encumbering possessions on the plank of Christ's cross.'[25] The terms in which he pictured conversion to Christianity come very close to the classic language of ascetic detachment and renunciation. They seem actually to echo words used by Jerome in a letter to Paulinus in praise of the ascetic life.[26] For all the ascetic colouring in which Paulinus presents Christianity in this letter, however, what is striking is that in the end he refuses to identify the two, and goes out of his way to assure Jovius that

---

[23] Waddell, *The wandering scholars*, 39, writing of *Carmen* 11. On the relationship see, most recently, Van Dam, *Leadership and community*, 303–9.
[24] Ambrose, *Ep.* 58.1; Sulpicius Severus, *Vita Mart.* 25.4, and the commentary by Fontaine, *Vie*, vol. 3, 1056–60. See Lienhard, *Paulinus of Nola*, 23; 29 on Paulinus' fame.
[25] *Ep.* 16.7–8. On the correspondence with Jovius, see Erdt, *Christentum*, 11–12, who regards Jovius' religious allegiance as uncertain.
[26] *Ep.* 58.2.

God does not ask him and his family to renounce their wealth, but rather to acknowledge that it is He who bestowed it on them.[27]

More often, however, this clarity eluded Paulinus. He had no firm and settled consciousness of a need to keep the Christian and the ascetic life distinct. Another correspondent, Crispinianus, was exhorted to exchange the life of a soldier of Caesar for that of a soldier of Christ. It is significant that Paulinus' language gives us no certainty as to whether Crispinianus was a pagan being urged to become a Christian, a catechumen awaiting baptism and full entry into the Christian life, or a baptised Christian being exhorted to undertake the ascetic life. He is reported to be a Christian 'in aspiration, not in his action' (*in uoto potius quam in opere*), a phrase which leaves all possibilities open, and Paulinus is urging him to follow his own example and to embrace a life of ascetic renunciation. It seems likeliest that Paulinus is summoning his correspondent to Christian baptism, but that in doing so is telescoping the two steps of becoming a Christian and becoming an ascetic.[28] This is characteristic of his view of Christianity: true Christianity, for Paulinus, is apt to melt into asceticism. He had kept their distinctness in mind writing to Jovius; but he forgot it when writing to Crispinianus, who is not offered the option of conversion without asceticism and is left no 'middle ground'. On another occasion Paulinus praised the achievement of a missionary bishop in Rouen: his preaching had multiplied the virgins and widows and the married couples who have renounced marital life.[29] 'Conversion', for Paulinus, could be either to Christianity or to the ascetic state. The two things were so close that he did not always feel a need to distinguish them. The cost of establishing a clearer Christian identity than was readily available in Paulinus' world was this confusion of Christianity with asceticism.

This ambiguity is as old as Christianity itself. The threads which went into the idea of the fully Christian life had coalesced

---

[27] *Ep.* 16.9. This crucial concession seems not to have been noticed by Lienhard, *Paulinus of Nola*, 137. For a corresponding distinction between the married state and that of virgins and widows, see *Ep.* 41.2.

[28] See *Ep.* 25 and 25*, with the excellent commentary by Lienhard, *Paulinus of Nola*, 44–7. Lienhard notes that *Ep.* 25* contains several allusions to a baptismal liturgy and creed, and suggests that Crispinianus is a catechumen or sympathiser contemplating baptism. Compare *Ep.* 7.3 and 8 (Licentius) with 16.1 (Jovius).

[29] *Ep.* 18.5.

over the centuries, and still formed a bundle; but in Paulinus' time the threads were beginning to come apart rather easily. Paulinus, Jerome and many of their contemporaries, were apt to see authentic Christianity in terms of some form of ascetic renunciation. The vanishing of the lines which marked out Christians in their society helped to reinforce the ancient appeal of monastic withdrawal and ascetic self-denial. Asceticism helped Paulinus and others to define an authentic Christian identity in a world in which ordinary Christianity seemed far from authentic to many. But alongside the growing appeal of asceticism, especially among upper-class Romans in Italy and Gaul, voices were beginning to be heard attacking the supremacy of asceticism. Jerome may have been not the most tactful advocate of the ascetic life; but even Paulinus met with some hostility in Rome, apparently from suspicion of his ascetic spirituality.[30] The careers of Priscillian and Saint Martin, in the preceding decades, provide ample evidence of the coolness that many of the clergy felt towards ascetics. Priscillian's esoteric brand of spirituality laid him open to accusations of heresy; and Martin's opposition to the condemnation of Priscillian by a secular tribunal made him suspect of being a sympathiser. Though Priscillian was, evidently, no Manichee,[31] the label was readily attached to him, as it was often applied to ascetics by their enemies.[32] St Martin's disciple and biographer, Sulpicius Severus, needed to take great care in commending Martin's asceticism to a generation deeply divided on this question.[33]

Opposition to asceticism had an ancestry almost as ancient as did asceticism. Differences of opinion on continence erupted as early as the second century.[34] At the Council of Nicaea the aged Paphnutius, who had himself suffered for his faith, defended the ideal of Christian marriage with the assertion that a married man's intercourse with his wife deserved the name of chastity.[35] It was in Jerome's time that this opposition swelled into protest

[30] *Ep.* 5.14.
[31] See Chadwick, *Priscillian*, 70–2, 98.
[32] E.g. Jerome, *Ep.* 22.13; *Adv. Iov.* 1.3. See below, ch. 4, n. 14.
[33] See Stancliffe, *St. Martin*, 289–312.
[34] See Eusebius, *HE* IV.32.7–8.
[35] See Socrates, *HE* I.11.

against the growing gap between the religion of the ordinary Christian and that of the ascetic elite. Asceticism and virginity came under repeated attack, not least by some of Jerome's enemies. In 383 one Helvidius affirmed the equal value of marriage and chastity. In 403 another target of Jerome's invective, Vigilantius, turned in revulsion from asceticism, perhaps partly as a result of what he had seen of it in the Holy Land in 395, when he visited, among others, Jerome.[36] These were no isolated voices. The most interesting among the protesters was Jovinian, turned into the 'first Protestant' by the partisan historiography of the sixteenth century. We have little information about him apart from what can be discerned behind Jerome's vulgar abuse. Jerome made fun of the well-washed, well-groomed, polished and well-fed figure, 'the Epicurus of the Christians', who rejected the asceticism Jerome had espoused.

Jovinian's attack on virginity and asceticism raised two questions which were not yet clearly distinguished. His mode of conduct questioned the extent to which asceticism was a necessary part of the monastic vocation. Jovinian was a monk, and, though he denounced ascetic practices and turned his back on his previously ascetic mode of life, he apparently continued to be celibate and to think of himself as a monk. This was a crucial moment in the history of monasticism, a time when monastic institutions were crystallising into accepted and recognisable forms. For Jerome, as for Paulinus, to be a monk was to be distinguishable by one's dress, mode of life, food and outward appearance. Paulinus, having decided on a life of monastic withdrawal, had turned to the expert, Jerome, for advice on how he should conduct himself and what pattern of life he should adopt.[37] Neither of them would have taken the view made popular in the Middle Ages, that it is not the habit that makes the monk. Dress, diet and appearance counted for much and in questioning this, Jovinian raised a fundamental

---

[36] See Stancliffe, *St. Martin*, 53, 301–9 for the possibility that the Vigilantius who carried Paulinus' letter to Jerome in 395 is identical with the carrier of Sulpicius Severus' first letter to Paulinus in 396 and a member, until c. 403, of Sulpicius' community at Primuliacum.

[37] See Jerome, *Ep.* 58, esp. para. 5. Cf. Paulinus, *Ep.* 22.2. On the whole theme, see Lienhard, *Paulinus of Nola*, 58–81, and Kelly, *Jerome*, 192.

question about the institution at a decisive moment in its evolution in Western Europe. We shall have to return to the problem he raised for monasticism (below, ch. 5).

The other question raised by Jovinian was, however, more fundamental: how much renunciation did being a Christian involve? How necessary, indeed, was asceticism to the Christian life at all? This is the challenge which made him notorious in Jerome's time. What Helvidius, Jovinian, Vigilantius and others were protesting against, often in confused ways, was the widening gap between what Norman Baynes called the 'two standards': 'one for the ordinary Christian living his life in the work-a-day world and the other standard for those who were haunted by the words of Christ: "if thou wouldst be perfect . . .".'.[38] Jovinian wanted to reduce the part played by this double standard in the Church of his day. If there were ascetics in the Christian community, they were not to be a spiritual elite. 'Be not proud', he said to virgins: 'you are members of the same Church as the married.'[39] The huge virginity of the Church overshadowed the chastity of the individual virgin, and dwarfed her eminence over the ordinary faithful Christian into insignificance.

The most articulate voice to raise the question of what 'conversion' meant in the conditions of around 400 was that of Pelagius. Pelagius did not in fact oppose the ideal of virginity, and may not have made his début in Rome – as has been thought – by rallying to the defence of marriage against Jerome's intemperate attack.[40] Jerome's advocacy of virginity and asceticism had, however, alienated public opinion in Rome; even some of his friends had been embarrassed. Pelagius was moving in circles of devout Christians, often aristocratic women, ascetics, virgins and widows – côteries of what Jerome, with ill-aimed sarcasm, called 'little women'.[41] It is among such groups that Jerome had first achieved notoriety in Rome. Augustine, Ambrose, and indeed almost every churchman, had extensive contacts with

---

[38] 'The thought-world of East Rome', 26. For a classic statement of the distinction, Eusebius, *Dem. Ev.* I.8. See now Brown, *The body*, especially the superb summary of this development, pp. 204–9.
[39] Jerome, *Adv. Iov.* I.7 (*PL* 23.228).
[40] The identification of the young monk of Jerome's *Ep.* 50, most convincingly by Evans, *Pelagius*, 31–7, has been undermined by Duval, 'Pélage'.
[41] *mulierculae*: *Ep.* 50.3; 133.4. Cf. *Adv. Iov.* II.36 on Jovinian. On Jerome's propensity to use the word for the audience of 'heretics', Duval, 'Pélage', 535–6.

members of the great families. The ramifications of these groups and their conflicts spread as far afield as the monastic establishments of the Holy Land,[42] into Gaul and Spain, and, especially after the Gothic sack of Rome in 410, into Sicily and North Africa, where many of the Roman nobility flocked for safety. Links of friendship, patronage, the giving and receiving of spiritual guidance, as well as, sometimes, suspicion and conflict, created a web of complex threads constituting what a recent scholar has called this international 'ascetic brotherhood'.[43] It is this brotherhood that was to be rent by the teaching of Pelagius.

Like Jovinian before him, Pelagius rejected the 'double standard' of the ordinary Christian and the ascetic elite. Unlike Jovinian, he sought to close the gap between the two not by rehabilitating 'ordinary' Christianity, but by demanding perfection of all, virgin or married, lay or cleric.[44] In 413 he wrote at length to a teenage girl, Demetrias, member of one of the foremost aristocratic families of whom he had become a family friend and mentor. Among the writings we can confidently assign to Pelagius, it is this letter that best reveals the mainspring of his thought. Demetrias had broken off her engagement for a marriage, arranged, as were most such marriages, with an eye to political advantage and social propriety, and vowed herself to virginity. Her mother and grandmother called in the experts: Jerome and Pelagius. Both rose to the occasion. Jerome wrote what has been described as 'one of his most impressive literary productions';[45] Pelagius' letter – which Jerome had seen and made use of in composing his own[46] – is the finest of his spiritual manifestos. Pelagius knew he was addressing a member not only of a leading aristocratic family, but also of a spiritual elite: 'she is not content to live according to the common manner, in mediocrity ... She wants her form of life [*conversationem*] to be no less admirable than her conversion; noble in the world, she

---

[42] Hunt, *Holy Land pilgrimage*, 155–248.
[43] Stancliffe, *St. Martin*, 48f.
[44] There is now a vast literature. I owe most to Evans, *Pelagius*; Brown, 'Pelagius and his supporters' and 'The patrons of Pelagius'; also his *Augustine*, 340–52. Bonner, *Augustine and modern research* is far more than a survey of the *status quaestionis*, though it does contain an excellent one. On attributions, see now Nuvolone, 'Pélage'.
[45] See Kelly, *Jerome*, 312 on Jerome's *Ep.* 130.
[46] *Ibid.* 313.

wants to be nobler with God.'[47] He was addressing no ordinary
Christian, and he went on to underscore the difference between
Christians who carry out what is commanded and those who do
more: who renounce, as counselled in the Gospel (Matthew
19.21), what the law permits.[48]

And yet, Pelagius insisted, there was 'one law for all'. 'I have
said and I will repeat', he wrote to Demetrias, 'in the matter of
righteousness we all have the same obligations: virgins, widows
or married women, men of high, middle or low class, are equally
bidden to obey the commandments'.[49] All alike are called to
fulfil the demands of the law of charity, and to aspire to Christian
perfection. Ascetic renunciation became secondary, or
irrelevant. On virginity and marriage Pelagius and his followers
came to take a variety of views. Some later Pelagian writers
would take an attitude towards marriage much more like
Jerome's than Pelagius', and held that 'all Christians of serious
intent will clearly see themselves summoned to the life of continence'.[50] This was perhaps to take Pelagius' demand for perfection to its furthest limit, yet also to perpetuate that 'double
standard' which disturbed Pelagius and Jovinian, among others.
Pelagius himself, in calling for perfection from all, whether
married or celibate, seems rather to have equated the two states,
disregarded their distinctness and treated them as equally imperfect and equally capable of being perfected. Perfection was
obligatory for all who claimed to be Christians, not for a chosen
few. The foundation of his spirituality, as he says in his letter
to Demetrias, is that 'in order to embark on a more perfect life,
the goodness of nature must be the more fully asserted, lest the
soul should be sluggish or negligent in the pursuit of virtue,
underestimating its capabilities'.[51] What Pelagius attacked was
the propensity of Christians to set their moral sights lower than
the powers given them by God require. We are not to protest
to the Lord, 'in the manner of proud and worthless servants,

---

[47] *Ep. ad Dem.* 1 (*PL* 30.16A). Cf. Augustine, *Ep.* 150, 188.1 and the anonymous *Epistola
ad Demetriadem*, 1. The *topos* of secular and spiritual nobility is frequent; e.g. applied
to the elder Melania by Paulinus, *Ep.* 29.6–7.
[48] *Ep. ad Dem.* 9 (*PL* 30.24D).
[49] *Ep. ad Dem.* 10 (*PL* 30.25A–B). Cf. *De div.*, 6.3 (*PLS* 1.1387).
[50] Evans, *Pelagius*, 38–42. On Pelagius' own views, see Tibiletti, 'Teologia pelagiana'.
[51] *Ep. ad Dem.* 2 (*PL* 30.16D).

"it is too hard, it is arduous, we cannot do it, we are only human, encircled by the weakness of the flesh!" What blind insanity, what profane pride: to charge the all-knowing God with a two-fold ignorance – with not knowing what he has made and not knowing what he has commanded.'[52] We can understand why Pelagius was impatient with the apparent passivity of Augustine's prayer in the tenth book of his *Confessions*: 'Command what you will and give what you command'.[53]

Pelagianism was an onslaught on the languid, second-rate Christianity which blurred the line between a conventional Christian and the ordinary, pagan Roman. 'God wished his people to be holy and free from all injustice and iniquity. He wished it to be so, so devout, so pure, so immaculate, so innocent, that the heathen might find nothing to revile in it'; a Christian whose conduct is indistinguishable (*aequalis*) from a pagan's is the beginning of blasphemy. 'There is no name without a corresponding reality ... A Christian is one who is so not in name only, but in action.' *Non nomine sed opere* – 'not in name but in action' is the ceaseless refrain of a Pelagian treatise on the Christian Life.[54] Baptism, a holy anointing, must be followed by holy conduct (*conversatio*).[55] For Pelagius and his followers Christianity is a demand for moral ardour and unceasing struggle with inertia: 'it is no better to do nothing than to do wickedly'.[56]

In the crisis of identity which afflicted Western Christians in this time of mass-christianisation of Roman society Pelagius' brand of puritanic revivalism offered a means of establishing one's Christian identity. Pelagius wanted his Christians to be as clearly defined and as distinct a group in society as the ascetics were in the Christian Church. His austere call for perfection offered his generation the most radical answer to the perplexity which haunted it: what is it to be a Christian? The wholesale evangelical reform Pelagius called for was a high price to pay; and Augustinian theology could offer an alternative.

---

[52] *Ep. ad Dem.* 16 (*PL* 30.30C–D).
[53] *Conf.* X.29.40; 31.45; 37.60; *De dono pers.* 20.53. It seems probable that Pelagius was not alone in this abhorrence: see Marrou, 'Les attaches', 470–2.
[54] *De vita chr.* 9. On the authorship, see Evans, 'Pelagius', and Liebeschuetz, 'Pelagian evidence'.
[55] *De vita chr.* 1; cf. 11, 14.
[56] *Ibid.* 10.

4

Augustine: a defence of Christian mediocrity

Long before the conflict with Pelagius in the years after 411, Augustine and the African Church had been touched by the anxieties of the European churches. In 401 Augustine recalled Jovinian's denial that virginity and celibacy had any superiority over the married state. The Church 'over there', in Italy, Augustine tells us, resisted his 'monstrous teachings' with utter faith and determination (*fidelissime et fortissime*); but an undercurrent of whisperings still remained to be dealt with.[1] Augustine therefore wrote a book, *On the good of marriage*. It is a significant title; and Augustine gives us the explanation why his answer to Jovinian's attack on the superiority of virginity took the form of a defence – not, as might be expected, of virginity – but of the married state. Such a treatise was necessary, Augustine says, because it was now being alleged that it was impossible to answer Jovinian without disparaging marriage.[2] The memory of Jerome's notorious and ill-fated attack on Jovinian was fresh in Augustine's mind. In 415, writing to Jerome, Augustine repeatedly praised Jerome's 'splendid treatise' against Jovinian;[3] but on each occasion he makes it clear that what he has in mind is Jerome's refutation of Jovinian's theses on the equality of sins and on original sin. He is coolly silent on Jerome's views on marriage.[4] Augustine's rehabilitation of the married state is a thinly veiled answer to Jerome's denigration (*vituperatio*) of it: his covert work *Against Jerome*.

---

[1] *Retract.* II.22.1.
[2] *Ibid.* Cf. *De nupt. et conc.* II.23.38.
[3] See *Ep.* 166.3.6, 7.21; 167.2.4, 3.10.
[4] *Retract.* II.45.

This work was accompanied by another, 'as was to be expected',[5] entitled *On holy virginity*. The two treatises between them amount to a re-statement of a central, moderate and traditional view on the two callings: marriage is good, virginity is better;[6] let the continent and the virgin not give themselves airs and despise the married; but let nobody place the two states on the same level. In words very similar to Pelagius', Augustine says that it is an error 'either to equate marriage with virginity or to condemn it'.[7] The twin treatises in effect re-assert, albeit in a humane and mitigated form, the differentiation which had given such anxiety to many of Augustine's contemporaries, between the ordinary Christian and an ascetic elite. Augustine here assumes the validity of this distinction, but tries to minimise the gap between the two. Both sorts of faithful belong within the one Church and both are called to serve God in faith and love. All who seek to follow the Lord are within his flock: 'and the married are certainly able to follow His footsteps [*vestigia*], even if their feet do not fit perfectly into the footprints, yet following the same path'.[8] This is Augustine's re-affirmation of the central Christian tradition, and it is significantly closer to Pelagius' and to Jovinian's than to Jerome's views on the subject.

This pair of treatises, however, stand on the threshold of a momentous change of direction. Already uncertain about some crucial points at the time of writing, Augustine was launched, within a few months of writing them, on a process of re-thinking which was to cause an upheaval in the whole intellectual landscape of his own mind and to leave its mark on the mind of Western Christendom. To understand this change of direction we need to place it firmly in the context of Augustine's spiritual pilgrimage, the intellectual restlessness and the ceaseless growth and development of his thought which mark him out among European thinkers.

---

[5] *Retract.* II.23.
[6] *De bono con.* 8.8; 9.9; 23.28; *De virg.* 18.
[7] *De virg.* 19: *vel aequare ... vel damnare* ... Cf. Pelagius, *Ep. ad Celantiam* 28 (*PL* 22.1217): *Apostolicae doctrinae regula nec cum Ioviniano aequat continentiae opera nuptiarum, nec cum Manichaeo coniugia condemnat.* On Jovinian see above, ch. 3, pp. 39–40 and below, ch. 5, n. 49.
[8] *De virg.* 28.

No reader of his *Confessions* can mistake the fiercely ascetic momentum behind Augustine's conversion to Christianity.[9] Ambrose's preaching had prepared the ground. Augustine's call to decision came to him, finally, in the form of a summons to break with his former life, in the manner of Saint Antony: 'You converted me to Yourself, so that I no longer sought a wife, nor any of this world's promise.' Of the things which have sometimes been suspected of having predisposed his mind towards ascetic renunciation Manichaean dualism – which could furnish a warrant for ascetic renunciation – can be ruled out. Conversion liberated Augustine from his lingering attachment to Manicheism.[10] The most powerful impulse behind Augustine's break with the religion of the followers of Mani, if we are to judge, as we must, by his account in the *Confessions*, was that the solution which it offered to the problem of evil was, in the last resort, unacceptable. Its image of the world as the product of two forces locked in permanent conflict, one good, the other evil, gave too easy an explanation of the inner conflicts within the personality. The self was seen as a spark of the world of light trapped within a world of darkness; man was a stage on which the cosmic warfare of the two principles was being played out, rather than an agent responsible for his own actions. Manichaean doctrine allowed the impersonal forces of darkness to be disowned as alien to the real self. Not long before his conversion to Christianity, Augustine says 'I still held the view that it was not we that sinned, but some other nature sinning in us ... I very much preferred to excuse myself and accuse some other thing that was in me but was not I.'[11] It was listening to Ambrose's preaching in Milan in the spring of 386 that Augustine discovered that 'in truth, however, I was one whole: it was impiety that divided me against myself'.[12] His inner reality is no longer a spark of the light struggling with and quenched by an alien force hostile to it. His

---

[9] Esp. VIII.6.13–12.30. The quotation is from the end of this section. On the importance of Ambrose, see Madec, *Saint Ambroise et la philosophie*.

[10] There is a vast literature. I have elaborated my view in *Conversion*, where some references are given. On the convergence of Christian and Manichaean asceticism, Lieu, *Manichaeism*, 143–9.

[11] *Conf.* V.10.18; cf. VII.3.5.

[12] *Ibid.* On the Ambrosian background, see Courcelle, *Recherches*, 100.

struggles are now within his self: 'It was myself', Augustine observes of his divided mind, unable to come to a decision, 'myself I was dissipated in.'[13] Many years later Augustine was to be accused of having remained a Manichee at heart. Such accusations were part of the standard vocabulary of denigration, frequently hurled especially at ascetics and their defenders.[14] But, whatever the grounds of Augustine's ascetic inclinations, lingering addiction to a dualism of the Manichaean type is not among them.

Augustine's conversion was accompanied by, and in part achieved through, his prior conversion to the philosophical tradition of Platonism as this was being interpreted among the avant-garde intellectuals of Milan in the 380s. This, too, pointed towards an ascetic life-style. In Ambrose's preaching in Milan Augustine discovered a Christianity deeply penetrated by neo-Platonic ideas. The step from the intellectual universe of 'the Platonists' to that of Saint Paul and the Fourth Gospel, as Augustine describes it in the seventh and eighth books of his *Confessions*, was a short one. The two sets of concepts fused into a single image in his mind. As a Christian Platonist, Augustine saw the world as an ordered hierarchy of beings, descending from their transcendent source through all the levels of spirit and body down to the lowest realms of inanimate matter. The human soul had to follow this order in reverse to ascend to its goal and reach its true home, where lay its origin. The body had its due place in the hierarchically ordered cosmos; its purpose was to enable the work of intellect – rational order – to be expressed in the lower reaches of the hierarchy. Far from being an object of loathing and hatred, it was an instrument of – though it could

---

[13] *Conf.* VIII.10.22.
[14] E.g. by Jovinian against Jerome: see Jerome, *Adv. Iov.* I.5; Augustine, *De nupt. et conc.* II.23.38: Jovinian had accused Catholics of taking the Manichees' side in exalting virginity at the expense of marriage. If Jovinian had attacked Ambrose personally on these grounds, as Augustine suggests (*ibid.* II.5.15 and *Op. imp.* IV.122), then Ambrose's counter-accusation of Jovinian and his supporters (*Ep.* 42.13) would be explicable as having only retaliatory significance. See now Clark, 'Heresy, asceticism, Adam and Eve', 359. On the tendency for 'Manichee' to become a denigratory *topos*, see Jerome, *Ep.* 22.13; Chadwick, *Priscillian*, 146, n. 2; for a fascinating parallel in medieval China, Lieu, *Manichaeism*, 222–3. Van Dam, *Leadership and community*, 78–114, raises more questions than it answers. On the necessary discriminations in the use of the terms, see Augustine, *De nupt. et conc.* II.3.9, *Op. imp.* III.170, etc.

also become an obstacle to – man's progress towards his goal, through virtue and wisdom, to his true fulfilment. Although the differences between Gnostic, Manichaean, neo-Platonic and Christian valuations of the body and of the material world were profound,[15] the ascetic morality towards which their doctrines pointed could in practice look very much alike. Augustine's ascetic ideas certainly show no Manichaean background. His distrust of sensual delight, of music, of sweet scents,[16] springs not from loathing but from a sharp sensitiveness to their beauty and their power, combined with a no less sharp concern not to allow them to run away with reason and judgement. This is why men need intellectual and moral effort and training in order to make right use of material things. Given a mind freed from slavery to sensuality by reason, 'order is that which, if we follow it in our lives, leads to God'.[17]

This moral discipline, like that enjoined by Diotima in Plato's *Symposium,* implied a certain degree of asceticism. The mind must be free of the fetters of subjection to its body and to the sphere of material concerns; rather, it must subject them to rational order. Too close an attachment to material things tends to deprive the mind of its ability to 'return to itself', to deprive it of its freedom to control, and to subject it to the power of the things 'to which it is stuck by the glue of attachment'.[18] 'To be caught up in perverse delights is to be estranged from our heavenly home [*alienaremur a patria*] whose delight alone is true happiness.'[19] Both in the philosophical tradition of Platonism and in the Christianity of the Cappadocian Fathers, of Ambrose and of Augustine, among many others, an ascetic morality of detachment is a means of achieving inner freedom, power over the body and its desires. Augustine was able to understand the

[15] The best discussions I know are a number of studies by A. H. Armstrong. See his 'The self-definition'; 'Gnosis' (especially the conclusion); 'Man in the Cosmos', and, above all, 'Neoplatonic valuations', which stresses the restraint that Platonism exercised on 'the tendency to a sometimes positively frenzied dislike of this world and of the body which seems to have curiously deep roots in the religion of the incarnation' (p. 38). On Plotinus, see also Armstrong's 'Plotinus', 250–63.

[16] E.g. *Conf.* X.33.49–50; 32.48.

[17] *De ord.* I.9.27. Cf. Rief, *Der Ordobegriff.*

[18] *De Trin.* X.5.7.

[19] *De doctr. christ.* I.4.4; cf. *De vera rel.* 54.104. For a discussion of these ideas, see Markus, 'Alienatio'.

Pauline command 'Do not be conformed to this world' (Rom. 12.2) without strain in this context.[20]

For some years Augustine's neo-Platonically inspired philosophical views and his ascetically coloured Christianity blended harmoniously in his mind. But around 400, when he was completing his *Confessions* and about to write the twin treatises on marriage and on virginity, a huge shift in his intellectual perspective was already well on its way.[21] His 'epistemological crisis' (I borrow the phrase from Alasdair MacIntyre; see below, ch. 14, p. 224) did not break upon him at the time of his conversion to Christianity, but some nine or ten years later. He re-read Saint Paul in the mid-390s, and his previous confidence in man's rational and moral capabilities vanished. He could not renounce his faith in some kind of order in God's world; but it was now no longer an order that could be so readily taken for granted, nor one which a well-trained and educated mind could be sure of discovering, or a disciplined will follow in its free decisions. For, as Saint Paul had written, 'inscrutable are His judgements and his ways are past searching out' (Rom. 11.33).[22] Augustine's belief that the final goal of human striving was attainable by human effort through rational resources was shattered. Salvation was now no longer an ordered progression towards a distant goal, but a sustained miracle of divine initiative. Human expertise, far from being a means of achieving it, was the chief among the obstacles man can place in its way. What had earlier seemed a short step from the universe of the 'Platonists' to that of Saint Paul, was now revealed to Augustine as a step across an abyss that had opened at his feet.

It was an intellectual landslide, and it transformed the whole configuration of Augustine's thought. Some old fragments survived, or re-appeared charged with a new meaning, but much had to be thought out anew, including the problems of sin and salvation. Saint Paul had given Augustine a sense of the power of sin in men's lives and of man's powerlessness to free himself

---

[20] *De Trin.* XI.5.8. A finely balanced statement of Augustine's view of the material world is given by Marrou, *The Resurrection.*

[21] On what follows see my discussion in *Conversion*, which I here condense. The most important discussions: Cranz, 'The development'; Fredriksen, *Augustine on Romans*, and her 'Paul and Augustine'.

[22] Cited in *De div. quaest. ad Simpl.* I.ii.22.

of its sway without God's grace. To Augustine sin now appeared no longer as a breach of right order or a surrender of reason to passion. At bottom, sin was a retreat into privacy. In 401 Augustine embarked on the vast project of a literal commentary on Genesis, where he set about to work out many of the ideas which underlay his later works. Among the questions his text made him face those arising from Adam's fall took a large share of his attention. He now searched for the roots of human sin in man's liability to close in on himself. His description of Adam's sin, and of sin in general, is punctuated by phrases such as 'pleasing oneself', 'to live according to oneself, for oneself' (*secundum se vivere, sibi placere*). Sin is seen as a withdrawal into a 'privacy' which is a deprivation. By it all community is fatally ruptured: man's community with God, community with his fellow-men, with his own self. It is in such terms that Augustine tends henceforth to portray pride, the archetypal and fontal sin, rather than in terms of violation of the right rational order.[23] This re-direction of his thought, begun in his meditation on the nature of Adam's fall as told in Genesis, underlies his vast panorama of the history of human pride which is the final section (beginning with book XIV) of his *City of God*.

By the time that Augustine encountered Pelagius and took stock of the nature of his teaching in the years following 411, the elements of the theology he would deploy against Pelagius were already to hand. Their germs had been sown in his reading of Saint Paul and matured in his meditating the story of Adam's creation and fall. In Pelagius' views Augustine came to recognise something of his own past: the past on which he had turned his back in the 390s. Moreover, he now had another long intellectual preparation behind him: his debate with Donatism, sustained over some two decades. When he received the reports of Pelagius' views as he had expounded them at the Synod of Diospolis, Augustine seized on the affinity he detected between Pelagian and Donatist teaching: both asserted belief in a pure Church, 'without spot or wrinkle'.[24] With such a claim Augustine

---

[23] *De Gen. ad litt.* XI.15.19–20; *De civ. Dei* XIV.5, 13.1; *Enarr. in Ps.* 131.5–7, etc.
[24] *De gest. Pel.* 12.27. On this see Evans, *One and holy*, 95–7, who exaggerates slightly the extent to which Augustine had already laid down in his anti-Donatist writings the basic lines of his reply to Pelagian perfectionism.

felt at home; it went to the heart of his views on the meaning of being a Christian, and he had long since learnt how to deal with it. The Donatists had made their own an older African tradition of thought about the Church as a pure, gathered elite, separated from the world. They had upheld the principle of a pure, unblemished Church in sacramental terms. They insisted on the necessity of an episcopate unpolluted by the crime of *traditio*, of compromise with the persecutor in the time of trial, and on the need for re-baptism for those entering their communion from outside. Pelagius and his followers called for *integri Christiani*, for 'authentic Christians'. Their overriding demand for holiness in the baptised Christian transposed the Donatist call for an authentic Church endowed with the 'fullness of the sacraments, unspotted wholeness'[25] into individual, moral rather than ecclesial terms. Donatism and Pelagianism 'both contended for a pure Church, the one by external separation, the other by internal migration'.[26]

Augustine was quick to see the affinities, and he diagnosed the roots of the two maladies in the same fundamental error: the impatient, peremptory anticipation here and now, before the time, of the Church's eschatological purity. Augustine rejected both versions of perfectionism with the passionate intensity of a man who had once come close to something akin to them. He had rejected Manichaean asceticism not only as an insult to the value of created nature, but because it implied too radical a dichotomy between the ordinary believer and a spiritual elite.[27] As a young Christian he had spoken with condescension of ordinary Catholics and even of uneducated clergy;[28] pastoral responsibility brought him a deepened sense of community with the half-educated, the superstitious and the sensual Christians of Hippo, and a poignant remorse for his brash *hauteur*.[29] His answer to both Donatist and Pelagian perfectionism was the same. It was the answer he had learnt from the dissident Donatist theologian Tyconius: the Church here on earth is a mixed body in which the holy rub shoulders with the wicked. The wheat

---

[25] *Gesta Conl. Carth.* III.102.
[26] Bonner, *Augustine and modern research*, 36.
[27] *C. Faust.* XXX.5–6.
[28] *De mor. eccles.* I.34.75.
[29] *Ep.* 21.1–2.

and the tares, as Augustine was always reminding the Donatists, must be allowed to co-exist until the harvest (Matt. 13.24–30). The Church cannot be an elite in the world; it is necessarily holy and worldly at the same time, to be purified only at the end.[30] The ecclesiology Augustine deployed against Donatism had been an attack on one brand of perfectionism. Pelagian perfectionism raised new problems and demanded new theological labours; but the direction of Augustine's answer to Pelagius was already settled. It had to be a vindication of Christian mediocrity.

One thing that 'being a Christian' was necessarily understood to involve in Augustine's age was some reference to baptism. A 'Christian' could not simply be equated with being a baptised person, for the label could be given to others known to have committed themselves to Christ, for instance, to those intending to receive baptism; but baptism was the universal point of reference.[31] To this extent Augustine and Pelagius agreed that baptism is what marks out a Christian among other men. Baptism establishes one as a new man, re-born in the Pauline sense, through Christ's death and resurrection into the circle of His grace and His new law. Where Augustine and Pelagius differed was in their views on what baptism achieved in renewing a man.[32] From the moment that Augustine perceived the affinity between Pelagianism and Donatism in their tendency to anticipate an eschatological purification, he also perceived that the nature of baptism lay at the roots of the problem. 'Which of us would deny that in baptism all sins are forgiven, that all the faithful emerge from the water of regeneration without spot or wrinkle? What Catholic Christian will reject, what the Lord himself approves and what is to be realised in the future, a Church enduring without spot or wrinkle?' – all could agree on that; what Pelagius took no account of – as Augustine, perhaps somewhat unfairly, complained – was 'the interim, the interval between the remission of sins which takes place in baptism, and

---

[30] On all this, Markus, *Saeculum*, 105–26. On the Catholic and Donatist interpretations of the parable of the wheat and the tares, p. 122. A fine statement: *C. litt. Pet.* III.2.3. On Augustine and Tyconius, Fredriksen, 'Tyconius'.

[31] See Lamirande, 'La signification'.

[32] On baptism, see Brown, 'Pelagius and his supporters', and Greshake, *Gnade*, 108–11.

the permanently established sinless state in the kingdom that is to come, this middle time [*tempus hoc medium*] of prayer, while [we] must pray "Forgive us our sins".'[33]

In Augustine's view baptism launched a Christian on a lifelong process of convalescence, rather than curing him at once and enabling him to make a clean break with his past. He had long ago learnt to appreciate the insidious force of habit.[34] The hold of his unregenerate past was condensed in the power of ingrained habit, and it was never wholly conquered in this life. In the last resort, the individual Christian, like the Church, remains always deeply infected with sin. For both the individual Christian and the Church, we must heed the Pauline prohibition of pronouncing judgement before the time, 'before the Lord comes, who will bring to light the things now hidden in darkness and disclose the purposes of the heart' (I Cor. 4.5). Augustine had learnt to come to terms with the dark layers within his own self in the tenth book of his *Confessions*, and had come to accept himself as ultimately problematic: 'here I am, weep with me and weep for me, all you who do anything good within your inner selves ... But You, O Lord my God, hear me, look upon me and see me; have mercy and heal me, You in whose sight I have become a question to myself.' [35] Pelagius' teaching, as Augustine understood it, would have left no place, in the baptised Christian, for God's merciful healing; Pelagius would replace Augustine's urgent prayer for grace with an austere call to cast off all weakness, a remorseless demand for perfection. 'A man of good works', Augustine wrote in answer to Pelagius,

who acts from the faith which works through love, who indulges his incontinence within the decent bounds of marriage, who both exacts and renders the debt of the flesh and sleeps with his wife – though only with his wife! – and does so not only for the sake of bringing

---

[33] *De gest. Pel.* 12.28. More precisely, Augustine points out that Pelagius passed over this crucial point trying to mislead his judges at Diospolis by refusing to come clean on it. See also Augustine's reply, *Ep.* 157.5.40, to the questions of the Sicilian bishop Hilary (*Ep.* 156).

[34] See *C. Fortun. Man.* 22; *De serm. Dom. in monte* I.17.51; 18.54; *Conf.* VIII.5.12, and the significant advice to Hilary (*Ep.* 157.5.40–1) on swearing. The distinction between baptism as renewal and penitence as cure occurs in the early *In Rom. inch. expos.* 19. On habit, see Prendiville, 'The development of the idea of habit'. I here follow, of course, Peter Brown's exposition of the issue between Augustine and Pelagius.

[35] *Conf.* X.33.50. See Markus, *Conversion.*

forth offspring, but even for sheer pleasure, . . . who will put up with wrongs done to him with less than complete patience, but burn with angry desire for revenge . . ., who guards what he possesses and gives alms, though not very generously, who does not take another's goods but defends his own in a court of law – ecclesiastical, not civil,

such a man, 'on account of his right faith in God . . ., acknowledging his own ignominy and giving the glory to God', such a man will depart this life and be received into the company of the saints destined to reign with Christ.[36]

Sibi tribuens ignominiam, illi gloriam – assigning the disgrace to himself, the glory to God – this is the bedrock of Augustine's tolerance of mediocrity, of unresolved tensions, both in the individual Christian and in the Church. This tolerance is the line which divides his theology from Pelagius' perfectionism. The two doctrines understood man's freedom to choose and to act in fundamentally opposed ways. A Pelagian bishop in Italy, Julian of Eclanum, stated the Pelagian conception of freedom with the most drastic clarity: 'The freedom of the will, by which man is emancipated [*emancipatus*] from God, consists in the possibility of committing or abstaining from sin.' Augustine's sharp rejoinder – 'if a man is emancipated from God, he is not within the father's family'[37] – reveals the springs of his impatience with Pelagianism. In the Pelagian programme he saw a sanction for that insidious pride which ruptures community.

Augustine entered this last debate of his career with ideas formed in his mind over some thirty years. Long ago he had discovered that for his salvation man was utterly dependent on God. Reviewing the debate at the end of his life he tells his correspondent that it was his reading of Saint Paul in the 390s that had brought about the upheaval in his mind and that the matters debated now, in the late 420s, had been solved then, in the answers he had written to Simplicianus' questions.[38] With hindsight, Augustine now realised that it was then, at 'the beginning of his episcopate', that the full import of Saint Paul's question had struck him: 'What have you that you have not

[36] *C. duas ep. Pel.* III.5.14. Cf. *Sermo* 4.19.20, on 'carrying the sinner'.
[37] *Op. imp.* I.78.
[38] *De praed. sanct.* 4.8, quoting *Retract.* II.1.1, referring to *De div. quaest. ad Simpl.*

received?' (I Cor. 4.7). He had then learnt from Saint Paul the meaning of his injunction to work out our salvation 'in fear and trembling' (Phil. 2.12–13): commenting on the verse Augustine wrote 'thus he sufficiently shows that good will is brought about in us by God's action'.[39] Pelagius also believed in grace, but interpreted it in a way which left man's power of self-determination intact. 'Nothing marks [Augustine] off more sharply from the Pelagians than the recognition of the fact that to have free will is not the same as to be free.'[40] In a way which Augustine acknowledged to be mysterious, the free exercise of his free will lay beyond man's power. Ignorance and weakness prevent his will from willing to do good; 'O Lord, I know that the way of a man is not within himself: it is not in man that walketh to direct his steps' (Jer. 10.23).[41] To regain the full freedom to love and to act which was mutilated by Adam's sin, the will needed restoring by grace. Grace liberates choice from the imprisoning power of egoism and pride, it endows choice with freedom, liberates nature and allows sin to be overcome.[42] To the cut-off, enclosed self which is the product of sin, grace brings 'a new dimension, whereby decisions in [and for] this world are given a qualitatively different consistency precisely because they transpire in an entirely new context of the ultimately important and the permanently valuable . . .; freedom is expanded because the objects of choice and decision exist in a new context of importance.'[43]

Augustine had rejected Manicheism because it offered too easy a resolution of the problem of evil (see above); he now rejected Pelagianism because it offered too simple a solution – theologically too simple, if morally demanding – of the problem of Christian perfection. Not surprisingly, adherents of the 'new heresy' accused Augustine of having remained a Manichee. His division of the human race into those predestined to be saved and those to be damned seemed to draw as stark a line across it as had Mani's division between an evil world of dark and a

[39] *De div. quaest. ad Simpl.* I.ii.12.
[40] Bonner, *Augustine of Hippo*, 385. On Pelagian teaching on grace, see also Bohlin, *Die Theologie*, 15–46; Greshake, *Gnade*, especially the summary on p. 153.
[41] *De pecc. mer. et rem.* II.17.26.
[42] *De gratia et lib. arb.* 14.27.
[43] Haight, *The experience*, 48.

world of light, and it appeared to pose no less of a threat to a belief in human responsibility. In much of the long debate with Julian of Eclanum which occupied Augustine over most of the last decade of his life, Augustine was concerned to refute the charge of Manicheism.[44] This gave him little difficulty; it was not hard to show that Julian had not understood the Manichees' teaching, and still less Augustine's, and misrepresented both. The debate came to be focused on sex. As Julian and Augustine both perceived, the whole cluster of problems concerned with nature, original sin and grace was brought to a sharp point in the questions about sexuality, marriage and virginity.[45] In attacking Augustine's views on marriage Julian wished to represent them as dangerously similar to radically dualist rejection of the goodness of created nature. But Augustine had rejected Manichaean dualism, and since writing his pair of treatises on marriage and virginity in 401, he had also re-thought his views on sexuality. Sexual activity now opened for Augustine a window onto the glory and the misery of the fallen human condition.

This re-thinking, like so much else in the last phase of his career, was prompted by Augustine's meditation on Genesis. Its upshot was to distance himself more firmly than ever from the religion of Mani, to underline the goodness of nature, including sex and marriage. Augustine embarked on his literal commentary on Genesis in 401, immediately after writing the two books *On marriage* and *On holy virginity.* It is hard not to wonder whether those two books did not contribute to a need he perceived to re-think traditional ideas on human nature, on the effect of the Fall upon it, on sexuality, as well as on other topics of major importance. At any rate, the commentary is Augustine's intellectual workshop, where we can observe him grappling with the concepts which would go into the writings of his old age. The work took him some thirteen years to complete, and though dating the progress of its composition is no easy task, it seems certain that he had reached a turning point in his understanding

---

[44] See *Retract.* II.62, and frequently in the anti-Pelagian writings; see especially *C. duas ep. Pel.* II. On Julian and Augustine's alleged Manicheism, Markus, 'Manicheism revisited'.
[45] On this see Brown, 'Sexuality and society', and now Fredriksen, 'Beyond the body–soul dichotomy'.

of sexuality before he had his first encounter with the teaching of Pelagius.[46] His new views were henceforth to underlie all his discussions of these topics, frequent as they are, especially in his anti-Pelagian writings.

Augustine had touched on these questions before, notably in the course of a commentary he had written on Genesis with the aim of refuting Manichaean interpretations of the book.[47] At that time (388/9) Augustine had shared the notions prevailing among Christian thinkers in the fourth century. According to these, Adam and Eve had been created sexless, in an innocence which some writers regarded as the innocence of childhood. Had they not sinned, sexual intercourse would not have been required for the increasing and multiplying of the human race. Maturity, puberty and sexual activity came with their fall from grace, along with pain, illness, death, slavery and all the other horrors that disfigure human life and the life of society. After some hesitation, by the time he came to write Book IX of his great Genesis commentary, Augustine had come to reject this view very firmly. 'I see no reason why there should not have been honourable marriage in paradise', he now writes;[48] and he defends in a long discussion the view that sexual partnership and reproduction are not a fall from some pre-sexual state of innocence, but part of God's original creative intention for his creatures. In rejecting his own earlier views on this question, Augustine was parting company with a wide Christian consensus among his contemporaries.

In the second century Melito, Irenaeus and others had held a very benign view of the body, of material existence and sexuality. But attitudes had come to diverge ever more widely since. Mainstream Christianity became infected by the strong undercurrent of ideas which accompanied it, sometimes as an overt rival, more often as its own, dark, shadow. Western Christianity, especially, thus acquired a pronounced streak of distrust of the body and of sexuality, a distrust which has been labelled as 'encratite'. In Africa this tendency, perhaps derived from the

[46] This has been persuasively argued by Clark, 'Heresy, asceticism, Adam and Eve'. Augustine was still undecided when writing *De Gen. ad litt.* III.21.33.
[47] *De Gen. c. Man.* I.19.30, with *Retract.* I.10.2, where Augustine says of the 'spiritual' interpretation there offered of Gen. 1.28 that 'this I can now in no manner approve'.
[48] *De Gen. ad litt.* IX.3.6. The discussion extends to IX.10.18.

tenacity of Jewish-Christian traditions and communities, appears to have been especially strong. Many of the ambiguities in fourth-century views about sin, holiness, the body and sex seem to arise from this sinister inheritance. Augustine's own views were formed within the context of a long native African Christian tradition deeply tainted by such attitudes;[49] and this tradition naturally continued to exercise a severe restraint on the development of his views. All the same, he did change his view about human sexuality, and his change of view is remarkable, an impressive result of the independence of mind which enabled him to break with some of the deep-seated ideas current in his circle. In changing his mind about sex, Augustine came to adopt a view very rare in the Church at the end of the fourth century. He was evidently aware of some division of opinion on this matter,[50] and, before long, he would come to turn his back on the prevailing consensus. At any rate, well before his encounter with Pelagius, he had come to assert that human sexuality was a part of man's created nature, not a result of its corruption through sin. Henceforth sexual existence was no longer a problem for Augustine. What had to be accounted for was no longer the existence of sex, but rather, now, its mode of functioning; and the effect of Adam's sin on the sexuality of his heirs.

In the demonology of the history of sexuality Augustine has found a high place. Much of the responsibility for the negative attitude towards sexual pleasure, for the strain in the Christian tradition which insisted, for centuries, that only a procreative intention can justify sexual union, is generally laid at Augustine's door. The power of his name is said to have given the dominant

---

[49] On this see Beatrice, *Tradux peccati*, whose central thesis I summarise in this paragraph.

[50] Augustine asserts (*De bono con.* 2.2) that opinion on this matter had been divided. His reticence on the question here may reflect both his own uncertainty at this time, and, possibly, reluctance to embrace a view apparently held by Jovinian – if the attractive suggestion made by Clark, 'Heresy, asceticism, Adam and Eve', is accepted. A view such as Augustine came to adopt may have originated with Jovinian, as Clark argues on the strength of Jerome, *Adv. Iov.* I.29, though some Antiochene exegetes – whom Augustine did not, of course, know – may have come close to it: see e.g. Theodore of Mopsuestia, *In Gal.* II.15–16 (Swete, I.26–7). Similar views may, however, have circulated in the West, e.g. the Ambrosiaster, *Q. vet. and novi test.* 127 (*CSEL* 50.399–416), esp. 2–5 (pp. 399–400) and, perhaps in Faltonia Betitia Proba's description of Eve as *iam matura viro, iam plenis nubilis annis* (*Cento Probae, CSEL* 16.577). I owe this reference to Moorhead, 'Adam and Eve'.

Christian view of sex a repressive, even inhuman stamp. How true is this? It is a good question, and one which the historian of sexuality and especially of the development of Christian thought on sex must take very seriously. To inherit a tradition is to possess a principle of selection among options: the more specific the content of a tradition, the more it excludes. In so far as the Christian tradition of thought on sexuality can be traced back to Augustine, it bears a different stamp than would a tradition moulded by Jerome, say, or Gregory of Nyssa. It would be pointless to speculate on other directions that a different tradition might have given to Christian attitudes. Our concern is with Augustine and his generation. To understand Augustine we need to disentangle what he was telling his contemporaries from that which he shared with them and questioned no more than did most of them. What we must listen to is the quiet debate between him and them, indeed a debate within his own mind, concerning the right attitude to take to questions on which his predecessors had already reflected deeply. To diagnose what is novel, what is personal to and distinctive of Augustine, it will be the shifts of emphasis we need to detect. And if we attend to these, paying particular attention to the shifts in Augustine's own thinking, what is striking is the very definite positive re-valuation of human sexuality that his later thought represents in relation to much of the earlier tradition and, indeed, to the prevailing orientation of Christian thought in his own time. We need hardly underline the gulf that divides Augustine from, for instance, Jerome, or even from Ambrose or the Cappadocian fathers on this subject. For Augustine sexuality was without question part of man's created nature. Sexuality was part of what it meant to be human. Whatever was wrong with sex was no more and no less than whatever it was that went wrong with being human.

The experience of sexuality – man's and woman's – now became Augustine's model for the understanding of fallen human nature, and its typical instance. The exercise and the experience of sex in man's fallen state is irrevocably infected with what Augustine calls *concupiscentia carnis*, perhaps still best translated as 'lust of the flesh'. It is important not to misunderstand this very central notion of Augustine's. He is not asserting a simple opposition between 'spirit' and 'flesh' or 'soul' and 'body', as if two elements in man's make-up were, by their nature, at war within himself. The disturbance set up within the personality is a turbulence within the soul itself, at the roots of its instinct to rebel against the will of God. The 'lust of the flesh' belongs to a whole genus of 'lusts' – for power, for domination, for renown – all brought about by the same disorder rooted in man's sin. 'It is not the corruptible flesh that made the soul sinful, but the sin of the soul that brought about the corruption of the flesh.'[51] This sin removes areas of man's own self from his control. Man ceases to be fully accessible to himself, just as Adam ceased to be accessible to God. 'In paradise the flesh would never have lusted against the spirit, but rather it would have obeyed the will in a wonderful harmony' (*pace mirabili*).[52] The Fall is re-enacted in the daily experience of the loss of this 'miraculous peace'.

The dislocation within the self results from and reflects the dislocation in the primordial community between man and God. In his sexual experience man's estrangement from God is re-enacted in the estrangement from his own body.[53] What is reprehensible in sex and the cause of shame in its exercise is not its existence, but its tendency to run out of control, to escape rational direction. Thus it reveals at its sharpest the break in wholeness, the ground of the inner conflict between the law of God in the inward man at war with the law of sin in the members (Rom. 7.22).[54] The disruption of the self as experienced in sex becomes Augustine's paradigm for the disruption of man's primordial community with God, with his fellows and with himself. The tension that Manichaean teaching projected onto two separate natures in permanent conflict was now transposed into terms of conflict within the self:

---

[51] *De civ. Dei* XIV.3.2. On the concept, see Thonnard, 'La notion de concupiscence'; Bonner, '*Libido* and *concupiscentia*' and *Augustine of Hippo*, 375–8, 398–401; and now Brown, *The body*, 396–423.
[52] *Ep.* 6*.8. On it, see Berrouard, 'Les lettres 6* et 19*'; and Bonner, 'Some remarks'. The date 421–2 advocated here seems much likelier than the editor's earlier dating.
[53] *De nupt. et conc.* I.6.7.
[54] *Ibid.* II.2.6. Cf. 7.17, 14.29 and *De pecc. orig.* 35.40. The fullest exposition is in *De civ. Dei* XIV.22–6. On Augustine's doctrine, see Gross, *Entstehungsgeschichte*, 257–376.

The fact that the flesh lusts [*concupiscit*] against the spirit is not something outside me, for I am not made up of a nature contrary to it; and that I do not consent to its urges, that too is something within me ... What I long for is to be healed as a whole, for I am one whole: not that my flesh were for ever removed, as if it were something alien to me, but that it be healed, one whole with me.[55]

What Augustine resented most in the imputations made against him by Julian of Eclanum was the suggestion that he condemned sex, marriage and procreation as a work of the Devil, not of God.[56]

His break with Manicheism, his gradual disenchantment with the image of a rationally ordered universe and the despair of imposing a rational order on himself, his growing sense of total dependence on Christ's healing grace, had finally brought Augustine to the threshold of the theology he was to deploy against Pelagius and Julian of Eclanum. His reflection on human sexuality was prompted by meditating on the text of Genesis, and it provided the paradigm in which he diagnosed the rupture between God and man and within man himself in his fallen state. This involved a rehabilitation of the flesh. The whole person, body and soul, restored from revolt to concord, was to exhibit holiness. And finally, this involved a rehabilitation of marriage: never again would it be possible, after Augustine's rebuttal of the charge of Manicheism, to write of marriage in the manner of Jerome. Equally, however, it would be harder to write of virginity in the manner of Ambrose or Gregory of Nyssa. Augustine's defence of marriage and of Christian mediocrity needed to be complemented by re-thinking the nature of ascetic renunciation and monasticism. To that we must now turn.

---

[55] *Sermo* 30.3.4. Cf. Markus, 'Manicheism revisited'.
[56] *De nupt. et conc.* I.1.1, and *Ep.* 6*.3.3–5.

5

'Be ye perfect'

The message of Pelagius was a call to the Church at large. Its appeal was strong, especially to Christian lay people of high social rank. It summoned Christians to a life of perfection. It preached an austere morality akin to the ascetic discipline of the monastic tradition. Monks were, by definition, dedicated to the ideal – the pursuit of perfection – which Pelagius wished to hold up to the lay world. It was not monks who needed to take note of this teaching, and not monks who were liable to be disturbed by it. It was Augustine's doctrine, rather than Pelagius', that raised doubts among them. If Augustine was right, the ground on which they stood would be undermined.[1] If salvation was a work of God's grace and not of man's effort, what was the point of their special exertions in the religious life? Would the condemnation of Pelagius in 418, and the triumph of Augustinian theology, not tend to sap the mainspring of ascetic dedication? Would trust in grace not paralyse effort? This problem was raised in acute form in African monastic quarters in 426–7, and not much later in Southern Gaul.

A copy of one of Augustine's most uncompromising statements against Pelagius, a letter (*Ep.* 194) written some eight years earlier to the Roman priest (later pope) Sixtus, who had been sympathetic to Pelagius, became known to the monks of Hadrumetum. Some were worried and the community was

---

[1] The general affinity between monasticism and Pelagian teaching has been noted by Lorenz, 'Die Anfänge', 36–8. See *ibid.*, n. 39 on Augustine's Pauline re-orientation of monastic theology. A clear and forceful statement of the difficulty is contained in Prosper's letter to Augustine, *inter* Augustine, *Ep.* 225.3; Cassian, *Conl.* XIII.2. On this, see Chéné, 'Les origines', esp. 82–109. For an exquisite recent sketch of the problem, see Chadwick, 'The ascetic ideal'.

deeply divided. At the request of its abbot, Augustine clarified his teaching on grace, trying to reassure them. How could he possibly have questioned the freedom of the will, he wrote, when it was to Timothy's free will that Saint Paul appealed when he exhorted him to be continent (I Tim. 5.22)? God gave men free will in order that they might live and act well. Without free will his correspondents would not have gathered in a community in which they live in continence, spurning marital bliss.[2] They have heard the word summoning them, and they have obeyed its call;

but it is not all that hear it, only those to whom it is given to hear it. Those to whom it is not given, either do not will, or fail to carry out their will. Those to whom it is given, will in such a way that they carry out what they will. So the fact that this word of summons is received by some but not by all, is both a gift of God and an act of free will.[3]

Augustine tried to reassure the monks of Hadrumetum that their life of renunciation and ascetic striving is not rendered null by the gift of grace. They have received two gifts: of being called, and of obeying the call. It is by their own free decision they obey and fulfil its demands. So, Augustine concludes, his defence of grace is not a denial of free will[4] and free will is not vindicated at the expense of grace – as it is by those who inflate and thus destroy it.[5] Augustine's answer to the troubled monks in effect places them, faced with God's call and his grace, in a position no different from that of any Christian awaiting God's grace and responding to it in freedom.

Augustine has turned Pelagius' universal demand for perfection[6] on its head: 'God would not command what he knew men cannot perform', he quotes the Pelagian slogan; Augustine replies,

of course, who does not know that? But he does command some things that we cannot carry out in order that we might know what we should entreat him for ... It is certain that we can obey his commands if we

---

[2] *De gratia et lib. arb.* 4.7.
[3] *Ibid.*
[4] *Ibid.* 1.1.
[5] *Ibid.* 14.27; cf. *Ep.* 194.13.
[6] See above, ch. 3.

will to do so; but because God prepares the will, we must entreat him that we might will in a manner which would suffice to enable us to carry out what we have willed, having willed it.[7]

The grounds for the distinction between the life of the ordinary Christian and the life of renunciation lie hidden in the mysterious workings of grace. Neither Augustine nor Pelagius could allow any line running across the human race to divide it into two classes. For both Pelagius and Augustine the division between the ordinary Christian and the seeker after perfection was overcome: for Pelagius in the universality of the summons to perfection, for Augustine by the universality of the need for grace. In the last resort Augustine could admit only one division, that between those destined to be saved and the reprobate; and this was hidden in the mysterious depth of God's will, not to be revealed before the end. Mediocrity and perfection were no longer on opposite sides of a great divide that cut through the Christian community, creating a two-tier Church. For Pelagius the whole community had to be perfect; for Augustine the ordinary Christian was no more remote from grace and salvation than the monk or ascetic. All are called to pursue perfection; none attain it here, but all are commanded to run so as to obtain the prize (I Cor. 9.24; Phil. 3.12). Perfection is the distant goal, imperfection the inescapable condition – for monk and lay person alike.[8] The pursuit of perfection could not, therefore, be the distinguishing mark of the monk. The Pelagian crisis and the Augustinian response thus fundamentally shifted the ground on which the theology of monastic life had to be re-thought.

Augustine was more interested in the general conditions of Christian living as such than in formulating a theology of the monastic life. But the provisions he made for his own communities, and the comments he occasionally made on monastic matters, do allow us to see the outlines of a theological approach to the meaning of the monastic life. It would be surprising, with a man such as Augustine, were it otherwise. His contribution to

---

[7] *De gratia et lib. arb.* 16.32.
[8] *De perf. iust. hom.* 8.19, and *De nat. et gratia* 70.84. On this subject, see Zumkeller, *Das Mönchtum*, 121–2 and 212–13.

monastic thought marks a decisive change in the direction of its development; more so than does the pattern of his monasteries, which are closely in line with the communal ideals recommended by St Basil. To assess the change of direction in the late fourth century, and the impact of Augustine's thought on it, we would need a fuller survey than is possible here of this much discussed and amply described institution. No attempt will be made to survey its development yet again; what this and a later chapter (see below, ch. 11) will explore is the meaning of monasticism, and its connection with the related notion of asceticism. It will try to disentangle from the variety of their embodiments the relation between the two ideas, rather than to describe the changing shape they were to assume in the course of their historical development.

To see what the idea of monastic life meant to Augustine's less reflective contemporaries in the early fifth century, we may begin with a statement by Augustine's disciple, Orosius. Orosius defined monks as 'Christians who, having renounced the multifarious activities concerned with worldly things, confine themselves to the one work of faith'.[9] We may take Orosius' definition – formal as it is, though certainly not deeply thought over – as reflecting generally current ideas. Monasticism is seen with two faces, one positive, the other negative. It is a life wholly dedicated to religion ('the work of faith'); this is combined with, or entails, by its very nature – it is not clear from Orosius' statement which; he merely says the two go together – renunciation of all worldly activities. In this statement Orosius is echoing the long-established tradition which linked the quest of perfection with asceticism. Orosius left in the shadows what worried so many of his contemporaries: the differences between being a Christian, being a seeker after perfection, being an ascetic, and being a monk. But in this group of overlapping religious types with complex relations among themselves we now need to consider what is distinctive of the monk.

The word could refer to so many different sorts of religious that some have despaired of defining its meaning before the

---

[9] *Hist.* VII.33: *monachi, hoc est, Christiani qui ad unum fidei opus dimissa saecularium rerum multimoda actione, se redigunt.*

end of the fourth century.[10] The ambiguities surrounding it reflect the richness of the meaning, and the complexity in its development. 'By one of those paradoxes in which the history of men and of the words they use abounds, it was this very word *monachos*, "solitary", which became accepted in the course of the centuries to denote someone whose state is linked, by his calling, to that of others in a community: the coenobite [i.e. monk living in community]'.[11] In Christian usage ideas of dedication to chastity and celibacy, of detachment from material things, of likeness and a relationship to God's 'only-begotten' Son, the *monogenes*, came to overlay the original sense of the word. In the course of the fourth century its primary meaning ('solitary') had come to be eclipsed to the extent that, if one wished to refer to the solitary monk, the epithet 'solitary' (*anachoretes*) had to be added to the word to qualify its meaning.[12] By the end of the fourth century the notion of a 'monk' had begun to take on a definite 'socio-political' connotation. What solitary ascetics shared with those living in organised communities was more than inner dispositions, attitudes, actions, or even some outward modes of life. To be a monk was definable only in social terms.

This is not to assert what would patently be untrue, that monks necessarily lived in social groups. Hermits, anchorites and solitary holy men were not only the predecessors of monks, but survived long after the emergence of communal forms of monastic living. What, then, defines the monk among the multifarious holy men and ascetics? In a now classic definition Karl Heussi identified the specific constitutive difference which marked off a monk among other ascetics as the creation of a *Sonderwelt* – a 'separate world' – inhabited by him.[13] This *Sonderwelt* could be the hermit's cave, the cell or the pillar as well as the cloister, or even, for that matter, a town house. Public vows came, eventually, to define the monk as distinct from the private ascetic. But long before the hardening of formal criteria, Augustine had known monastic communities in Rome and Milan: 'a praiseworthy *genus*

[10] Prinz, *Askese und Kultur*, 12.
[11] Morard, 'Monachos', 334–5.
[12] *Ibid.* 402. See also Judge, 'The earliest use'. I consider below, ch. 12, the further momentum given to this development by Cassian.
[13] *Der Ursprung*, 53. Public vows make the monk: *Vita Fulgentii* 2 (of the late fifth century); and Faustus of Riez, *Ep.* 10, on Ruricius as *miles Christi secretus*.

of Christians who live in cities but are far removed from the common way of life'.[14] The monk has detached himself from the social pattern of the ordinary community. Unlike the ascetic or the holy man – or, more often, woman – who continues to exercise his special mode of life or to cultivate his personal virtue anonymously within the community, the monk has seceded from his social group and entered a world defined by different principles. This 'separate world', marked off from the community at large, is the 'desert' of monastic literature, set apart from society by the common dedication of its members expressed in its institutional form, whether in the city or the wilderness.

Such a definition of monasticism takes us a long step beyond Orosius. It marks clearly what the monastic ideal adds to far older Christian (and, for that matter, as we shall see, non-Christian) aspirations; and it also indicates what it has in common with them. The monk is thus necessarily also an ascetic, at least to the extent that monastic life involves some renunciations. In this specific sense monasticism – a creation of the third century – includes the idea of asceticism – as old as, and even older than, Christianity itself. Heussi described it as a life wholly based on religion and prayer, accompanied by abstinence from, or restricted enjoyment of, a whole range of human goods: property, sex, bodily comfort, the pleasures of food and drink or the less tangible pleasures of self-assertion and the free pursuit of personal choice;[15] and to these we might add renunciation of status and prestige. Monastic groups, when they began to emerge in the third century, thus perpetuated more ancient ideals: the ideal of self-abnegation and prayer at its core, and of contemplation, generally assumed to be its culmination, all comprehended in a conception of Christian perfection. By its nature, monasticism was committed to these ideals, with varying emphases and, of course, variously interpreted; but there could be no question that the monastic profession committed one to the pursuit of Christian perfection. The converse, however, did not necessarily follow: Christian perfection might be sought in other than

---

[14] *De mor. eccles.* I.33.70. Cf. Jerome, *Ep.* 24.4: *in urbe turbida [Asella] invenit eremum monachorum.* See also ch. 3, n. 21.
[15] *Der Ursprung.*, 13. On fasting, see Musurillo, 'The problem'; and generally, Strathmann and Keseling, 'Askese', and Chadwick, 'Enkrateia'.

monastic ways. Neither perfection nor the quest for it could be assumed to be the monk's monopoly.

We considered in the last chapter the uncertainties in the decades just before and just after the turn of the fourth century about the meaning of the Christian life and the demand for perfection. Now we must consider how the tidal waves of that crisis in their turn affected the institution of monasticism. I shall suggest that their overall effect was not so much to give a new direction to monastic endeavour, nor to set it new ideals or give it new forms, but rather to reinforce some among its inherited cluster of aspirations and to attenuate others. For this purpose we must distinguish, as briefly as possible, the separate strands in the medley of aspirations which had poured from various quarters of the ancient world and set in the mould of the monastic ideal.[16]

Until comparatively recent times a scholar as great as Adolf von Harnack, or a writer once as widely read as Montalambert, could confidently relate the growing appeal of monasticism to a widespread sapping of Christian moral standards consequent upon Constantine's adoption of Christianity. Harnack had said of the final outcome of Constantine's conversion that it left 'the world in possession of all except its gods'.[17] He saw monasticism as the result of a crisis in the Christian conscience precisely like that which we have observed at the end of the fourth century, only extended over a longer period, the whole of the fourth century. Now there is no reason to doubt that many of those who swarmed into the Egyptian desert in imitation of Antony did so in order to find scope for the exercise of a Christian heroism no longer demanded of them in the great urban churches of Alexandria and their like.[18] To understand how the monk came to take the place of the martyr in the post-Constantinian world we need to go behind the myth about monastic

[16] The literature is enormous. As there is no single work that is entirely satisfactory, and nothing remotely approaching this in English, I refer here only to Heussi, *Der Ursprung*. Lorenz, 'Die Anfänge', though concerned with the emergence of Western monasticism, has some penetrating remarks on this theme. Some other important studies are referred to in the sequel in connection with specific points.

[17] *Das Mönchtum*, 28; cf. his *History*, III.127–32.

[18] See Athanasius (attr.), *Vita Ant.* 47. Cf. Sulpicius Severus, *Ep.* 2.9, 12; John Chrysostom, *C. oppugnatores* 1.7 (*PG* 47.327).

origins propagated in monastic circles and accepted by some modern writers, expressed, for example, by the Rev. H. B. Workman three-quarters of a century ago: 'Monasticism ... in its origin was the effort of the nobler spirits in a dissolute age to recover more completely the lost ideal of renunciation.'[19]

The cessation of persecution taken by itself is no explanation of monasticism, if only because monasticism began earlier; but in the post-Constantinian world it nevertheless received added impetus from the relaxation of the sense of insecurity and the emotional tension 'which [before Constantine] profoundly affected Christian corporate life and the development of Christian thought. Though an individual Christian might never himself be persecuted or harassed, the Church [was] a church of the martyrs.'[20] The profound upheaval in the social and psychological conditions of being a Christian after Constantine made it natural for monasticism to succeed martyrdom as a form of Christian *militia*.[21] In the middle of the fifth century Salvian assured one of his correspondents of the mercy 'of our kind and tender Father, who would rather have us show our faith in these times of peace by the works of religion than to prove it by the suffering of our bodies in persecution'.[22] The emotional energies previously absorbed by the duty to rise to the demands made on a persecuted Church were largely re-directed towards disciplined ascetic living. Unsatisfied desire for martyrdom was sometimes attributed to ascetics; and so 'peace, too, had its martyrs'.[23] Caesarius, bishop of Arles in the early sixth century, thought the Christian's fight with fornication was the hardest of all his struggles and gave him a title to 'martyrdom'; but as the holy martyrs would intercede for anyone in whom they recognised something of their own virtue, those who resisted drunkenness could also qualify.[24] The vocabulary previously applied to the trials of the martyr would now find its way into the repertoire for the monk's spiritual struggle: with sin, with

---

[19] *The evolution of the monastic ideal*, 54. On the myth of origins, see below, ch. 11, pp. 165–6.
[20] Barnes, *Tertullian*, 163. This subject is further explored below, ch. 7.
[21] On this see Malone, *The monk and the martyr*, and Harnack, *Militia Christi*.
[22] *Ep.* 9.
[23] Hilary of Arles, *Sermo de vita Honorati*, 8.37–8, echoed by Caesarius of Arles, *Sermo* 41.1. Cf. Beck, *The pastoral care*, who provides a wealth of Gallic examples, 286–9.
[24] *Sermo* 41.2; 44.1; 47.2, *inter multa*.

temptation, with the Devil. 'Look at the whole world, brothers': said Gregory the Great at the end of the sixth century, 'it is full of martyrs.'[25] The story of St Martin's giving up *militia* in the emperor's army for the *militia* of Christ gave wide currency to a dramatic image, and helped to encourage the notion of a vicarious martyrdom.[26] From the fourth century on Christian literature abounds in the commonplaces of martyrdom equated with monasticism[27] and of virginity represented as a bloodless martyrdom. The vocabulary of military life found in so much monastic literature[28] is a permanent reminder of the extent to which the monk's fortitude shown in the battle with the demon, with pride, with lust and with avarice, came to be seen as equivalent to the martyr's courage in rendering faithful witness in his fight with the adversary.

Behind the commonplaces of the fourth and later centuries there was an earlier tradition, reaching back to Clement of Alexandria and Origen, in which there could be substitutes for martyrdom as a way to Christian perfection. Virginity was the foremost among the alternatives already acknowledged in the third century. With the ending of the age of persecution, monasticism came to absorb the ideal of the martyr. Like the martyr, the monk freed himself from the world for God and found the fullness of freedom in his death. In his fidelity and commitment to Christ the monk, like the martyr, participated in the death of the risen Lord and in the renewal of his life.[29] Monastic writers loved to make Christ's obedience even unto death (Phil. 2.8) a model for the monk.[30] In terms which recall the description of Polycarp's martyrdom as a *holocautoma*,[31] Gregory the Great was to draw out the moral basis underlying the parallel between

---

[25] *Hom. in Ev.* II.27.4. The theme is an *ostinato* in Augustine's sermons on the martyrdom of St Stephen: e.g. *Sermo* 315.9: 'The Devil has made us all martyrs.'

[26] Sulpicius Severus, *Vita Mart.* 4.3, and Fontaine, *Vie*, 1214–23.

[27] E.g., Ambrose, *Expos. in ps.* CXVIII.20.47; Jerome, *Ep.* 108.31; Augustine, *Enarr. in Ps.* 132.6; Leo, *Tract.* 47.1; Gregory, *Dial.* III.26.7–8, (and de Vogüé, *ad loc.*); *Mor.* XXIX.7.16–17; *Hom. in Ev.* I.3.4; II.32.4; 35.7–9. Salvian, *Ep.* 9 contains a striking discussion of the idea, which is, of course, much older. See Delehaye, *Sanctus*, 109–21.

[28] E.g. Augustine, *De op. mon.* 16.19; *Reg. Ben. Prol.*3, 2.20, 61.10; Cassian, *Conl.* VIII.16; Arnobius Iunior, *Ad Gregoriam* 11, *inter multa.* Cf. Harnack, *Militia Christi*, 28f.

[29] On the components of the concept of the martyr, see Lods, *Confesseurs*, esp. 18–27; on its development, Campenhausen, *Idee des Martyriums*, esp. 124, 129, 139–44, 174.

[30] E.g. *Reg. Ben.* 7.34 = *Reg. mag.* 10.49; *Reg. Ben. Prol.*, 50, and the commentary by de Vogüé, vii.148–52 and 396.

[31] *Mart. Pol.* 14.1.

the martyr's death and ascetic self-denial: 'there are some who keep nothing for themselves but offer [*immolant*] to the almighty Lord their sense, their speech, their life and all the substance with which they have been endowed. Their offering can be nothing other than the "whole sacrifice" [*holocaustum*]; indeed they are themselves the holocaust.'[32] Isidore of Seville summed it all up thus: 'many who bear the attacks of the adversary and resist the desires of the flesh are martyrs, even in the time of peace, in virtue of this self-immolation to God in their heart: they would have been martyrs in the time of the persecutions'.[33]

It would be easy to see in all this no more than metaphor, a rhetorical assimilation of Christian ardour to the 'heroism' of the martyr. But this would be to miss what, already in the third century, made more thoughtful Christians honour the martyr: not heroism,[34] but constancy, loyalty and a fidelity which, in the end, were God's gift. We shall be considering in a later chapter the image of the martyr and the way in which it came to stand for the epitome of all the aspirations of fourth-century Christians.[35] The central importance of the martyr in the Christian cult as it took shape in the post-Constantinian world was one of the most powerful of the pressures behind the wide appeal of asceticism and monasticism. Much of the appeal of virginity and monastic renunciation rested on their equation with martyrdom. Chastity, self-denial, monasticism became the mould into which the old ideal of the martyr would now set. In this sense the idea of martyrdom, far from becoming attenuated and dissolved,[36] actually remained deeply embedded in Christian self-awareness and contributed to the haunting power of the call for total self-surrender, for perfection.

The figure of the martyr thus remained one of the Christian types gathered up in the figure of the monk. But it was not the

---

[32] *Hom. in Hiezech.* II.8.16.

[33] *Etym.* VII.11.4.

[34] The martyr's 'heroism' was greatly attenuated in the course of the third century, especially in the writings of Tertullian, who was anxious to divest the concept of its pagan associations. See Campenhausen, *Idee des Martyriums*, 128: 'Tertullian wanted no Christian heroes, but the supremacy of God's law.' See *ibid.* 101–2. But cf. Augustine, *De civ. Dei* X.21; XIII.4. Rordorf, 'Aux origines', 325–31.

[35] See below, ch. 6, pp. 92–5.

[36] *abgelöst und verflüchtigt* – Campenhausen, *Idee des Martyriums*, 174, who holds that it was to be re-vitalised in the Catholic Church only in the emergence of the crusading ideal.

only one. The monk also came to sum up the ideal of contemplative living, to represent the type of human ideal of which the philosopher had been the chief representative in Greco-Roman antiquity. For Augustine, to take a central example, an unbroken progression linked his conversion to philosophy at the age of eighteen to his adoption of a monastic mode of life. 'Quite definitely', he wrote of his reading Cicero's exhortation to philosophy as a young man on the threshold of a career, 'it changed the direction of my mind, turned my prayers to You, O Lord, and gave me a new purpose and ambition. Suddenly, all empty hope withered in me, and with an unbelievably burning heart I began to long for the wisdom of immortality.'[37] The experience remained for Augustine the gateway of his journey to God. The first months after his conversion to Christianity some thirteen years later were spent in the company of a few like-minded friends in philosophic retirement. This *Christianae vitae otium*, as he later referred to it,[38] 'the leisure of the Christian life', combined something of the ease of the country villa with the contemplative repose of the community of philosophers, and served as a preparation for the communities which Augustine was to found on his return to Africa. 'Leisure for reading' remained a central objective of the 'service of God'.[39]

Augustine's progress fitted into a pattern well established in the ancient world. The ideal of the philosophic life was among the most important of the sources which nourished Christian monasticism. It was especially well suited for this because it was often associated with some degree of self-denial. In contrast with Judaism, where asceticism played only a minor role and one largely confined to the fringes of orthodox circles, the whole Hellenistic and Roman philosophical tradition offered a rich store-house of commonplaces extolling the ascetic life. The pursuit of wisdom had a religious quality and demanded detachment, simplicity of life, even poverty, and emancipation from wants and needs (*autarkeia*); thus it offered a way to real freedom. It was a 'training' (*askesis*) in virtue. Aristotle thought the company of the right sort of friends could help, and some philosophic

---

[37] *Conf.* III.4.7.
[38] *Retract.* I.1.1.
[39] *Ep.* 184A.1. Cf. *De op. mon.* 29.37, where the mixture includes 'some manual labour'.

schools adopted the common life for the 'school'. The followers of Pythagoras were reported to have lived together in a community as *koinobioi*, sharing a 'common life' and their goods, just as Augustine was to set out to do with his friends.[40] Christians were not the first to combine the notions of self-denial and of the life of contemplation; even communal dedication to these ideals had been anticipated in Antiquity. Athanasius was not forcing the career of Antony, 'the first monk', into a mould unsuited to it in calling it the 'philosophic' life, nor Eusebius that of Pamphilus or Narcissus or others.[41]

Thus 'philosophy' had long ago pointed to much of what became distinctive of monasticism. The essentially contemplative character of the 'philosophic' life as it was conceived in Antiquity made the philosopher an ideal human type readily available for adoption by Christians. The idea of self-mastery, of an inner combat in which the self had to emerge victorious over itself, had long been articulated by classical thought. Christians, like other Late Antique men, were apt to see perfection in terms of freedom from the passions and from mundane concerns that disturb the serene pursuit of wisdom by a cultivated mind.[42] The hospitality of the ancient philosophic ideal to some degree of renunciation could also encourage the streak of asceticism inextricably woven into the fabric of Christianity. The distance between the philosopher, the *mousikos aner* – the 'man of the Muses', of cultivated intellect and devoted to the life of the spirit – and the *theios aner* – the 'divine man', close to the divinity – was never very great and could easily be crossed. The life of contemplation (*bios theoretikos*) spiritualised its practitioner and lifted him to a higher level of being.[43] Here was a widely current secular model for a whole cluster of virtues admired by Christians: more than ordinarily exacting norms of conduct, detachment, otherworldliness, self-denial, contemplation of and union

---

[40] *Conf.* VI.14.24.
[41] *Vita Ant. passim*; Eusebius, *HE* VII.32.25; VI.9.6, etc. On this theme, see Leipoldt, 'Griechische Philosophie', and Bieler, *Theios aner*. Fowden, 'The pagan holy man', on a similar rapprochement between the pagan holy man and the philosopher.
[42] On this, see Foucault, *L'usage des plaisirs*, 79–90. On the Christian applications of the imagery, see Marrou, *Mousikos aner*, 269–87.
[43] Cf. Bieler, *Theios aner*, 78. On the theme of the active and the contemplative life, see further below, ch. 12.

with the divine. Thus in the later third and fourth centuries, the creative age in the development of monasticism, traditions of asceticism reaching back to the origins of Christianity combined with traditions of secular origin about the shape of the life of virtue to outline an ideal of human perfection. The stereotype of the 'philosopher' came to be applied to the virgin, the martyr, and the uncouth and often uneducated holy man; and these overlapping models found institutional form in monastic withdrawal from the secular world. But the crisis of conscience about the nature of Christian identity at the end of the fourth century and the beginning of the fifth led to a disentangling of some of the threads in this conglomerate of ideas.

Jerome, Paulinus, and their contemporaries would have assumed, almost universally, that asceticism in some form was an essential ingredient in the monastic life, even though they might differ – as Jerome and Paulinus differed[44] – on the forms it might take. The severity of ascetic observance was subject to a good deal of variation. Even in the Egyptian desert attitudes ranged from that of the Father who said he was killing his body because it was killing him[45] to that reported of an old monk who, urging a penitent to spare himself, assured him that just as he would mend a worn garment rather than throw it away, so God will have mercy on his own image.[46] Basilian monasticism in the later fourth century laid a far greater stress on practical charity in the brotherhood than on asceticism,[47] and ascetic notions were being played down in circles close to Saint Martin in Gaul.[48] Even here, however, as generally, monasticism remained a vehicle for the life of renunciation, at least to the extent that it involved renunciation of marriage, family and property.

The first to raise questions about the precise connection between self-denial and the monastic life was Jovinian (see above, ch. 3). Jovinian, as we have seen, had attacked the strong

---

[44] See above, ch. 3, p. 39.
[45] *Heracl. Parad.* 1.
[46] *Verba seniorum*, ed. Rosweyde, IV.30 (*PL* 73.1019).
[47] On this, see Meredith, 'Asceticism'.
[48] See Sulpicius Severus, *Dial.* I.4.6.

emphasis that was being laid on virginity, and on ascetic life-styles; but no less important for the future, if less immediately apparent to his contemporaries, was his attack on the assumption that asceticism was a necessary ingredient of the monastic life. Jovinian had once followed a rigorously ascetic manner of living, but abandoned it for the relaxed and comfortable style which provoked Jerome's vitriol; but he remained celibate and still called himself a monk.[49] Jovinian's challenge to the current assumptions about monasticism were eclipsed by the impact made by his wider attack on asceticism. He was condemned by a Roman synod under pope Siricius[50] – no lover of ascetics – and by Ambrose.[51] But he was the first to raise a question which was to trouble others: was the pursuit of perfection through self-denial the essential substance of the monastic life?

Although Jovinian vanished from the scene, his teaching had evidently set up ripples which reached monastic circles such as the community at Vercelli, one of the earliest monastic groups known in the West, sufficient to worry Ambrose. It appears that the phenomenon of monks denouncing asceticism was not uncommon; and we should be on our guard against assuming, as is too often done, that such monks were necessarily apostate monks.[52] We have seen (above, ch. 4) that Augustine still felt it necessary nearly ten years after the event to deal with the problems about marriage and virginity which Jerome's debate with Jovinian had left unresolved. This may be a measure of the extent to which Jovinian was the mouthpiece of a widely felt malaise. Jovinian's ideas may have prompted Augustine to re-think some of his views on sexuality; but it was not Jovinian's ideas that stimulated him into re-thinking the theological foundations of the monastic life. That appears to have taken place under the momentum of his own developing thought. The

---

[49] Lienhard, *Paulinus of Nola*, 123, 127, is mistaken in thinking of Jovinian as a former monk: Jerome's assault only makes sense if Jovinian continued to consider himself a monk. See esp. Jerome, *Adv. Iov.* I.40; and Haller, *Iovinianus*, 123; Valli, *Gioviniano*, 22–3, and now Hunter, 'Resistance'.

[50] *Ep.* 7.4 (*PL* 13.1171).

[51] *Ep.* 42.14.

[52] *Ep.* 63.7; cf. *Expl. super Ps.* 36.49: the monks referred to were almost certainly disciples of Jovinian. Augustine was reserved about ostentatious asceticism: see *De serm. Dom. in monte* II.12.41.

direction of Augustine's thinking about monasticism helped to deprive asceticism of the dominant place it still occupied in many circles.

Augustine could never have gone as far as Jovinian in emptying monasticism of its content of asceticism. His own conversion to Christianity had been a conversion to asceticism, and he never ceased to place the highest value on virginity and self-denial.[53] They were bound to remain important for his conception of what constituted Christian perfection. But the way to thinking of monastic life in terms of the pursuit of perfection was barred for him. His instinctive suspicion of any form of spiritual elitism was reinforced by the thrust of the theology of human action and divine grace which he developed in the course of his debate with Pelagius and his followers. Thus Augustine came to realise that he had to abandon the old idea that what distinguished the monastic life from other forms of Christian living was the pursuit of perfection through self-denial. The quest of perfection could not be allowed to be the monopoly of one group of Christians. The Christian community could not be allowed to be divided by a double standard, one for the ordinary Christian, another for an ascetic elite (see above, pp. 40–1): there is a single final end all must strive to attain, and a single Christian morality all must follow. The basis on which monastic groups were to be distinguished within the Christian community had to be re-defined.

Augustine's own approach to Christian communal living had been through the group of friends devoted to the search for wisdom: this coloured his subsequent views on monasticism more than did his ascetic inclinations. In his re-valuation of the received monastic traditions he came to lay all the stress on charity within the community, the sharing of possessions 'according to the manner and rule laid down by the Apostles',[54] 'the love which promotes the common good for the sake of the heavenly society'.[55] Among the things he laid down to be observed within the monastery, he placed first 'that on account

---

[53] E.g. *Ep.* 157.39.
[54] Possidius, *Vita Aug.* 5. On this see Lorenz, 'Die Anfänge', 39.
[55] *De Gen. ad litt.* XI.15.20.

of which you have been assembled together: that you might live in concord in the house, and have a single heart and a single mind in God'.[56] So much importance did Augustine attach to this Apostolic model of a Christian community that on one important (and painful) occasion he chose to repeat, before delivering his sermon, the passage of Acts 4 just read by the deacon: 'to read these words gives me more delight than anything I could say to you myself'.[57] Renunciation of private property is, naturally, central to this conception of monastic living; fasting still has its place, and chastity is assumed without question; but comparison with existing monastic practice leaves no doubt that Augustine shifted much of the stress previously laid on asceticism towards the values of communal living and the virtues which foster it. 'With the Rule of Saint Augustine Western monasticism embarks on a road which leads to Benedict.'[58]

The community living in concord and singlemindedness, with all property shared, is Augustine's favoured model of the monastery. These are the qualities which make it a microcosm of the City of God. The most insidious form of pride, the root of all sin, was 'privacy', self-enclosure. The 'private' was the opposite of 'shared', 'common', 'public'; and the Heavenly City was the community in which full sharing would be had. In the presence of God with the saints,

we shall experience none of the necessities of society [*nullas societatis angustias*], in loving what we have as private possession [*rei nostrae quasi privatae*]. For when that most glorious City has come into its promised inheritance, its citizens will have nothing in which to rejoice as if it were their own, for God will be all in all. Anyone who in this earthly pilgrimage is earnestly and faithfully seeking community with Him,

---

[56] *Ep.* 211.5. I by-pass here the controversies over the 'Rule' of Saint Augustine. See now Lawless, *Augustine*, for an up-to-date account (based on the work of Luc Verheijen) of Augustine's monasticism. Sage, *La vie religieuse*, 45–6, has traced the shift of emphasis from detachment towards fraternal charity (*anima una et cor unum*) in Augustine to the years after 401, and to his greater interest, developed in the course of the Donatist controversy, in baptism. Zumkeller, *Das Mönchtum*, 121–51, also places the idea of the loving community at the centre of his account of the development of Augustine's *Mönchsideal*, without, however, considering the chronological development of Augustine's views. See also Verheijen, 'Saint Augustin'.

[57] *Sermo* 355: see also 356, preached on the same occasion.

[58] Lorenz, 'Die Anfänge', 61.

must accustom himself to prefer the common to the private, not seeking what is his own, but what is Jesus Christ's.

The two poles of social living were, at one extreme, to be enclosed in an isolated self, and, at the other, to live in full community with God and one's fellows. All human societies fell somewhere between these two poles; but the monastery had a privileged relation to the community of the Heavenly City.[59] Once Augustine had written a short treatise on the monk's duty to work for the common good of the community. In a crucially significant paragraph he referred to the monastery as God's *res publica*, the City of God: if even among the Romans, in the earthly City, some placed the common good before their own private interests (Augustine is referring here, as he was to do in the *City of God*, to the great models of pagan Roman virtue), 'what should be the attitude of the citizen of that heavenly City of Jerusalem in his own commonwealth [*res publica*]?'. The commonwealth Augustine is speaking of here is the monastic community.[60] It is not through oversight or by coincidence that he is writing of the monastery in the same terms as he was to use of the City of God.

In his long controversy with the Donatists over the nature of the Church and its relation to the unredeemed world Augustine had come to relinquish the image of the Church as a spiritual elite set in the world.[61] Like any other society of men, it was irretrievably tinged with sin and contained within itself both the City of God and the earthly City, inextricably interwoven. Only at the end, beyond their historical careers, would the two Cities be distinct, made visible in their separate realities by the divine judgement. The Church is for ever caught in the inescapable tension between what it is here and now, and what it shall be: *qualis nunc est, qualis tunc erit.*[62] In speaking of the monastic community in terms of the 'City of God' Augustine seems to be identifying a particular institution within the Church with this eschatological vocation of the whole Church. The monastic life

[59] *Enarr. in Ps.* 105.34; cf. 103.ii.11; 131.6.
[60] *De op. mon.* 25.32; cf. *De civ. Dei* V.15. *De bono con.* 18.21 makes the point explicit, though in a condensed form.
[61] On this and what follows, see Markus, *Saeculum*, especially 105–26.
[62] *De civ. Dei* XX.9.1; see Markus, *Saeculum*, 120f.

displays, in a special way, the Church's calling to be the perfect community which can be realised only in the City of God *qualis tunc erit,* beyond history. It is a privileged anticipation of the Church's eschatological realisation. The Church could be no alternative society in which men could take refuge from the dislocated and tension-torn society in which it was, always and inevitably, placed; but the monastery was called to be a visible anticipation, a showing forth here and now, of the shape of the society that would be embodied in the Church in its final state, no longer the 'mixed body' (*corpus permixtum*) but purified on God's threshing floor.[63]

Augustine was, especially in his later years, intensely conscious of the power of sin in human society. The bonds between men had become drastically dislocated, no human group could hope to escape the tension and disorder which was endemic in the society of Adam's heirs. But the monastery, though not exempt from the universal human condition, was to be the nearest that men could get to a society in which the bonds between its members were restored to their original integrity. To become a monk was to undertake a commitment to uphold an image of social cohesion different from that of society – even a Christian society, if such were possible – at large. It was to associate with others on a basis of free rational decision, to take on obligations which would conform to the Pauline command to owe no man anything but to love one another (Rom. 13.8), and transform all duties into works of love. In this synthesis of Pauline theology and monastic tradition Augustine incorporated some of the ideas in which the social thinkers of Antiquity had outlined images of the perfect society. Thus the Stoic ideal of friendship found its fulfilment in monasticism: meditating in an early work on the question why men wish to live with those whom they love, Augustine had written: 'that we might seek our own souls and God in concord together'.[64] The monastery embodies this 'sociological function of the love of God'. In shifting the emphasis from asceticism to the renewal of unspoilt human relationships as the core of the monastic life Augustine focused a direction

---

[63] *Gesta Conl. Carth.* III.261, 265, 273; see Markus, *Saeculum*, 122.
[64] *Sol.* I.12.20, referred to by Lorenz, 'Die Anfänge', 40, n. 22. The phrase quoted is from *ibid.*, p. 40. I here lean heavily on Lorenz's pages 38–42.

already implicit in the development of fourth-century
spirituality.

To become a monk now came to mean more than the adoption
of a new personal identity. To undergo *conversio* to the monastic
calling was at the same time to proclaim the possibility of a new
social identity. This was the image of a society withdrawn from
the 'social necessities', a society constituted by the free association
of its members to create a community of love, ruled by humility
not power, living in concord without exploitation. In the monastic community the shape of the final society of the saints was
made actually visible, to the extent that it could be anticipated
on earth. Its existence here and now proclaimed a permanent
challenge to all other forms of social existence, a question mark
placed against the structures of domination inherent in the
society of fallen men, an ideal Augustine held up to his lay
congregations to imitate in 'building the temple of God'.[65] The
monastery was a living proclamation of a social organisation
alternative to that of any possible form of association of human
beings in large-scale societies, liberated from their tragic
'necessities'. Augustine's re-definition of the monastic ideal is
drawn in terms of a new kind of society and the meaning of
new human relationships within it.

The explosion of asceticism in Late Antiquity is not explicable
in terms of that 'contempt for the human condition and hatred
of the body' which E. R. Dodds diagnosed as 'a disease endemic
in the entire culture of the period' (of his 'age of anxiety', from
Marcus Aurelius to Constantine, and, in fact beyond).[66] Revulsion from the body, and difficulties in articulating a sense of the
wholeness of the embodied person, inherited from a variety of
traditions, certainly continued to dog the development of Christian thought. All the same, Christians understood sexual union
as a joining of two persons, not of two bodies; and they understood virginity as the joining of a whole person to God. We have
learnt, most recently and luminously from Peter Brown,[67] that
the appeal of renunciation, virginity and asceticism in its widest
sweep is more than a neurosis of men alienated from their

[65] *Enarr. in Ps.* 131.5–7.
[66] Dodds, *Pagan and Christian*, 35.
[67] See now his *The body and society*.

society, 'introjecting' – to use the Freudian term adopted by Dodds – their hostility towards the world, turning it into 'resentment against the ego'.[68] A gulf separates the Gnostic's resentment of the body and of the material world from the stress that comes increasingly to be laid by Christian writers on the body as the 'temple of the Holy Spirit'.[69] For them the line between the real self destined for salvation and the alien, irredeemable residue ran not between soul and body, but between the self as a whole and the sin-infected world in which it was struggling for freedom. The good wife, Ambrose wrote, 'is tied by conjugal bonds; [the pious virgin] is free of these bonds. The former is under the law, the latter under grace.'[70] To embrace a life of virginity was to assert a freedom to withdraw from the web of bonds which kept the self captive in a very imperfect society, through the structures of marriage, property, succession and the attendant and endlessly varied forms of domination. A 'Mirror for wives' addressed to a noble Christian lady reminded her of the obligations she had incurred: 'You have been purchased, bought by the marriage contract, bound by as many knots as you have bodily parts.'[71] To renounce marriage was not to reject the body; it was to take the whole, undivided self across that line which divides sin from holiness. Like the virgin, the monk embraced this freedom from the bonds on which the fabric of secular society depended; but the monk found this freedom within a community in which mutual service replaced 'social necessity'. In his social disengagement and his entry into a community created by free decisions the monk was proclaiming the existence here and now, not as a mere ideal possibility, of an alternative mode of social ordering, anticipating the life of the saints in the City of God *qualis tunc erit.*

[68] Dodds, *Pagan and Christian*, 27–8.
[69] E.g. Paulinus, *Ep.* 24.6, *inter multa* (see *Ep.* 16.13 for a fine image of slavery to and rebellion against God).
[70] *Ep.* 42.3
[71] Arnobius Iunior, *Ad Gregoriam* 7. (On its authorship, Morin, 'Arnobe le Jeune', 332–40). Cf. Ambrosiaster, *In Ep. ad Cor. I* 7.27 (*CSEL* 81/2.83); Basil of Ancyra: 'with your dowry you have bought yourself servitude' – quoted by Aline Rousselle, *Porneia*, 176, a book which contains, among other remarkable things, a fine account of the restrictions hemming in the freedom of the partners in marriage and concubinage, and outside them; see especially 136–7. Augustine, *Sermo* 37.6.7, on *tabulae matrimoniales* as the *instrumenta emptionis suae*. On 'the traditional bundle of duties that went with marriage', see Shaw, 'The family', 32.

Augustine's re-interpretation of the monastic life is rooted in the development of his own theology; it also reflects the development within the monastic and ascetic tradition. In turn, Augustine's re-valuation of that tradition helped to open monasticism to the demands of the ecclesial community and strengthened the forces which led to its integration in the life of the Church.[72] In later chapters we shall have to return to ask what contribution it made to the understanding of the triple relationships between religious community, Church and society at large.

---

[72] See Lorenz, 'Die Anfänge', 42. I return to this subject below, chs. 11–13.

II

KAIROI: CHRISTIAN TIMES AND THE PAST

The central problem for fourth-century Christians was their own past. A continuous biography is the core of our sense of personal identity. This is true no less of a group's sense of identity. It needs to be able to recognise itself as one and the same group enduring through time, the heir of its own past.

This, however, was difficult for the larger part of the Christians in the fourth century. Dissident groups like that of the Donatists in North Africa, or the Nicene opposition under arianising emperors, were more exposed to pressure from the government, denied the privileges and the prestige of its support, sometimes exposed to persecution by the authorities. On the face of it, it was such groups rather than the 'Catholics' who had the most direct and obvious claim to be the heirs of the martyrs. They made the best of that claim, and in the conditions of the post-Constantinian Empire it was not easy to dispute it.[1] The past seemed, clearly, to belong to them. (See below, pp. 92–3.) The future belonged to the Great Church; but it could hardly remain content with only the future. To be universal, 'catholic', it had to annex the past, too. It had to wrest the legacy of the persecuted Church from more plausible claimants.

[1] For a sample of the debate, see Augustine, *Ep.* 185.2.9–11, or Gregory Nazianzen, *Or.* 43.6 (*PG* 36.500–1).

6

The last times

Long before the fourth century Christians had known that with
the coming of Christ the world entered a new age. The Promised
One expected by the Jews had come; the definitive end of world
history had been anticipated in events that took place in a Roman
province in the reigns of Augustus and Tiberius. The prophets
and the biblical writers had singled out one strand of history.
Interpreting it in the perspective of God's saving acts done
among His people, they turned it into 'sacred history'. In submit-
ting itself to a fixed canon of scripture comprising the books of
the Old and the New Testaments, the Christian Church accepted
a strictly limited understanding of 'sacred history'. The scriptural authors not only told a particular strand of the history of
the ancient Near East, that of the Jews and of Jesus; they were
'inspired' by God in telling it, that is to say, they were giving,
along with their narrative, an interpretation; and to their interpretation the Church was prepared to assign divine authority.

The sacred writers, prophets and evangelists were presenting
God's action in their narratives within the framework of the
history of salvation. Their interpretative scheme was inspired
and authorised, so Christians held, by the Spirit Himself. Of
course, God had been active outside this particular and narrow
stream of historical narrative; of course, He would continue to
act in all history and nothing would be remote from His providence. But nowhere else could the Church be bound to an
authoritative insight into the meaning of any historical event
or process in the scheme of salvation. God's purposes may,
occasionally, be disclosed to some later prophet *quasi privatim*,

as Augustine would say,[1] 'personally'; but His revelation of His purposes in the public history of salvation was closed. Christian history would show, not least in the fourth century, that even more necessary than the prophets – true and false – who would claim to discern God's hand in events, in societies or cultures – or in political programmes or utopian visions – is the prophet who will remind his Church that outside the narrow bounds of the scriptures no one is authorised to proclaim what God is up to.

This sacred history reached its decisive climax in the life, work and death of Jesus; but, as Christians gradually came to realise, the 'end' was not yet. They, and later generations after them, would have to await the return of the Lord in glory to gather His faithful from the four corners of the world, and to wait without a clue as to the time of its coming, but in the knowledge that the decisive event of their salvation had already been accomplished. The division of time into 'BC' and 'AD' which represents this consciousness, crystallised only in the sixth century and came into widespread use only in the eighth; but in one way or another the various divisions of history into 'ages' current in Christian Antiquity all marked the crucial divide that Christ's coming had inserted into the flow of time. This it was that separated all that came before – even if that happened to be further sub-divided into a sequence of 'ages' – from all that followed, including the present. The Incarnation of the Word transformed the ontological conditions of Christian existence and overshadowed all other landmarks between any other epochs that might be distinguished in world history.[2]

This strained time-scheme was reflected in the rhythm of Christian worship. The life of the faithful unfolded between two 'ends', the one already achieved, the other still in the waiting. Their worship constantly recalled them to a sense of the tension between the 'already' and the 'not yet'. In the recurrent cycle of celebrations, the faithful were summoned to carry out God's command: 'Thou shalt remember what the Lord Thy God did.' At the same time they were bidden to look to the future, waiting

[1] *De vera rel.* 25.46. On all this see Markus, *Saeculum*, Appendix A.
[2] The classic is, still, Cullmann, *Christ and time.* On the misguided contrast often drawn in the wake of Cullmann's work between Christian 'linear' and allegedly 'circular' time in classical paganism, see Momigliano, 'Time in ancient historiography'.

in hope: 'Come, Lord Jesus.' These were the 'last times'. Whatever world-shaking events, disasters or revolutions intervened,
nothing could now have a decisive significance in the history of
salvation. In this long perspective – and nobody could say how
long it might be – events could henceforth only be neutral,
devoid of sacred significance. There was no room for further
'epoch-making' events. The 'sacred history' of the last times was
a blank, an open space between the Lord's two comings.[3]

These immense simplicities of their faith and prayer were,
however, confused for Christians by new uncertainties brought
by the post-Constantinian era. The conversion of an emperor,
followed by the large-scale christianisation of their society within
a few generations, seemed to transform the conditions of Christian existence dramatically, and certainly more visibly than the
great divide of the Incarnation. The miracle which turned a
persecuting empire into the political embodiment of their
religion, into its protector, promoter and enforcer, almost succeeded in seducing Christians from their sense of the
homogeneity of these 'last times'. They were almost lured into
believing that a new messianic age had dawned with Constantine's conversion. The era inaugurated by Constantine and,
especially, the decades around 400, following the great strides
made by the Theodosian establishment in imposing Christian
orthodoxy on the empire, seemed to mark a new divide in the
seamless fabric of this last age. How could such a miraculous
triumph of their only recently oppressed religion be anything
other than God's mighty work? To the mass of Christians, their
clergy and their bishops, as well as to their increasingly
apprehensive and reproachful non-Christian opponents, these
'Christian times' seemed to have inaugurated a new dispensation
in the world. The collective euphoria of the post-Theodosian
generation was deflated by the theological critique of Augustine's
City of God;[4] and, perhaps more effectively, by the troubles to
which the empire was subjected in the early fifth century.

---

[3] I summarise here what is more fully expounded in my *Saeculum*, ch. 1.
[4] See my *Saeculum*, chs. 2–3, where, however, I failed to appreciate the importance of
Julian's attempted restoration of the Temple and its failure for the emergence of the
consciousness of a 'Christian world'. This is well brought out by Wilken, *John Chrysostom*,
138–48.

Ultimately, what was at stake in the fourth and fifth centuries was the historical unity of the Church through time. It was this unity, the identity of the triumphant Church with the Church which had not long before been persecuted by the emperors, that had come under threat in the 'Christian times'. Fourth-century Christians were sharply aware of a generation gap. It was given voice in the first post-Constantinian Christian generation by Eusebius. At the end of his life, after more than two decades of the first Christian emperor's rule, Eusebius wrote:[5] 'We, although not held worthy to have struggled [*agonizasthai*] unto death and to have shed our blood for God, yet, being the sons of those who have suffered thus and distinguished [*semnunomenoi*] by our fathers' virtues, pray for mercy through them.'

To bridge this generation gap, Eusebius and his contemporaries and successors had to convince themselves that, essentially, nothing had changed and that their Church was still the Church of the martyrs. Somehow the homogeneity of these last times between the coming of Christ and His return in glory had to be rescued. No radical break could be allowed to divide the triumphant Church of the fourth and later centuries from its persecuted predecessor. The past had to be kept alive in the Church's mind, and not only alive, but renewed in the novel conditions of its existence. This is what gave urgency to the heated doctrinal debates of the fourth century. The perplexities concerning God's fatherhood and the sonship of Jesus sprang from a need perceived to safeguard the continuity of Christian belief, and to do so at a time when the Church's mode of existence was itself undergoing drastic change. Fourth-century Christians had to run very fast indeed to stand still: 'to reject all innovation was simply not a real option', as has recently been observed,[6] if the historic continuity of belief was to be maintained. What was at stake in the debates around Nicaea was the question of what new theological formulation would best serve to articulate that

---

[5] *Comm. in Ps.* 78.11 (*PG* 23.949A). The permanence of the 'generation gap' between the age of the martyrs and the times of peace is, of course, well attested in later Christian literature, e.g. Hilary of Arles, *Sermo* 8.38. For the seventh century, good examples are *Passio S. Leudegarii* I.1 (*MGH SRM* 5, p. 283) and *Vita Audoini* 6 (*Ibid.* 557). See also n. 20 below.

[6] Williams, *Arius*, 235.

continuity. The theologians of the Constantinian era were faced with the need to clarify the Church's self-awareness with total faithfulness to the Gospel and to the experience of the worshipping Christian community. The Christians needed every device of intellect, imagination and devotion to help them accommodate themselves to their present without an acute sense of having betrayed their past.

The fourth century had two chief means of closing this permanent generation gap. One was the work of the ecclesiastical historians.[7] Eusebius had been the great pioneer of the *genre*. His *Ecclesiastical history* was begun towards the end of the long period of peace enjoyed by the Church before Diocletian's persecution;[8] when Eusebius completed his last revision of it the world had changed. Throughout the work Eusebius laid the greatest possible stress on the constant, the enduring and the continuous in the Church's past: the permanent features that its fourth-century descendant inherited. Hence the importance he gave to the succession of bishops in the principal sees; hence also the insistence – somewhat oversimplified – on the enduring orthodoxy of the Church's doctrinal tradition. Until the time of the emperor Trajan the Church had remained a pure virgin, uncorrupted by the 'deceit of false teachers'; and so, Eusebius insisted, she remained thereafter, through the faithful handing on of the Apostolic traditions, unblemished, though attacked, by heresy.[9] Unlike another of Eusebius' central themes, the stories of the persecutions and the martyrs, which belonged to a heroic age now recollected in tranquillity, orthodoxy and the succession of bishops were the threads on which the Church's continuing identity rested.

Eusebius' *Ecclesiastical history* was what a pioneering work rarely has the good fortune to become: both definitive and successful. It had many imitators and continuators. It met a deeply felt need, and met it so adequately that no ancient author ever thought it necessary to cover the same ground again. The book became canonical, and served as a model for ecclesiastical

[7] The following summarises Markus, 'Church history'.
[8] I accept the chronology established by Barnes, 'The editions', and used by him in *Constantine and Eusebius.*
[9] On the problem of orthodoxy and heresy, see Markus, 'The problem of self-definition'.

history writing. Its form and its choice of themes both set the pattern for all the Church historians at least until the end of the sixth century, even though the Church's history as it was taking shape was beginning to press on the conventions uncomfortably. In the very *genre* they adopted, its unchanging consistency and almost monolithic uniformity, the Church historians were proclaiming the identity of the Church of the fourth, the fifth and the sixth centuries with the persecuted Church of the first three.

Reading Eusebius and the translations and continuations of his *Ecclesiastical history* was thus one way by which later Christians could convince themselves that they were the true descendants of the martyrs. This way was available to those who could read, and was widely followed among the educated upper classes. There was an alternative with a far wider appeal: the cult of the martyrs. Long honoured in the Church, as had been heroes among the Jews and in wider circles in the ancient world, the cult of the martyrs came into its own when martyrdom was a thing of the past. The martyr was the human image of perfection, a model to follow. To be persecuted for the Lord's sake was the hall-mark of the true Christian. But as the fourth century wore on, this heroic image was slipping into a past ever more remote. In the fifth century a bishop who lost his life in a riot over the destruction of a pagan sanctuary was described as 'fortunate in having been given the opportunity to die for God'.[10] The picture of the Christian persecutor as a martyr is not only a supreme irony of history: it is also the measure of the need felt to share vicariously in the martyrs' struggle and their victory.

The cult of the martyr conflated the present and the past in the martyr's abiding presence at his shrine. Groups on the edge of orthodoxy which at times found themselves subject to more or less fierce official repression, such as the Donatists of North Africa in the fourth century, naturally saw themselves as the heirs of the Church of the martyrs. 'We rejoice in being hated by the world', one of them said,[11] and others sought out opportunities for violent death at the hands of the authorities or, if necessary, even their own. In the fourth century the Donatists

[10] Sozomen, *HE* VII.15.12–15. Compare the express prohibition by the Council of Elvira (c. 60) of receiving such people as martyrs.
[11] Gaudentius, quoted by Augustine, *C. Gaudent.* I.26.2.

led the way in multiplying celebrations of the martyrs' anniversaries and bringing to these celebrations unprecedented exuberance.[12] But apart from some of the more extravagant forms of devotion to the martyrs of their own sect, there was little that Donatists could not share with Catholics. Catholics were not actually exposed, as were the Donatists and, at times, other dissidents from the religion of the imperial establishment, to pressure from the authorities, landowners and even armies. For such men, living in respectable security, the need to identify themselves with the Church of the martyrs was even more imperative. Everywhere in the fourth century the cult of the martyrs came to meet this need in the most effective way: by taking a far greater place in the annual cycle of the celebrations which shaped the Christians' sense of their sacred time. Africa led the way here, as in so many respects. 'Full of the bodies of the blessed martyrs', Augustine wrote of Africa;[13] and on their lamps and tableware African craftsmen transformed traditional decorative themes to turn them into yet more reminders of the glories of the martyrs' victory over death.[14]

The martyr stood for the possibility of victory: man's victory over death, *our* victory over the frailty of our bodies, over the waywardness of our labile wills, the instability of our resolve, the weakness of our faith and our bondage to sin. The Christian was summoned to a daily battle in his heart: 'It is an august theatre, God is the spectator of your fight.'[15] On the festivals commemorating St Stephen Augustine liked to remind his congregations of the call to daily martyrdom, addressed to all believers: for had he not been one of us, of the same flesh and blood and the faithful servant of the same Lord?[16] Even when you are ill in bed, resisting the offer of healing by magical potions, witnessing to your Lord, 'you are in the arena: lying down, you are fighting'.[17] The martyr's presence in the city, his annual commemoration, and, especially, the arrival and solemn reception of his relics, were reminders to the faithful Christian that

[12] See Schindler, 'Sur l'attitude des Donatistes'.
[13] *Ep.* 78.3.
[14] See Salomonson, *Voluptatem spectandi non perdat sed mutat.*
[15] Augustine, *Sermo* 315.7.10.
[16] *Ibid.* 317.2.3.
[17] *Ibid.* 318.3.

his life had to be a struggle – now as in the heroic days of the faith; and that victory was within his reach. The healing power of the relics commend the martyr's faith:[18]

Stephen the martyr has spread his light in the regions of his suffering, in ours by visiting us in death. But he would not be visiting us dead, if in death he were not alive. How so little a handful of dust can draw so great a multitude! The [power of the] dust is hidden; the merciful gifts bestowed through it are manifest. Think, beloved, of what God mercifully grants us in the land of the living, who has given us so much through the remains of the dead. Saint Stephen's body has been made famous the world over: but it is the merit of his faith that is commended to us.

A relic, especially one newly discovered or newly arrived, was a potent reminder of the great works of God done for the salvation of men. It recalled 'at a particular time and place, the immensity of God's mercy'.[19] In Augustine's sermons the miracles attributed to the virtue of the relics, meticulously catalogued by the local clergy, achieved a peculiar transparency: he gave them a voice that spoke of God's saving acts done in the past, even more than of the power displayed in the present. Here was the assurance, anxiously sought by post-Constantinian Christians, of the ever-present possibility of martyrdom and the crown of victory to be won. The distance that separated their present from the past was abolished in the cult of the martyrs.

In the closing years of the fourth century, when persecution was a distant memory, far away in the North of Gaul a bishop was receiving relics of the martyrs sent from Italy, more fortunate in possessing her own, in great abundance. Nothing, perhaps, in the literature of Late Antique Christianity evokes as poignantly both the gulf that had opened between the persecuted Church and its triumphant successor, and the power of the martyr's relic to bridge it, as does his exultant address. Leading his congregation in welcoming the relics' arrival the bishop gave voice to the feelings of his congregation – shared with congregations from one end of the Mediterranean to the

---

[18] *Ibid.* 317.1.1.
[19] Brown, *The cult*, 92.

other: 'No oppressor's sword has been drawn against us; we have free access to God's altars; no savage enemy lies in wait for us . . . no torturer has attacked us . . . no blood is shed now, no persecutor pursues us; yet we are filled with the joy of triumph.'[20] The struggle for the past was won over the bodies of the martyrs.

[20] Victricius of Rouen, *De laude sanct.* 1. See also below, ch. 10, n. 21.

7

The martyrs and sacred time

'There, in that heavenly City of Jerusalem', Augustine wrote, 'whence we are wandering, the angels await us wanderers.'[1] That vast community of angels and saints is there, expecting Christ's faithful on earth:

the body of that Head is the Church; not the Church which is in this place, but the Church which is here and in the whole world; nor the Church which is now, but that which is from Abel to those until the end of time who are still to be born and to believe in Christ: the whole people of the saints that belong to the one City, the City which is Christ's body and whose head is Christ. There the angels are our fellow citizens. We, wanderers, labour still; there, in that City, they await our arrival.[2]

A faithful Christian's death is a triumphal entry – an *adventus* – to that City. In his funeral cortège its earthly members accompany him along the first stage of his triumphal procession, a celebration of a 'cosmic Easter'.[3]

Of this community that straddled heaven and earth the martyrs were honoured members. Greco-Roman paganism gave honour to the community's heroes; late Judaism recognised the claim of its martyrs to veneration, though without making their tombs places of public commemorative celebration. Christian eclecticism, giving the martyrs a place in public worship, had to guard against the danger of turning the martyr into a cult hero: we do not venerate our martyrs, Augustine warned,[4]

---

[1] *Enarr. in Ps.* 62.6: *unde nos peregrinamur, attendunt nos peregrinos.*
[2] *Enarr. in Ps.* 90; *Sermo* II.1. See above, ch. 2, n. 3.
[3] See Sicard, *La liturgie de la mort*, 257.
[4] *Sermo* 273.7. Cf. *De civ. Dei* XXII.10; on the whole theme, see Rordorf, *Aux origines*, 329–31.

as gods; we do not build temples to them, no altars, nor do we sacrifice
in their honour. Our priests make no offering to them – God forbid!
... Even at their shrines [*memoriae*] when we make our offering, it is
to God. The martyrs have their place of honour; look, at the commemoration at Christ's altar, they are given precedence; but they are
not adored instead of Christ.

The martyrs were, after the Apostles, the supreme representatives of the community of the faithful in God's presence. In
them the communion of saints was most tangibly epitomised.

Whenever a Christian took part in a public act of worship,
especially of the eucharist, he was brought into the presence of
the martyrs. But it was in the fourth century that the Church
went to the greatest lengths to keep this presence vividly before
his mind. Up to then the calendar of worship had taken little
note of the martyr. The anniversary of his 'birthday' or his
'deposition' was commemorated by each community at the site
of his burial. But the cycle of Christian festivals developed
independently, and remained based on the Lord's resurrection:
'for the faith of the early Church the Resurrection of Jesus was
so decisive that in the last resort only one festival seemed essential
to it'.[5] The Resurrection was thus the hinge on which the cycle
of sacred time turned. The year and the week both revolved
around it. Every Sunday was a weekly celebration of Easter,
every Friday a weekly Good Friday.[6] A second cycle came to
cluster around the festival of the Lord's birth and went on
developing in the fourth century and beyond. (On Sunday and
Christmas, see below, pp. 103–6.)

The development which overshadowed all others, however,
was the huge expansion of the cult of the martyrs. Commemorations of the 'depositions' of its own martyrs had been added
to the principal feasts in each church from the earliest times.
Individual churches kept records of such dates and celebrated
their anniversaries. Sometimes these dates might be communi-
cated to a sister-church with which contact was kept up, thus
spreading the celebration of the martyr's anniversary more
widely. The Roman Church had such a calendar within Constantine's life-time. It contained some thirty anniversaries of the
deposition of its own martyrs, together with a few others. Within

[5] Klauser, 'Der Festkalender', 380.
[6] Innocent I, *Ep.* 25.4.7 (*PL* 20.553).

the space of two or three generations commemorations of the martyrs came to fill the interstices in the calendar, especially the longer spells of summer unrelieved by feasts of the life of Christ. 'Hardly a day can be found in the circle of the year on which martyrs were not somewhere crowned', said Augustine; we only space out the celebrations to avoid the tedium of habit.[7] By the end of the sixth century the Christian year was almost swamped by the new festivals. On a large number of the year's days, a Christian who attended a church service would be liturgically thrust back into the age of the martyrs. At mass, he was united with them, caught up in the perpetual liturgy which embraced him within the society of the angels and the saints. Here, supremely, he was at one with the martyrs and shared in their glory. The martyrs were assured of survival in the post-Constantinian world, and Christians of living in their continued presence; of living, as it were, in the age of the martyrs.

The gradual development of this liturgical cycle may mislead us into underestimating its significance. To be sure, there is no denying the continuity. In the age before Constantine, to honour the martyr had been a duty. Clergy were enjoined to record the dates of their death in order to ensure proper celebration of the anniversaries;[8] the anniversaries were to be celebrated with seemly restraint and discipline, unlike the pagans' 'junketings' (*laetitiae*) at the graveside. The emphasis was subtly shifted in the fourth century: to honour the dead, especially the martyr, remained a duty, but its discharge was now the satisfaction of a new need. This was the need to be able to see the post-Constantinian Church as the heir of the Church of the martyrs (see ch. 6, above). It accounts for the greatest novelty in the fourth-century cult of the martyrs, the quantitative leap in the scale and speed of its expansion.

This need gave the impetus to the vast elaboration of the annual cycle of the Christian scheme of sacred time. But another shift was also to contribute to the creation of this time-scheme. Until, in the course of the third century, Christians began to

---

[7] *Sermo Denis* 13.1. Of the rich literature on the cult of the martyrs, I refer only to the classic discussion by Delehaye, *Les origines*, and Saxer, *Morts, martyrs, reliques*. On the swamping of the calendar, see Klauser, 'Der Festkalender', 383.

[8] E.g. Cyprian, *Ep.* 12.2; 39.3.1; 80.1.4, *inter multa*.

enter the mainstream of Roman life in sizeable numbers, their
main need was for a calendar of religious observance which
would set them apart from the Jews. Thus the earliest surviving
Church order tells the faithful not to fast at the same times as
do the 'hypocrites', on Mondays and Thursdays, but on Wednes-
days and Fridays.[9] The Lord's day superseded the Sabbath and
Easter the Passover. The date of Easter was, eventually, to be
reckoned in such a way as to make coincidence impossible.[10]
Their calendar thus assured Christians of a group identity distinct from the Jews. There was much less danger, until much
later times, of their group melting into the pagan society around
it, and therefore nothing like the same necessity to replace pagan
festivals with their own alternatives.

A current of thought apparently hostile to the importance of
celebrating set festivals can be detected, running alongside the
growing importance of the calendar of celebrations, in the
apologetic literature of the first three centuries. 'All the days
are the Lord's' is a thought often to be found, usually as a
justification for abstaining from Jewish, sometimes from pagan,
festivities.[11] The idea seems to undermine the importance of
festivals; but this was not the intention. An exchange between
the pagan Celsus and the Christian Origen turns a sharp momentary beam of light on the problem: why do Christians avoid the
public feasts and observe their own instead? After all, as Celsus
observed, they are all intended to celebrate the One supreme
God, who is in need of nothing. In his reply, Origen does not
dispute this; indeed, in doing one's duty, he says, and 'continually offering bloodless sacrifices of prayer', one is celebrating
an unending festival. The man who is 'always engaged in the
words, works, and thoughts of the divine Logos who is by nature
his Lord, is always living in His days and is continually observing
the Lord's Day'.[12] What matters is communion with God, which
is achieved by upright living and contemplation of the truth.
For the wise man all days are, as they are in God's sight, the

[9] *Didache.* 8.1.
[10] See Zerubavel, 'Easter and Passover'. For a fine study of a sacred calendar serving
to define group identity, see Tedlock, *Time and the highland Maya*.
[11] E.g. *Didasc. Ap.* VI.18.16, ed. Conolly, 237; *Ad Diognet.*, 4; and Origen, cf. n. 12 below.
[12] Origen, *C. Celsum*, VIII.21–2, trs. H. Chadwick, 467–8. For a perceptive commentary,
see Dihle, 'Zur spätantiken Kultfrömmigkeit'.

same – celebrations are otiose. Origen's notion of worship and festivals has much in common with the philosophical tradition of Late Antique religiosity on which his pagan opponent's argument also depended. Origen was a sophisticated Christian, acquainted with much Greek thought; we may not assume that his fellow faithful shared his views on the nature of Christian festivals. Educated pagans as well as Christian thinkers might spiritualise away the significance of particular moments of time; but there is no real doubt about the cardinal importance of Sunday in the Christian week and of Easter in the year. This was enough to set them apart from the Jews as well as from the pagans.

When Origen wrote the problem of defining a Christian group identity in pagan society was only just arising. For the first two centuries of its existence the Christian group was only too clearly and sometimes even painfully divided from the pagan milieu in which it existed. As in the course of the third century the cross-section of the ordinary Christian community in a Roman town came gradually to reflect the social composition of the world around it, its identity came to need sharper outlines to define it.[13] The need was to grow from the middle of the third century. Christians had to guard against the threat to their identity by becoming too assimilated, to dissociate themselves from the calendar of traditional Roman public festivals, and the celebrations, circus games, banquets, shows in the theatre and the hippodrome, associated with many of them. As the number of Christians grew and as they came to be drawn from a wider and more representative cross-section of society, many of them flocked to the circus and the theatres, in Rome and in Carthage and elsewhere, there to enjoy the spectacles along with their pagan neighbours. Everyone was aware of the religious origins of these shows and celebrations, but few thought such participation amounted to compromise with idolatry. Both Tertullian's and Novatian's diatribes against Christian participation in the shows leave no doubt that those who favoured them did so with a clear conscience, regarding them as occasions of secular

---

[13] See Markus, 'The problem of self-definition'. For a meticulous case-study, see now Schöllgen, *Ecclesia sordida?*

rejoicing without religious significance. 'They usurp the authority of the name of Christian', ran the denunciation.[14] It was against such conformists that Tertullian and Novatian upheld an older and stricter rule: whatever a Christian who frequented the shows believed, his actions proclaimed him a pagan. 'By this shall they know a man for a Christian', Tertullian wrote, 'that he has repudiated the shows.'[15] The pagan cycle of sacred time had to be shown up as idolatry, vain delusion: 'pick out each festival of the pagans, set them in a row, and they won't make up one single Pentecost'.[16]

Christians had already gone a long way in appropriating the culture and life-styles of their pagan contemporaries before the time of Constantine. The emperor's conversion to their religion did nothing to reverse this trend. In the third century the thunder of Tertullian and Novatian seems to have fallen on deaf ears; around the middle of the fourth, there were no Tertullians or Novatians to recall Christians to a more intransigent standard. In the 350s high-class Christians cele-brated ancient Roman festivals along with their own feasts and anniversaries, without apparent embarrassment or rebuke. Around AD 400 Faustus the Manichee taunted Augustine: the Christians, he said, celebrated kalends and solstices just as do the heathen; their Church, therefore, he argued, was no more than a 'schism' from its pagan 'matrix', having nothing essential of its own in cult or manner of life to distinguish it from its pagan milieu. So it was no more than a separate 'conventicle' (*conventus*), a hived-off congregation, of pagans.[17] Faustus' argu-ment was aimed against Christian holy days celebrated on the same days as were pagan festivals. The same point could be made even more tellingly against Christian participation in pagan celebrations, and it was not lost on Augustine. If Christians are to be *con*gregated in a Church, he preached, they must be *se*gregated from the heathen – the *gentes* – separated from the pagans and their festivities.[18] The sacred calendar, he appreci-

[14] Novatian, *De spect.* 1–2: *vitiorum assertores blandi et indulgentes patrones ... christiani sibi nominis auctoritatem vindicantes*; cf. Tertullian, *De idol.* 14; *De spect.* 20.
[15] *de repudio spectaculorum* – *De spect.* 24.3.
[16] Tertullian, *De idol.* 14.7.
[17] Quoted by Augustine, *C. Faust.* XX.4, 1.
[18] *Sermo* 198.2.

ated, was one of the principal rituals of exclusion: it identifies
the Christian – as Tertullian had said – by the celebrations which
he has renounced.

The problem posed by one rival sacred calendar, the Jewish
religious week and year, had long ago been dealt with. The
problem posed by the traditional Roman calendar was more
difficult. Its celebrations were rooted in a distant religious past;
but they were also the rites which governed the rhythm of public
life, and they articulated a corporate civic and municipal consensus. Many Christians were deeply involved in public life, and
found it easy to persuade themselves that the religious overtones
of public celebrations were faint enough not to offend their
piety. Could one distinguish between celebrations that retained
a religious significance and had, therefore, to be shunned, from
those that could be regarded as secular and thus tolerable?

Some festivals were clearly religious in nature. Among them,
in the fourth century, the day of the Sun[19] and the winter solstice,
25 December, which had since the later third century been
celebrated as the birthday of the Unconquered Sun, offered
little difficulty. They needed no more than re-interpretation in
a Christian context.[20] 'The world itself proclaims [by its darkness
yielding to returning light] its own rebirth with the birth of
Christ': Maximus, bishop of Turin, liked to dwell in his Christmas sermons on the displacement of the old festival of the Sun
by the 'new Sun'. The Lord's day and Christmas could suitably
replace the pagan days. Their place in the Christian sacred
calendar would establish and underpin their new meaning.
Others, such as the Kalends of January, posed a problem less
tractable.[21] This feast had developed over a long time, and came
to mark the ending of the old year and the beginning of the
new. On 1 January took place the solemn inauguration of the
new consuls; but the three-day celebration was also an occasion
for private observances: of rejoicing, of the giving of presents
and good wishes, devotions to secure an auspicious year. The

[19] See Rordorf, *Der Sonntag.*
[20] See Dölger, 'Das Sonnengleichnis', 23–30. Maximus of Turin, *Sermo* 61a.1; cf. 61b.1
(of dubious attribution); 62.
[21] On this see Meslin, *La fête des kalendes*, a fine example of the manner in which
'survivals' should be, but rarely are, studied. The bare and selective summary I give in
the text is based on this full and perceptive study.

suppression of the traditional sacrifices which 'gave the public ceremony of the opening of the year its profound religious sense'[22] turned the festival into a secular, civic celebration, though one occasionally marked by some later pious consul with some act of Christian devotion. It had been left untouched by the legislation of Christian emperors, and thus became one of the few great occasions on which the remaining pagans could express their devotion freely and openly.

But Christians celebrated it equally, without anxiety on the score of its possibly 'pagan' character. Shorn of its overtly religious ceremonial, the sacrifice, and the supremely valued circus games, 'the foundations – along with the baths – of all civilised living',[23] the first of January continued to be celebrated by pagan and Christian, by poor and rich, in town and in countryside. More than any other, it was a day for healing rifts, of establishing and celebrating social cohesion. It would thus appear to be a perfect example of a festival in which civic and religious elements had originally blended to form an indivisible unity, which, allowed to survive purged of its pagan content, might have been well on the way to developing into a purely civic celebration. But, though permitted by the law, it was fiercely opposed by churchmen from Ambrose and Jerome in the fourth century, to Maximus of Turin and Peter Chrysologus in fifth-century Italy, Caesarius of Arles in Gaul and Martin of Braga in sixth-century Galicia.[24] The virulence and the unanimity of their attacks comes not of bitterness against the pagan outsider: it is an attack on widespread and large-scale participation by Christians; Christians, moreover, who saw nothing wrong in taking part: 'we commit no sacrilege, these are only games ... – it is the gladness over the new, rejoicing over the start of a new year; it is not the falsehood of the [pagan] past, nor the sin of idolatry'.[25] But the bishops would have none of it: 'he who

---

[22] *Ibid.* 58.
[23] *Ibid.* 67; cf. *CIL* VIII.17938, an inscription (from the forum in Timgad) which Marrou liked to think of as an epitome of Roman urban civilisation.
[24] Details in Meslin, *La fête des kalendes*, 71–5. John Chrysostom, *Hom. in Kalendas* (*PG* 48.953–62) and *Hom. c. ludos et theatra* (*PG* 56.263–70) are noteworthy.
[25] Peter Chrysologus, *Sermo* 155 (*CC* 24B.964, quoted by Meslin, *La fête des kalendes*, 96). Compare Jacob of Seroug, *Homily on the Spectacles* 5, ed. C. Moss, 109: 'I do not go that I may believe, but that I might laugh', say the defenders of the practice. See above, n. 14.

would play with the Devil cannot rejoice with Christ'. Their indignation and horror of such festivities as simply incompatible with being a Christian calls for some explanation.

The reason undoubtedly lies in the significance they instinctively attached to their own festival of renewal. Only a week before the Kalends of January Christians celebrated the incarnation of their Lord. It first appeared in the Christian calendar in the middle of the fourth century, when Christians, like all their fellow-Romans, had long been accustomed to celebrating the New Year a week later. But for Christians there could only be one festival of renewal, and the merry-making a week after Christmas jeopardised the uniqueness of the renewal offered by the incarnate Lord. 'The mystery [*sacramentum*] of our salvation promised us in the beginning, given us at the end, destined to last for ever, is renewed for us by the revolving year', preached pope Leo I in one of his Christmas sermons.[26] 'In celebrating the Lord's birth', he said in another 'we are celebrating our true beginning; for the birth [*generatio*] of Christ is the source and origin of the Christian people; the birthday of the Head is also the birthday of His body.'[27] Thus Christmas had to be made the single festival of the new beginning, without rival. In Late Roman times it had scarcely had the chance to establish itself securely as the Christian successor of the ancient festival of the year's dark midnight, the winter solstice. The cycle of cosmic renewal had to be given its new meaning, and its new meaning had to be firmly established in the minds of the faithful. But the elemental power of celebrating the returning light at the darkest moment of the year could not be wiped out so easily; though appropriated and re-interpreted by Christians in the framework of the story of the Incarnation, its new meaning could never be wholly secure, would always be apt to slide back into a pre-Christian past. Men would always be liable to remember the re-birth of the year, the returning of the Sun, and to forget the birth of a Saviour in squalor and wretchedness. Christian bishops needed every possible device to strengthen in their congregations a sense of the one true birth commemorated at this time.

---

[26] *Tract.* 22.1.
[27] *Tract.* 26.2.

Hence the perpetual anxiety over any other celebration of renewal. There could be no true annual renewal but the commemoration of the one and only new Beginning. When, eventually, the Church began to take over the celebration of 1 January, it was in relation to that of Christmas.

The festivals linked with the cult of the Sun were quickly absorbed. The Kalends of January remained suspect for much longer. But there were many other traditional celebrations more troublingly ambiguous in character. What was to be the fate of those which were not re-interpreted and not absorbed into the cycle of Christian sacred time?

8

Secular festivals in Christian times?

From the time of Polybius, Roman religion had often been seen as the secret of Roman power and greatness. The Roman governing classes never doubted that proper discharge of the city's duties to its gods was essential to its success. Public life and official business was embedded in traditional religious ceremony to ensure that success. Varro, the great Roman antiquarian, had labelled this aspect of Roman religion the 'civic', and said of it: 'this is what the citizens, and especially the priests, must know and practice'.[1] Religion and civic life were deeply interwoven at every level. This axiom is what gave urgency to the problem raised for Christians, especially as they took a growing part in public life and a greater share of office, by the traditional celebrations surrounding public life. Throughout the third century, from the time of Tertullian (see above, pp. 101–3) to the council which met in Elvira in Spain soon after AD 300, high-class – and not only high-class – Christians were exposed to conflicting pressures on this score. One way of reconciling the claims of public life and those of Christian exclusiveness was through de-valuing the religious significance of traditional civic celebrations. If a case could be made for treating these as no more than secular in nature, they could be celebrated without the stain of idolatry. But could such a case be made?

The question has been much debated. The luxurious almanac for the year 354 executed for a Christian patron, which contains the fullest information at our disposal for the middle of the fourth century, has been seen as 'pagan', as 'neutral', even as a

[1] Quoted by Augustine, *De civ. Dei* VI.5.3.

107

'Christian' document.[2] In part such uncertainties are accounted for by assumptions made by twentieth-century historians about what is to count as 'Christian', what are 'pagan survivals' (discussed in ch. 1, above). But even when allowance has been made for the confusions imported by unfounded prejudice, there is still no simple answer to these questions. A profound ambiguity clung to these traditional celebrations, an ambiguity spotlighted by the two different descriptions offered of them by the most perceptive of modern students: they are said both to have carried 'a heavy charge of diffused religiosity',[3] and to belong, along with the artistic traditions of Late Antiquity, to a 'neutral technology of life', 'part of the hard-won skill of living in a Mediterranean environment', to the 'secular life' of the Late Antique city.[4]

Their roots lay deep within the pagan past. Christian writers in earlier days denounced the circus games, and especially the *pompa circensis* with which they opened, the solemn procession from the god's temple to the circus. They knew the ancient religious symbolism they carried, and duly condemned them as the image of the Devil's seductive display.[5] Had they now been sanitised, and allowed to survive in the calendar of festivals celebrated by Christians, shorn of their religious significance? Could religious cult, perhaps, be dissociated from purely secular celebration, in the way Constantine had in mind when he allowed the inhabitants of Hispellum to honour him with games and a temple, but without 'the pollution of any contagious superstition'?[6] This certainly was the view taken by the Christian emperors who continued to safeguard what they saw as the traditional amusements of their subjects, even while seeking to eliminate the religious context with which they had been traditionally associated. In 399 they rounded off a series of enactments by formally prohibiting the abolition by local authorities of the festivities on the pretext of their association with the

---

[2] For a summary, see Stern, *Le Calendrier*, 94–6.
[3] Brown, *The cult*, 43, with n. 104.
[4] Brown, 'Art and society', 23.
[5] E.g. Tertullian, *De spect.* 4.1–3; 10.2. Salvian adds *spectacula* to *pompa* – *De gub.* VI.6: see below, ch. 11. On the festivals celebrated with circus games, see Stern, *Le Calendrier*, 110.
[6] See above, ch. 3, p. 32, n. 10.

'profane rites' which had accompanied them and were now prohibited:

Just as we have already abolished profane rites by salutary law, so we do not allow the festal assemblies of citizens and the common pleasure of all to be abolished. Hence we decree that, according to the ancient custom, amusements shall be furnished to the people, but without any sacrifice or any accursed superstition, and they shall be allowed to attend festival banquets, whenever the public desires [*vota*] so demand.[7]

The festival of the Maiouma was restored 'provided that decency and modesty and chaste manners shall be preserved', and theatrical shows were allowed to be given 'lest sadness may be produced'.[8] The Christian government evidently took the view that secular festivities, rejoicing, shows and banquets could be dissociated from their religious origins. The emperors limited such secular jollification, in line with the complaints of churchmen, to avoid clashes with the principal Christian festivals and Sundays, for, as they sensibly observed, 'there is a time for prayer and a time for pleasure'.[9] Pope Gregory XIII was to echo their attitude faithfully in 1575 when he permitted bullfighting in Spain except on the Church's holy days.

The government complied with the clergy's wishes in trying to rule out unseemly conduct and in restricting the coincidence of Christian and secular festivals; but this was not enough for many of the clergy, who were not convinced that secular celebrations could be so clearly dissociated from their ancient religious significance; and they would have preferred (see below, p. 118) their flock to be more assiduous attending church services on many more feasts – especially those of the innumerable martyrs – than the emperors decreed to be set aside for worship.

The government's, and many lay Christians', approval of participation in secular festivities and the opposition of churchmen has generally been presented in terms of religious conflict: clerical attempts to 'christianise' more fully a half-Christian

---

[7] *CTh* XVI.10.17 (399); previous legislation on similar lines: *CTh* XVI.10.3; 8 (342; 382).
[8] *CTh* XV.6.1; 2 (392; 399); the government was still anxious to avoid sadness in 414/15: *CTh* XV.7.13.
[9] *CTh* XV.5.5 (425); previous legislation: *CTh* II.8.19; 20; 23; 25. *CJ* III.xii.6 (389) on *feriae* and *spectacula*. Cf. *Reg. eccl. Carth.* 61 (*CC* 149, p. 197).

society, in competition with 'pagan survivals' to which their flock clung tenaciously. But how 'pagan' were the festivals which were still being celebrated by Christians? Could it not be that there is substance behind the plea recounted in sermon after sermon (see above, ch. 7, nn. 14 and 25; and below, n. 22) according to which lay people saw no harm in enjoying 'secular' festivities to which they attached no religious significance? That, in other words, they recognised an implicit distinction between 'sacred' and 'secular'? Such questions are not answered by merely listing festivals found surviving in Christian calendars or in other evidence of Christian practice, and labelling them 'pagan survivals', as if such survival proved anything.[10] What is needed is searching investigation of what exactly the celebration of such traditional festivals involved, and what those – pagans as well as Christians – who took part in them thought they were doing, and what those who tried to prohibit participation in them accused them of doing. This enormous task has hardly been attempted,[11] and can probably not be carried out systematically anyway for lack of sufficient information on the precise circumstances and the views of those involved in each case. What we can hope to do is to consider the relatively few occasions when conflicts about Christians taking part in the celebration of festivities gave occasion to statements which yield some insight into what was at stake.

One such moment occurred in 399, when Augustine, five years a bishop, was preaching in Carthage. He had touched on the matter of celebrations, festivities, banqueting and revelry, especially around tombs (see above, ch. 3, pp. 33–4) before now. What concerns us here is his attitude to civic festivals and to the shows, races, games – *spectacula* – and the feasting which was their accompaniment; and not his views on pagan religious ceremonies, sacrifices, divination and astrological magic, or for that matter, on gladiatorial combats – 'licensed cruelty', as he

---

[10] E.g. Stern, *Le Calendrier*, 103–9; MacMullen, *Christianizing the Roman Empire*, 151 n. 9; Geffcken, *The last days*, 233.
[11] The following can be singled out as fine studies of the kind that are needed: Meslin, *La fête des kalendes*; Duval, 'Des Lupercales'; Halporn, 'Saint Augustine Sermon 104'; Andresen, 'Altchristliche Kritik'; Baus, *Der Kranz*; and Weismann, *Kirche und Schauspiele*. The fullest survey of Latin Fathers' knowledge of, but not of their attitude to, the theatre is Jürgens, *Pompa diaboli*.

called them.[12] All these were universally abhorred by bishops
and for the most part outlawed by emperors, though occasionally
still practised, and even by Christians. The shows, however, were
another matter. Augustine was sensitive to drama, just as he was
sensitive to physical beauty and to the power of music. On his
own testimony, as a young man he was moved to tears by
theatrical shows.[13] Though often hardest, in later life, on what
he saw as his own youthful failings, and impatient with the
impulses of his passionate nature, he was notably mild in the
views of theatrical performances that he came to hold later as
a priest and a bishop. He had valued the rhythms of dance and
music: they attuned the human mind to the universal rhythm
and cosmic harmony implanted by God in His creation. Augustine's youthful enthusiasm for them never quite vanished,
though it came to be toned down. Of shows of all kinds, banquets
and festivities, he took a somewhat less favourable view; but his
hostility must not be exaggerated.[14] In a sermon he preached,
probably in 393, on the occasion of a banquet in honour .of
Venus – and probably rather a respectable affair in 'celebration
of a life of harmony and fullness' – he said 'these things are to
be tolerated, not loved': a statement rightly described by its most
careful commentator as 'so mild a comment'.[15]

The comment is typical of what Augustine is repeating time
and again in the first years of his episcopate. The same attitude
is strikingly expressed in a sermon which unfortunately cannot
be dated. Augustine was preaching on the duty his congregation
had to conform with God's word: they must abstain from detest-
able pagan practices, divination, astrology, haruspication, sor-
tilege, auguries and the like – from all sacrilege; and, Augustine
adds for good measure, with significant indulgence towards his
audience, 'abstain, as far as you can, from worthless spectacles'.[16]
It was characteristic of Augustine not to make an issue of things

---

[12] *Enarr. in Ps.* 101.i.10.
[13] *Conf.* III.2–4. On this theme, see Weismann, *Kirche und Schauspiele*, 123–95.
[14] See Weismann, *Kirche und Schauspiele*, 175–6. Andresen, 'Altchristliche Kritik', 374–6
notes Augustine's positive views on dance, but fails to notice the change they underwent.
[15] *Sermo* 104 (*Morin Guelf.* 29) 7, with the comment by Halporn, 'Saint Augustine
Sermon 104', 102, whose dating I adopt.
[16] *Sermo* 9.11.17. See Additional note below, on the chronology of Augustine's sermons
on these subjects.

he regarded as unimportant among the things that really mattered. Thus he raised no strong objection to the growing practice of using the astrological week-day names, though he observed that Christians had 'their own language' and that 'it is more fitting that the ecclesiastical style of speech should flow from the mouth of Christians; yet, if anyone be drawn by the force of habit in such a way that what proceeds from the lips is that which is condemned by the heart', then to that there was no objection; only let the heavenly bodies mentioned by the words not be adored by the heart.[17] In contrast with Tertullian (see above, p. 102) who thought 'spectacles' to be idolatry, Augustine did not place them among the human institutions which belong to the 'superstitious institutions of men'. His refusal thus to classify them in what was his most formal division of institutions, worked out with every deliberation, is immensely significant. Though we may suspect that Augustine would have grouped them with the things which are 'superfluous and extravagant', rather than with the 'useful and necessary', they are not placed among the signs of communion with the Devil.[18] Vain and idle they may be, but idolatrous they are not.

His tone changed sharply in 399. We can catch him in the process of changing his mind in April 399, when he was the visiting preacher at Carthage. Relations between the pagan and the Christian communities in Carthage had suddenly and very recently become tense: imperial commissioners had arrived 'to destroy the temples and overturn the idols'.[19] Some of his congregation had been taking part with pagans in a civic celebration, apparently in honour of the 'genius of Carthage'. Others objected; some were carried away by anti-pagan zeal and were bent on taking the law into their own hands, trespassing on private property, on a rampage destroying cult statues. Augustine urged restraint:

Do not do what you are not authorised to do ... Many pagans have these abominations on their properties; are we to invade these in order

---

[17] *Enarr. in Ps.* 93.3–4. In polemic, to meet the taunts of Manichaean opponents, Augustine would take a stronger line: *C. Faust.* XVIII.5.
[18] Tertullian, *De spect.* 5–13; Augustine, *De doctr. christ.* II.25.38. For fuller comment on this important chapter, see below, p. 121.
[19] *De civ. Dei* XVIII.54.1.

to destroy them? No – let us rather act so as to break the idols in their hearts; when they are converted to Christianity, they will either invite us in to help them with the good work, or even carry it out themselves, before we get there to help. But now, we must pray for them, not burn with anger against them.

Then a significant change of tack:

If I am weighed down by one great sorrow, it is sorrow over Christians, over my brothers, who enter the church in their bodies but leave their hearts outside ... All must come within the church, body and soul; why should the body, which is seen by men, be within, while that which is seen by God is left outside? ... We certainly do preach against the idols: it is from their hearts we want to uproot them.[20]

Augustine's sermon is a masterpiece of crowd management: a plea to avoid violence and an effort to deflect his congregation's enthusiasm into their interior, spiritual lives: they must persecute the idols in the heart, their own no less than the pagans', by total devotion, body and soul. It was a highly charged moment, and had Augustine been content to condemn his flock's actions, or fudged the line which divided pagan from Christian, his plea could well have fallen on ears deafened by passion.

This is the clue to the other part of his sermon, the words addressed to those of his congregation who had taken part in the civic banquet to celebrate the local festival. Augustine knew that their example could only inflame the passions of the mob; in the heat of conflict they could only be seen as traitors. Well might they plead that the festivities were harmless, that the genius of Carthage was no god and the banquet no idolatry; but, Augustine pleaded with them,

[You say] 'we know he is no god' – would that they [the pagans] knew it too; but for the sake of the infirm who do not know this, you must not trouble their consciences ... How do you think you can avoid people being taken in by idols whom they assume to have been honoured by Christians? You may say 'God knows my heart'; alright, but your brother does not know it. If you are infirm, beware of falling into more serious illness; if you are healthy, beware of causing your brother to fall ill. Seeing you [taking part in the civic banquet] they

---

[20] *Sermo* 62.11.17; 12.18. For Augustine's concern with legality, see the striking example of *Ep.* 47.3. The situation appears to have been typical: see Libanius, *Or.* 30.9, 21, and Fowden, 'Bishops and temples', 68.

may be inspired not only to share in the banquet, but to sacrifice to idols.[21]

While participation could offend weak Christian consciences, it could also, conversely, reassure wavering pagans:

> We want to bring in the remaining pagans; you are rocks in their path. They will say in their heart: why should we leave the gods whom Christians worship along with us? You say, 'God forbid that I should worship pagan gods': I know, I understand, and I believe you. But what will you do about the consciences of the infirm which you have troubled?[22]

A few days later Augustine was preaching about the Lord's promise to bring not peace but a sword: the sword which would separate the Christian not only from his pagan family and friends, but from his 'evil habits'; and the 'evil habits' he was thinking of appear (from a later paragraph of the sermon) to be 'rejoicing with the impious', 'drinking, feasting, theatres and spectacles'.[23]

These sermons are richly informative on the new tensions within the civic community of Carthage, and within the local Christian community itself. The tense situation created by the repressive legislation of the 390s reached a climax with the despatch to Carthage of the imperial commissioners charged with carrying out the most recent severe anti-pagan measures. The more or less peaceful co-existence of Christian and non-Christian in the local community came under severe strain. It was the mirror-image of the situation created in many towns with a sizeable pagan population by Julian's restoration of paganism in 362, when pagan enthusiasm flared into civil disturbance.[24] In Carthage now, as in Gaza and elsewhere then, the threat of violence was in the air, and created further tension between groups of Christians: on the one side those who were intent on continuing the previous, easy-going civic community

---

[21] *Sermo.* 62.6.9–10; 4.7.
[22] *Ibid.* 6.9. In contrast, people who thought they could continue to frequent idols, to consult magicians and soothsayers, and yet boast 'I have not left the Church; I am a Catholic' received a very different answer from Augustine: *Enarr. in Ps.* 88.ii.14.
[23] *Enarr. in Ps.* 96.7, 19.
[24] Sozomen, *HE* V.9; Theodoret, *HE* III.6–7.

with its own ceremonies and festivities, which they saw as harmless secular occasions without religious significance; on the other
those to whom such an attitude seemed betrayal. Augustine's
attempt to restrain violence and to prevent a rift within the
Christian congregation marks the beginning of a swing away
from his earlier, easy-going attitude, a move towards the harsh
tone familiar from the polemical pages of the *City of God*. Significantly, however, he still believed – as he assured his flock in
this very sermon (see above, n. 22) – in the innocence and clear
conscience of those who had taken part in the banquets. He still
thought it possible, though inadvisable, for Christians to participate in civic celebrations without idolatry.

The years 399 to 401 were the climax of the forcible repression
of paganism in North Africa. The tensions created in Carthage
were not without parallel elsewhere. At Sufes in Byzacena a
Christian mob broke up a statue of Hercules. Sixty of them lost
their lives in the ensuing riot.[25] Some years later, after another
wave of repressive legislation,[26] similar unrest troubled Calama.
When outraged Christians tried to prevent a pagan celebration,
turmoil erupted; the authorities did nothing to prevent anti-
Christian violence.[27] We cannot know whether this was another
case of zealous Christian mobs taking traditional municipal festivities for pagan demonstrations, or pagans taking advantage
of such festivities to express their own religious loyalties through
them. They were certainly as ready to take to the streets in
protest against Christian shows of strength in defence of what
they saw as their injured rights as were the Christians.[28]

Augustine's sermons preached during the first crisis of 399–
401 give some impression of the variety of tensions that could
be encountered in different North African towns. On his way
back from Carthage in the summer of 399 he preached at Bulla
Regia. It was a small town, very different from Carthage, as
Augustine reminded his congregation: in Carthage, he said,
they can excuse themselves for taking part in civic festivities; it
was a large place, with a mixed population. 'There they can say:

---

[25] Augustine, *Ep.* 50.
[26] *CTh* XVI.5.43; 10.19; *Sirm.* 12, posted at Carthage in the forum on 5 June 408.
[27] Augustine, *Ep.* 91.8.
[28] *Enarr. in Ps.* 30.iii.11.

"It is done by the pagans, by the Jews": here, whoever takes part, is a Christian.'[29] What may be inevitable and excusable, if not appropriate, in a large mixed population, seems to be unacceptable in a small, wholly Christian town such as was Bulla, and neighbouring places including his own Hippo, where the shows had 'nearly ceased', and the little town of Simittu, which Augustine held up to his congregation as a shining example of a place 'where no-one enters a theatre, where all foulness has been banished'.[30] Bishops could evidently make sure that small and for the greater part Christian places conformed with norms which were beginning to be thought appropriate for lay people no less than for the clergy;[31] but a large town of mixed population was a different matter. There the admixture of Jews and pagans could protect and shelter the independence of Christian lay conduct.

Relations between people and their bishops could also become strained during these years of crisis. A sermon preached by Augustine in 401, again at Carthage, casts an interesting sidelight on the intercommunal tensions that had again flared up. A council had just been meeting at Carthage (see below, p. 117 for the measures agreed) on 16 June 401. On the Sunday following Augustine was the visiting preacher at the evening service. The Christian mob, infuriated by the easing of the government's repression of paganism, had taken the law into its own hands. They shaved off the recently re-gilded beard from a statue of Hercules. The situation was explosive, rioting between pagans and Christians imminent. Augustine preached another masterly sermon, carefully designed to curb the mob's fury without risking the loss of the clergy's fragile control. He praised their zeal 'for the house of God'; but they must heed the voice of their pastors – after all, Augustine reminded them, they, too, are among God's faithful people – 'God forbid that we [your clergy] should turn out to be reprobate, while you are righteous. What we want in this matter that you are agitating about is the same as what you want, though the manner of acting we want cannot be the same ... You must await our counsel in

---

[29] *Sermo Denis* 17.7.
[30] *Ibid.* 9.
[31] *Ibid.* 8.

fulfilling your wishes.' Having made his plea for restraint, Augustine launched into a harangue against pagan gods which can only have earned the applause that African Christians so readily gave to his sermons.[32] The bishops were not to be upstaged by the mob in their anti-pagan zeal.

The bishops had been acting under pressure. What they had just agreed to were demands to be put to the government: to 'cut off' the idols still remaining in the province, and to order the destruction of their shrines even in fields and in remote rural spots; to prohibit the banquets 'which accompany pagan falsehood in such a manner that Christians are nowadays forced [*cogantur*] by pagans to take part in such celebrations'; adding, somewhat disingenuously, that 'in this way a new persecution has covertly come into being in these times of the Christian emperors'.[33] The bishops stopped short of identifying banqueting and the shows with pagan idolatry; they could hardly have done so in the face of the emperors' insistence on distinguishing the two things (see above, p. 109, n. 7). Their objection to banqueting was that it brought a danger of inducing Christian participants to do more than feast: as Augustine had put it in a sermon two years before, not only to eat, but to sacrifice.[34]

These years of crisis following the active intervention of the authorities in Africa (principally in Carthage) were the time of Augustine's most uncritical endorsement of the Theodosian ideology and of his most enthusiastic approval of the official enforcement of Christian orthodoxy.[35] During these years his preaching settled into the shape it was to assume for the next eighteen years or so, after which he seems to have lost interest in the subject.[36] He will lament over Christians who fill the churches on the festivals of Jerusalem and the theatres on the

---

[32] *Sermo* 24.5–6.

[33] Council of Carthage, 401, in *Reg. eccl. Carth.* 58, 60, 84 (*CC* 149, pp. 196, 197, 205). The first two requests were made by a council held on 16 June; the first repeated on 13 September. By 'coercion of Christians by pagans' the bishops seem to have been alluding to the risk run by Christians of being taken off to the circus, well fed and well drunk, by their pagan friends: see *Enarr. in Ps.* 80.11. Abduction by pagan friends to the circus (and, conversely, by Christian friends to church) is an important theme in Augustine's preaching: see *Enarr. in Ps.* 85.15; 90.10.

[34] *Sermo* 62.4.7: does 'sacrifice' here mean the circus?

[35] On Augustine and *tempora christiana*, see Markus, *Saeculum*, 22–44.

[36] On his preaching about festivals, shows, etc., see Van der Meer, *Augustine the bishop*, 47–56, and on the chronology see the Additional note below.

festivals of Babylon;[37] over the fortunes squandered by the rich
on the shows 'while Christ's poor go hungry';[38] and he is constantly exhorting Christians to turn from the enjoyment of the
great civic occasions (*munera*) to the enjoyment of spiritual
delights: 'Give yourselves this treat: do not enter the theatre.'[39]
They have a better show awaiting them in the church: 'we have
heard that to-morrow there is to be a sea in the theatre: we have
a safe port here in Christ'.[40] So let them come to the finest show
on earth, the celebration of the blessed martyrs. In the words
of his disciple, Quodvultdeus, let them 'divert their passion for
spectacles, not give it up'.[41] Thus will the tables be turned on
the devotees of the spectacles. The Christians' true spectacle,
Augustine once said, is Jerusalem, 'the vision of peace', and
Sion, 'contemplation'; so let the pagans not imagine that they
only have spectacles. Christians should fast for the few remaining
pagans on their feast days 'so that the pagans themselves might
become their own spectacle'.[42]

Confrontation had turned Augustine's preaching into a summons to the Christian people to take sides. Until the crisis years
of 399–401, neither they nor their clergy had thought this
necessary. The public celebrations had served to articulate a
civic consensus and legitimated a mixed community's limited,
but none the less important, urban value-system. They attested
a continuity in the unchanged traditions of urban living. In
celebrating an essentially secular tradition they also helped to
secure its survival, without invoking any religious ideology, even
uniting adherents of opposed religious ideologies in the celebra-

---

[37] *Enarr. in Ps.* 61.10; 30.ii.2; 99.12; 80.2; 84.15; *De cat. rud.* 25.48; *Sermo* 51.1, and
the sermons discussed by La Bonnardière, 'Les "Enarrationes in Psalmos"', esp. 71–5.
Likewise, Leo, *Tract.* 84.1. On Antioch, Natali, 'Tradition ludique', who shows that
churches became the alternative *loci* of 'sociabilité'. See also Patlagean, *Pauvreté*, 208–15.
[38] *Sermo* 32.20; *Enarr. in Ps.* 102.28.
[39] *Sermo Denis* 17.7.
[40] *Enarr. in Ps.* 80.23.
[41] *Sermo* 3.2 (*De symb.* 1); *vide contra nostra sancta, sana, suavissima spectacula, ibid.* Cf.
Gloria sanct. 13.15–17. In *Sermo* 5.5 (*De symb.* 3) the spectacle is the passion. On
martyrdom as a *spectaculum*, see Prudentius, *Perist.* X.463, 701; Augustine, *Sermo* 49.11;
In Ioh. Ev. Tr. VII.6; *En. in Ps.* 39.9; *Sermo Denis* 14.3. Novatian had written of the
beauties of nature and the scriptures as the Christians' *spectacula meliora . . . vera*[*e*] *et
profutura*[*e*] *voluptates*: *De spect.* 9–10. On the iconography see Salomonson, *Voluptatem
spectandi non perdat sed mutat.* Leo I in 442: *Tract.* 84.1; on Salvian, see ch. 11, on
Quodvultdeus ch. 14, below.
[42] *Enarr. in Ps.* 98.5, 147.8.

tions. They had helped to mask conflict and tension, collapsing into the broadest and most inclusive categories groups in urban society divided by class and, especially, by religion.[43] But the government's heavy-handed intervention brought this consensus, and with it Augustine's conciliatory attitude, to an end. Under the new pressures the civic celebrations lost their integrative function. Some places, such as Madauros, appear to have remained under almost wholly pagan municipal government;[44] in some small towns like Simittu, perhaps Hippo and no doubt elsewhere (above, p. 116), the clergy were able to establish their authority over the citizen body and to re-create a civic consensus on a new, and now Christian, basis. In others, Carthage, Sufes, Calama among them, conflict replaced consensus. The mixed citizen body dissolved into the rival religious groups which still survived within the flourishing municipal life of many African towns,[45] now to be increasingly 'tribalised' in a sudden reversal of the trend towards co-existence. Communal celebrations became engulfed in conflict and served as its symbols and as mechanisms of division in the community. The result was that rival sets of festivals came to define alternative systems of *kairoi* running parallel in mutually exclusive cycles of sacred time.

Augustine's reluctance to condemn festivities, banquets and their like has to be assessed in the context not only of circumstances, but also of the thrust of his own deepest instincts concerning the nature of social existence. Like every Late Roman townsman, he knew very well that the circus, the theatre, the hippodrome and the baths were always apt to serve as the arena for displaying tensions in the citizen body, as well as its cohesion. Naturally, it was in such public spaces that tension flared into disturbance and violence. Such conflict had always been apt to accompany the excitement generated by the shows and the races,

[43] 'Dissensual patterns of belief are more often explicit and systematic, that is more ideological, than the consensual patterns which affirm the existing central institutional system' – Shils, *The centre and the periphery*, 172. It will be evident that I owe much to Shils' discussion of ritual, ceremony, and consensus. See esp. his essay (with M. Young) on 'The meaning of the coronation', 'Ritual and crisis' and 'Charisma, ritual and consensus' in this collection, esp. 139, 155–62. See also the essay by Victor Turner in *Secular ritual* and the editors' introduction. For Antioch, see now Brown, *The body*, 305–22.

[44] Augustine, *Ep.* 232.

[45] On this see Lepelley, *Les cités*, esp. 352–414.

and could sometimes amount to incipient 'civil war'.[46] Byzantinists have devoted much labour to elucidating the nature of these conflicts, which happily do not concern us here, especially in the period from c. 500 onwards. But to see Augustine's views in sharper relief, it is worth dwelling for a moment on the contrast between his preaching around 400 with that of Severus of Antioch more than a century later. In one of his Cathedral Homilies Severus began with a routine denunciation of the celebration of his city's 'Fortuna' – something like the genius of Carthage (see above, p. 111). It is idolatry; he weeps and trembles at the thought – a thought that had occurred to many others, including Augustine – that the lips which in church send mystic praise to the Father in heaven should utter demonic words at the spectacles. (We should take note that even in this expression of a commonplace of Late Antique preaching Severus, like Tertullian but unlike Augustine, instinctively thinks of the circus as a place of communication with the demonic world. We shall consider the contrast with Augustine below (p. 121). Severus then went on to denounce the passions released by the races and – in line with a long tradition of sacred rhetoric – lamented the wealth spent on them at the expense of Christ's poor. Then, in passing, something strikingly unusual: 'Let us grant that no idolatry takes place in the horse-races, that they are nothing but amusement and refreshment for the soul ... Even so: God gave us horses not so that we may subject them to such excessive strain, to make them turn round and round themselves, to the point of breaking their hoofs', and so on. Only after this remarkably sensitive outburst of humanity towards animals, does Severus finally narrow his focus to his most immediate worry: 'Let us, if you wish, even concede that making horses race is devoid of sin ...; but why let it become a cause of division and agitation, a source of harm to the whole people?'[47]

Severus' homily reveals his preoccupation with the risk of bloody civic strife. In Augustine's Carthage the evidence does not suggest that the games and races had become occasions of

---

[46] Civil war: Isidore of Pelusium, *Ep.* V.185 (*PG* 78.1433D). On factions and fighting, Cameron, *Circus factions.*

[47] *Cath. Hom.* 26 (*PO* 36.541–57); quotations from pp. 545, 549, 551–3. On cruelty to horses, see Quodvultdeus, *Sermo* 3.2 (*De symb.* 1).

civic discord and disturbance, and in fact suggests the contrary. That perhaps helps to explain why Augustine tried, for as long as he could, not to be too harsh in denouncing them. This, at bottom, may be the reason why Augustine insisted that they belonged among those human institutions which could serve the laudable ends of securing greater cohesion among men (see above, p. 112, n. 18). The paragraphs he devoted to these institutions in his *Of Christian teaching* are interestingly complex: as we have noted, even the theatres, actors, dancers, mimes and pantomimes – the most reprehensible people in episcopal and even in imperial eyes[48] – were carefully placed not among the institutions through which men communicate with demons, but among those which are means of human communication. To be sure, he placed them among the useless and extravagant, not the useful and necessary. But in this key passage his silence about the circus and the hippodrome and the spectacles in general is notable. Did he perhaps want to allow himself elbow-room to think, or to allow his readers to think, that such celebrations and amusements are, unlike those of the theatre, even 'useful and necessary'? There may be a premonition here that these things are capable of helping to bring about that cohesion of human wills on which social harmony rests, whose fostering he commends in the very next paragraph and – with vastly greater urgency – in the *City of God.*[49]

The circumstances which forced him to abandon from April 399 the indulgence he had shown towards civic festivals did not reverse his acute sense of the need to foster by all possible means whatever promoted the 'coherence of wills' which lay at the roots of any tolerable society.

ADDITIONAL NOTE ON THE CHRONOLOGY OF AUGUSTINE'S STATEMENTS ON SPECTACLES

It is surprising that apparently no chronological study has been made of Augustine's sermons and writings on the question of

---

[48] For their reputation, see Cameron, *Porphyrius*, 230–2, and Patlagean, *Pauvreté*, 212. Legislation: *CTh* XV.7.1; cf. the Council of Carthage (401) in *Reg. eccl. Carth.* 63 (*CC* 149, p. 197).
[49] Especially XIX.6; on it, see Markus, *Saeculum*, 94–104.

pagan celebrations, festivals, banquets and shows. Weismann, *Kirche und Schauspiele*, notes only a general change from Augustine's early views to their later hardening (e.g. p. 154). Halporn, 'Saint Augustine Sermon 104', notes that 'one of the major difficulties with any such studies . . . is that statements on paganism made by Augustine are drawn at random from the texts without regard for the time [and, I should add, the place] when they were delivered or written' (106, n. 142). He does not undertake such a survey, but asserts – rightly – that 'so mild a comment' on paganism as that of sermon 104 must belong to a period before 399, and plausibly dates the sermon to 393. Chadwick, 'Augustine on pagans', sets some key episodes into their proper context without undertaking a full chronological study. La Bonnardière, 'Les "Enarrationes"' does this for *Enarrationes in Psalmos* 147, 103, 80, 146 and 102. The fullest account, Van der Meer, *Augustine the bishop*, 47–56, takes no account of chronology or circumstance.

Apart from *Sermo* 104 (*Morin Guelf.* 29), I have found no dateable text on this matter from before 399 except the following: *Ep.* 9.3 (389); *De vera rel.* 172, 270 (390) and *Confessions* IV.1, VI.12 (397–9). These contain only the 'mild' *topos* of the shows as 'vain', 'carnal' pleasures.

The remaining texts are:

Sermones 24 (16 June 401); 32.19–20 (403); 34.6 (25 May 418); 46.8 (409–11); 51.1 (417–18); 62 (399); 153.10 (13 October 418); 159.2 (after 418); 311.55 (14 September 405); 332.1 (410–12) Denis 11 (?399); Denis 14.3 (September 401); 17 (summer 399); Morin 1 (401); Caillau II.19.7 (December 399).

(*Sermones* 9.10–17, 179.8, 196.4 and 198.2–3 are not dateable.)

In Ioh. Ev. Tr. 7.6 (406–7); 10.9 (406–7); 97.3 (?418). *Enarrationes in Psalmos* 30.iii.11 (411); 32.ii.5 (13 September 403); 38.2 (September 416); 39.6–9 (411–15); 50.1 (?411); 53.10 (412–13); 57.7 (17 September 403 or 409?); 61.10 (415/16); 76.14 (?416); 80.2, 11, 23 (409–11); 84.15 (after 418); 90.i.4 (?412); 96.7, 19 (April 399); 98.5 (?411); 99.12 (412/13?); 102.13, 28 (409/11); 103.i.13

(409); 119.5 (406–7); 127.10 (December 412); 136.9 (December 412); 146.4 (?409); 147.2,3,7,8,15 (?409); 149.13 (411–13).

(18.ii.1 and 33.ii.6 are apparently not dateable.)

It is noteworthy that a very high proportion of these sermons were preached at Carthage.

Other texts: *C. Faust.* XX.4 (397–9); *De civ. Dei* II.4, 26, etc. (after 413); *De cons. ev.* I.33.51 (399–400); *De op. mon.* 13.14; 17.20 (401); *De cat. rud.* 25.48–9; 7.11 (399). *Ep.* 91 (408); 120.5 (410–11); 138.14 (412).

I have tried to include all the texts I have come across, but my inventory is likely to be incomplete, and my criteria of relevance inevitably subjective. For dating I have usually given most weight to Perler, *Les voyages,* and to the studies of Mlle La Bonnardière. For the Psalm commentaries, I have also considered the (often somewhat impressionistic) datings proposed by H. Rondet, 'Essais'.

In the absence of a fuller study, I can here only sum up my opinion based on these texts in the observations (1) that the few texts before April 399 show no trace of the harsher views to be found in Augustine's later preaching and writings; (2) that there is a noticeable hardening of attitude in 399; and (3) that, despite this hardening, the texts from the post-399 period often also express the same milder views as are to be found in the earlier period.

9

The christianisation of time

In the last chapter we examined the co-existence of Christian and non-Christian in a civic setting, the pressures to which it was exposed, and the various ways in which it could survive or break down. In the end, however, this diversity was smoothed out into a uniformity spreading over Christian Western Europe. What we have seen happening in some of the smaller towns of North Africa with a fairly homogeneous Christian population was to set the pattern for the future. In such places the clergy could impose their norms without much difficulty. Religion swallowed up the secular civic consensus, citizenship merged with membership of the community of the faithful, and municipal affairs came to be dominated by the Church.

Rome, though always a law unto itself, underwent a development very similar to what happened in the tiny town of Simittu. The City's history in Late Antiquity is dominated by the disproportion between the supreme place it continued to occupy in educated Roman imaginations, and the comparatively unimportant part it played in the political and economic life of the Empire. This paradox facilitated its premature emergence as a Christian city. Its bishops were precociously energetic in exploiting the possibilities that they perceived for turning their city into the head and centre of the Christian world, the ancient capital renewed by its two martyr–Apostles and re-born as a Christian Rome.[1] Its new self-awareness was celebrated by Christian poets and artists; a series of fine churches, built in a classicising architectural style, long neglected in the imperially

[1] Kantorowicz, '*Puer exoriens*'; Pietri, *Roma christiana*, book III; and Huskinson, *Concordia apostolorum*. On Leo, see McShane, *La romanitas*, 53–232.

sponsored programme of church-building during the fourth century, proclaimed in physically visible form the Christian re-birth of a genuinely classical past. The churches built in the 430s and 440s under the popes, working in close alliance with the recently christianised urban aristocracy, announced their adoption of a classical tradition within the City, and together they staked out a Christian, papal, area in it, well removed from the ancient civic centre, still heavy with memories of the unexorcised pagan past.[2] Although emperors continued to spend some of their time in Rome, and though Valentinian III (425–55) even appears to have favoured it as a residence half a century after the court had moved to Ravenna, the City had long ago ceased to be an effective centre of government. In the course of the hundred years from the pontificate of Damasus (366–84) to that of Leo I (440–61) the physical aspect of the City had altered: it had become a fitting backdrop for the exercise of a new kind of authority by its bishops. The ecclesiastical claims elaborated by the popes during this period found a counterpart in the municipal authority gradually taken over by them. The process is well epitomised in the famous stories of the embassies led by pope Leo, accompanied by representatives of the local nobility, to save the City from destruction by Attila the Hun in 452 and again by Geiseric the Vandal three years later.[3]

The physical transformation of its townscape and the emergence of its bishop at the head of the local aristocracy as the City's supreme representative and authority, combined to create the conditions for pope Leo to give moral and religious content to the ideology of Rome's Christian renewal. Leo liked to dwell on this theme in his sermons preached annually on the occasion of the feast of Rome's twin Apostles. One year he apostrophised[4] the City as a

holy people, an elect nation, a priestly and royal city, become, through the see of St Peter established here, the head of the world; ruling more widely now through divine religion than it ever did by worldly dominion. Though enlarged by many victories, you have spread the

[2] Krautheimer, 'The architecture of Sixtus III'; *Rome*, 46–58; and *Three Christian capitals*, 104–21.
[3] Prosper, *Chron.*, s.a. 452, 455; ed. T. Mommsen, *Chron. min.* 1, 482, 483.
[4] *Tract.* 82.1.

authority of your rule over land and sea. What your warlike labours
have obtained for you is less than what the Christian peace has brought
you.

But Leo was not the man to mouth the slogans of empty
ideology, even that of the Christian City renewed by the
patronage of its Apostles. His pontificate has rightly been seen
as a sustained effort to give moral substance to this ideology.[5]
Characteristic is the stress he laid, for instance, on the duty to
give alms, in no less than some forty out of his ninety-eight
surviving sermons. Much recent study has taught us to see
this substitution of almsgiving – preferably anonymous! – for
the ancient competitive and conspicuous works of public
munificence as one of the profoundest aspects of a new conception of society, one in which the contrast between poor and rich
superseded the ancient dichotomy between citizen and non-
citizen.[6] Here is one facet of Leo's programme of turning Rome
into a new and radically Christian civic community. His determined effort to rid Rome of Manichees and other heretics also,
perhaps, formed part of a programme of establishing the City
as a *theopolis*;[7] and his exercise of episcopal authority in what
should have been matters of secular justice has been seen as a
step on the road towards papal domination of the City. Rome
and its bishop may have been ahead of other Western towns,
but not unique. What gave form and structure to these new
communities will occupy us later.

Leo was one of the first churchmen to appreciate the importance of a Christian civic time. What Leo's preaching to his Roman
congregations reveals is an overriding concern to draw them
into the rhythm of the Church's public worship. Time and again
he is trying to awaken in his audience a sense of the moment
in the sacred time-scheme whose deep rhythms he wishes to
reverberate in the hearts and minds of his hearers. Take fasting:
the pope is always exhorting his congregations to fast. It is a
meritorious activity, it purifies the mind as well as the body, and
subjects corporeal passions to the control of reason;[8] it restores

---

[5] Lepelley, 'Léon le Grand'.
[6] Patlagean, *Pauvreté*, 181–96; Veyne, *Le pain et le cirque*, 44–66, esp. 58–9.
[7] The suggestion is made by Lepelley, 'Léon le Grand', 137, 147.
[8] *Tract.* 46.1; cf. 81.2; 87.1; 90.1–4; 93.1; 91.1.

the right order of things;[9] it is good against heresy;[10] by 'spiritual fasting ... man discovers his dignity, made in the image and likeness of his creator'.[11] Above all, in countless sermons, Leo associates fasting with almsgiving: 'God wishes us to be the stewards of his gifts'; by excluding earthly loves through fasting and giving alms, the integrity of our nature is restored.[12] All the traditional armoury available for the praise of fasting is deployed; but even so central and so commendable a Christian activity as fasting is best carried out at the right seasons assigned to public fasts: 'the public [fasts] are to be preferred to the private';[13] the 'marching columns of the Christian army [*castra militiae christianae*] must keep in step with the rhythm of the public fasts'.[14] And, similarly, charitable almsgiving, too, though a permanent duty, was especially and solemnly binding on the days set aside for the 'collections', when the offerings of the more affluent were to be brought to the churches for redistribution among the poor. So it was a wise institution of the Fathers, Leo preached on one such occasion,[15]

to have laid down that there should be special days set aside in each season which would act as a call to the faithful people to the public collection. And because those in need of assistance flock, mainly, to the church, provision should be made through the care of the clergy to dispense what is needed from what has been provided out of the wealth of the many, contributed by them willingly to the holy collection.

One of these 'collection' days occurred at the time that the ancient Apollinarian games had traditionally been celebrated each July to commemorate Rome's deliverance from calamity after the battle of Cannae. The 'collections' may have been instituted as a deliberate counterfoil; but in Leo's time the games were no longer held, and there was thus no need for a Christian substitute to obliterate a rival pagan celebration. Yet in these sermons Leo loved to dwell on the juxtaposition of these seasons

---

[9] *Ibid.* 50.2.
[10] *Ibid.* 91.2; 42.5.
[11] *Ibid.* 94.2.
[12] *Ibid.* 90.3–4.
[13] *Ibid.* 89.2.
[14] *Ibid.* 88.2; 81.1, *inter multa*. Similarly, Maximus of Turin, *Sermo* 50.1.
[15] *Tract.* 11.2. See also the sermons *De collectis*, *Tract.* 6–11, especially 9.3 and 10.1.

of public and concentrated charitable effort with the pagan festivals they had superseded:[16]

We are invited to celebrate this day by apostolic institution, this day on which the fathers have prudently and profitably ordained the first of these holy collections; because at one time the pagan people used to render superstitious cult to their demons at this time, [the fathers intended] that our most holy offering of alms should be celebrated against [*contra*] the profane sacrifices of the impious.

This is all of a piece with Leo's worries about people who turned towards the East to greet the sun before entering Saint Peter's for mass.[17] It may be that this practice, which had been common in the cult of the Unconquered Sun as well as among Manichees, was being adopted by Christians in perfectly good faith, guilty of no more than trying to give a sound Christian meaning to a traditional pagan gesture. The pope's objection may in fact have been not so much to what these Christians were doing as to the private nature of their action. The church's answer was to turn the private ritual gesture into public worship: liturgical turning to the East for prayer, or the rapidly spreading practice of orienting churches, were more effective than attempts to suppress private orientalism.[18]

More than any of his predecessors, Leo wanted the lives of his people to be shaped by their public liturgical worship. His sermons are carefully designed to remind his audience of the significance of the moment. *Hodie* – 'to-day' – is their constant refrain: what is always true, always right and always devout, is especially so 'to-day' – 'no day more so than to-day', he preached one Christmas.[19] With apparently deliberate allusion to the *vota* of the New Year, Leo insists: 'let the vows [*vota*] be renewed in

---

[16] *Ibid.* 9.3; cf. 8, 10.1, etc. Leo here speaks of the games in the past tense, apparently implying that they were no longer held. Boethius, however, writing in 510, gives the Apollinarian games as an example of things which are in a time determined by the tense (here the present) of the statement asserting their being (*In Cat.* III, *PL* 64.263A). I am not convinced that his use of the present tense here can be taken as evidence of their actual existence in 510. If they were held, it may have been one of the revivals of Theodoric's reign. On this, and on the survival of the games in general, see Ward-Perkins, *From classical antiquity*, 92–109. Horse-racing is mentioned in seventh-century Sicily in the *Life* of St Leo of Catania, 29 (*AA. SS*, Feb., iii. 226–8. I owe this reference to Brown, *Gentlemen*, 17, n. 32.)

[17] *Tract.* 27, 22.

[18] Dölger, *Sol salutis*, especially 257.

[19] *Tract.* 26.1; cf. 28.1, *inter multa*.

us at the right time [*cum tempore*]; these festivals are moments of justified rejoicing'.[20] Preaching in Lent, he once said 'the signs of God's mercy are placed before us; no part of the year is empty of the sacred mysteries'.[21]

It is right and fitting and a work of true piety that on the days commemorating the works of God's mercy we should rejoice with all our hearts and honourably celebrate the things done for our salvation; being called to this by the law of the recurrent times [*recurrentium temporum lex*], which brings us the feast of the Epiphany close on the heels of [Christmas].[22]

There is a right time for baptism;[23] not to be overridden by 'undisciplined capricious choice', even on the pretext of celebrating martyrs' feasts, for everything has its correct day.[24] 'There should be nothing that lacks right order [*inordinatum*], nothing allowed to be confused, the rationale [*causae*] of feasts should be carefully discerned and . . . kept distinct', otherwise we would have 'every season assigned to indiscriminate continuation of all festivals [*omnia tempora continuatis erunt deputanda festis*]'.[25]

The middle of the fifth century, that is to say the time of Leo's pontificate in Rome, of Peter Chrysologus in Ravenna, and of Maximus, perhaps a little earlier, in Turin, seems to mark the climax of the century-old effort to create a cycle of Christian sacred time.[26] The evidence of a heap of humble inscriptions suggests that the effort had at least some success: Italian Christians were assimilating the habit of reckoning their days by the liturgy. 'A conquest of time': so a careful study describes the way ordinary Christians came to live in a time 'not unlike the time which regulates the life of the cleric, the monk and the penitent'.[27] Even when they used the astrological names of the week's days, they had learnt to forget their astrological implications and to recall, as Ambrose urged, that 'this is the

---

20 *Ibid.* 5.1.
21 *Ibid.* 49.1.
22 *Ibid.* 34.1.
23 *Ep.* 16.2–6.
24 *Ibid.* 16.2.
25 *Ibid.*
26 For details, see Pietri, *Roma christiana*, 617–24; Sottocornola, *L'Anno liturgico*; and Mutzenbecher, 'Der Festinhalt'.
27 Pietri, 'Le temps', 81.

day the Lord hath made' (Ps. 117.24).[28] Christians were becoming as conscious of the weekly cycle as they were made conscious by the annual rhythm of festivals of the history of their salvation.

'The increase in righteousness has consumed impiety', Leo said in one of his sermons (8.1) on the 'collections', in a triumphant reference to the eclipsed pagan festivals. His sense of triumph had some justification. Christian sacred time was acquiring a momentum of its own. The remaining traditional festivals came under growing threat, especially in Rome, where the bishops were forging a new Christian and Apostolic identity for what was now more and more *their* city. One of the celebrations which survived into the last years of the fifth century was the Lupercalia. Its fate provides another illustration of one of the ways in which the Late Roman world was being drained of its 'massive secularity'.[29]

Like the celebration of the genius of Carthage a century earlier, this, too, appears, by this time, to have lost most of its religious associations. Christians had taken part in it without hesitation or reproof until then. It was thought to be sufficiently harmless for at least one Christian lady to have had herself buried, probably in the 330s or 340s, in a (re-used) sarcophagus adorned with a scene representing the Lupercalia.[30] It had been celebrated by Christians in 354 and it still appeared in a Christian calendar for 448/9. Its origins and development are not our concern here; its fate in the Christian empire, however, illustrates another way in which neutral civic festivities could suddenly become contentious matters of religion. Far from being a pagan custom recently revived, perhaps by Christians, the celebration had been carried on by uninhibited Christians for over a hundred years. The open letter addressed by pope Gelasius I (492–6) or his predecessor, Felix III (483–92),[31] to

---

[28] *Ep.* 23.4. On Augustine's views on the practice of using the astrological week-day names, see above, ch. 8, n. 17.

[29] Brown, 'Art and society', 23.

[30] Solin and Brandenburg, 'Paganer Fruchtbarkeitsritus'.

[31] On the authorship and date, see Nautin, 'Felix III', and Duval, 'Des Lupercales', esp. 249, whose analysis of the circumstances and dating to before 489 are convincing. The letter may, of course, have been written for the pope by Gelasius in his capacity as a papal secretary. Numbers in brackets in the sequel refer to the paragraphs of *Ad Andromachum*.

the Roman senator Andromachus reveals that it had been tolerated by the pope's predecessors (29); Christian participation in
the rites had been usual, and evidently unaffected by the pope's
prohibition 'earlier in my pontificate' (23). Tolerated by their
bishop and by the government, the festivities clearly had no
overt religious import in the eyes of its Christian participants.
In the pope's own words, the rite had become 'toned down,
abridged, cheapened',[32] carried out no longer by honoured
noblemen but by low-born persons hired for the occasion: de-
valued by its very supporters, who 'are the first to have taken
action against it'.[33]

It is plain from the pope's invective that to its supporters, as
to previous popes, the rites were a harmless civic indulgence
permitted to lay people, if not to clergy (7). What he took
exception to was this very neutrality, its lack of any positive
religious identity. He was determined to force a choice on its
participants – whom he called 'neither Christians nor pagans'
(19) – a choice where none had been expected before: 'take
your stand', he challenged them:[34] either celebrate the rites in
the full-blooded manner of your ancestors (17; 26), or give them
up as 'vain superstition which is manifestly incompatible with
the profession of a Christian' (29). Therefore, the pope insisted,
no baptised person, no Christian, must celebrate the festival:
'let pagans only, to whom the rite belongs, carry it out' (30).
The reasons for the pope's brutal intervention forcing a choice
on Roman Christians are not wholly clear, but are evidently
linked with the uneasy relationship between himself and the
Roman aristocracy. His attack on the Lupercalia is an episode
in a running battle whose earlier stages have left only dimly
visible traces.[35]

To appreciate the significance of the pope's attempt to prohibit
Christian participation in the Lupercalia it is instructive to contrast it with Augustine's efforts to dissuade his congregation
from taking part in festival banquets in Carthage. (See above,
ch. 8, pp. 112–23.) In the 390s official pressure drove a wedge

[32] *cur decoloratis, cur eliditis, cur ad vilia quaeque deducitis* – 25.
[33] *vos ea depretiatis . . . vos ergo primi in Lupercalia commisistis* – 16.
[34] *figite gradum* – Ad. Andr. 23.
[35] On this see Duval, 'Des Lupercales', 247–52.

to widen the gap between two communities which had begun to settle into civic co-existence in Carthage, as in other towns. Augustine's first concern was to calm newly inflamed passions and to restrain violence. Only then, in the divided world in which the shows had come to be identified with paganism, was he determined to wean his flock from taking part in them. Unlike Augustine, the pope was not faced with a civic community recently split by religious conflict. In his attack on the Lupercalia and its devotees, he sought to divide a civic community which had travelled much further than had Carthage ninety years before along the road towards absorption of the pagan groups in a predominantly Christian urban community. By labelling it as 'pagan superstition', the pope tried to eliminate the easy-going self-indulgence hitherto sanctioned for lay people by local tradition. The attack was part of a concerted campaign: in the papal masses the congregations were taught to pray that 'those who profess the Christian faith might reject all that is contrary to it'; that 'God, who has commanded those who partake of his table to abstain from the Devil's banquet, might grant His people to throw off their taste for deadly profanity'; that He might grant 'that His Church, cleansed of profane vanities, might not profess one thing in words and express another in its actions'.[36] The congregations will have had little doubt as to the identification of the 'profane vanities'. Many of them would have wondered about the reasons which had so suddenly transformed their harmless if perhaps *risqué* self-indulgence into nothing short of apostasy.

The attack on the Lupercalia is not so much an attack on 'remnants of paganism' as on traditions of Roman urban living. It marks the end of a partnership between the papacy and the Christian aristocracy of the City which had reached its zenith during the pontificates of Sixtus III (432–40) and Leo I (440–61).[37] It is one symptom of the ascendancy the Roman Church was hastening to establish over an independent civic life with its own momentum and rhythm, a step towards absorbing its

[36] Quotations from masses VIII.xx_{BIS} and XVIII.xVIII, two of the eighteen attributed to Gelasius (i.e. probably Felix III) by Pomarès, *Gélase Ier*. These are the two masses whose attribution to Felix III (or perhaps Gelasius) is least doubtful.
[37] On the circumstances see Pietri, 'Aristocratie', 421–3.

remnants in a sacralised Christian order which had no place for the 'secular'. The different fate of the Lupercalia in the Byzantine world reveals a parting of ways between Greek and Latin Christendom: in the tenth century the Lupercalia were celebrated in Constantinople, as a mobile spring festival in which civic, political and religious elements were combined without the least tension.[38] It contrasts sharply with the papal attempt to impose on the lay world clerical norms which left no room for a neutral realm of the 'secular'.

These case histories shed some light on the fate of celebrations which had survived, at least for a time, alongside the gradually evolving cycle of Christian sacred time. The ambiguity which hovered over them was tacitly, though only temporarily, resolved. Though rooted in an increasingly remote pagan past, they were de-valorised and the associated amusements left as a residue: still the target of puritanical moralists, but no longer idolatrous. This erosion of their religious meaning allowed them to serve as secular celebrations in which Christians could affirm, together with their pagan fellow-citizens, their solidarity in an urban community. But then the conditions, and with them the status of these celebrations, suddenly changed. They became suspect, identified with pagan practice or idolatrous worship. In the cases we have examined, this transformation came about in the wake of crisis; in the first, a crisis induced by imperial repressive measures; in the second by papal ambitions to complete the transformation of Rome into a holy city. The trichotomy which had prevailed before the crises – of Christian (or sacred), secular (neutral, civic), pagan (profane) – vanished, to be replaced by a simpler dichotomy: sacred and profane, or, simply, 'Christian' and 'pagan'. Augustine's theology had carefully kept a space for an intermediate realm of the 'secular' between the 'sacred' and the 'profane';[39] his own inclinations, hinted at in his treatise *On Christian teaching* (see above, ch. 8, p. 121) and elaborated in the *City of God*, were to defend this area from encroachment by the 'sacred', from clerical interfer-

---

[38] See Duval, 'Des Lupercales'. The alleged substitution of the feast of the Virgin's Purification or 'Candlemas' (2 February) to replace the Lupercalia (15 February) rests on myth and is a much later development.
[39] Markus, *Saeculum*, and above, ch. 8, n. 49.

ference and ecclesiastical domination. But Augustine's differentiated and complex vision faded from the world of his successors.

At any rate in the West. How far the Greek East developed along similar lines is beyond the scope of this enquiry. Many of John Chrysostom's pronouncements,[40] or those of Severus of Antioch (see above, ch. 8, pp. 120–1) can read very like those made by Western churchmen. And yet, to at least one serious student, their thrust appeared to point in another direction.

> The preachers hardly ever give religious motivation to their condemnations. They criticise the excesses, as had before them the pagan moralists. Sometimes, in passing, they recall that hellenistic feasts had been celebrated in honour of idols, false gods, demons, that they served as vehicles of paganism. But this is not the principal point. They are condemned above all, if not wholly, for gross indulgence in eating and drinking, in laughter, dancing, sex and so forth ... It is the atmosphere of sensuality and license in the pagan ceremonies that are denounced.[41]

Perhaps we have here stumbled on one fundamental reason for the survival of festivals such as the Lupercalia in the Byzantine world: Greek Christianity was, somehow, less hospitable to sharp discontinuities which cut across the texture of Christian existence.

---

[40] E.g. the Homily in *PG* 56.263–70: cf. Augustine *Enarr. in Ps.* 61.10, etc. (above, ch. 8, n. 37); Leo *Tract.* 84.1.

[41] Harl, 'La dénonciation des festivités', 130. This, however, underestimates a distinctively monastic current of bitter hostility: see, e.g. *Barsanuphe et Jean de Gaza: Correspondence*, 837 (ed. L. Regnault *et al.*, Solesmes, 1972), p. 504. For Western ascetic views, see further ch. 11 below.

III

TOPOI: SPACE AND COMMUNITY

The 'Constantinian revolution' not only forced Christianity to re-assess itself in relation to its own past. It also raised other, far-reaching, questions about the nature of the community and the communities that it considered itself to be, and their inter-relationships. Christians experienced their Church both as a single community spanning heaven and earth, past and present, and as a multiplicity of communities, each in its way mirroring the one Community which, collectively, they constituted. The universal intersected with the particular in their own, local, groups. How were these individual 'churches' to see themselves in relation to the 'great Church', past and present? How were they to conceive of themselves in relation to the social world around them? How was the sense of their personal Christian calling reflected in the group identity of their church, or of other groups generated to give it expression?

10

Holy places and holy people

If it was in their history that Christians saw themselves as distinct
from all others, their geography was the projection of this history
on the ground. Here was a sharp departure from Late Antique
religiosity. The classical world was full of holy places. A traveller
in the region of Corycus in Asia Minor wrote of a cave he visited
there:[1]

Inside it there is a space which inspires such terror that nobody dares
to advance further; so it has remained unexplored. The whole cave
is venerable and truly sacred; it is worthy to be a habitation of the
gods, as it is, indeed, generally held to be. There is nothing there that
is not venerable, that does not in some manner manifest divine
presence.

This profound sense of holiness associated with a particular
place is not one that received much encouragement from Christianity. How could it?

He who hears [your prayer] dwells within. Turn your eyes not up to
the hills, do not lift your face to the stars, the sun or the moon. Do
not think you will be heard when you pray to him over the seas; rather,
let this sort of prayer be detested. Clean out the chamber of your
heart; wherever you wish to pray, that is where He will abide. He who
hears you is within you.[2]

Augustine was perhaps uniquely conscious of God's inward

---

[1] Pomponius Mela, *Chorogr.* I.13. Fox, *Pagans and Christians*, now offers a goldmine
on this as on other aspects of second- and third-century paganism. 'On a strict definition,
there were no pagan "holy men", for in pagan Greek the word "holy" applied to places,
but not to people' (253). On the tendency of 'canny men' to make use of 'uncanny
places', 204–5.
[2] Augustine, *In Ioh. Ev. Tr.* X.1. For reservations on the contrast drawn by Jonathan
Z. Smith between 'locative' and 'utopian' religions see ch. 2, *Additional note*, above p. 26.

presence to the self; but he was expressing what all Christians knew from the beginning: 'The God who made the world and everything in it, being the Lord of heaven and earth, does not live in shrines made by men' (Acts 17.24): so Saint Paul was reputed to have told the Athenians, looking over his shoulder at the great shrine of their patron goddess on the hill behind him. In its attitude to places and buildings Christianity cut right across the grain of ancient religion.

The gap between the two is hardly disguised by one streak in ancient religiosity which appears to anticipate Christian indifference to place: the philosophical piety which sometimes stressed the inwardness of true religion. Seneca, for instance, had insisted in almost Augustinian terms that 'There is no need to lift our hands heavenwards, nor to beg admission by the temple-keeper to the god's ear in order for our prayer to be heard. God is close to you, with you, within you.'[3] Seneca's spirituality was that of a philosophic counter-culture, lying oblique to the mainstream of ancient piety.[4] It was the protesting voice of that counter-culture, not the general consensus of Late Antique religiosity, that pointed in the direction of Christianity. Augustine, unlike Origen on the subject of holy days (see above, ch. 7, pp. 100–1 and n. 12), was expressing the shared conviction of Christians that for them no place was inherently sacred, for, as Saint Paul had said, they themselves were the temple of the living God (II Cor. 6.16). Their churches were not temples of a divinity, only the gathering places of his worshippers. 'As this building', Augustine said, preaching at the dedication of a church, 'was made for the purpose of congregating us bodily, so that building which is ourselves, is built spiritually for God.'[5] It was the community that was holy, not the church that housed it. The building had a sacredness only derivatively. 'These temples of wood or stone are built so that in them the living temples of God may be congregated and gathered into one temple of God.'[6] For centuries the church building

---

[3] *Ep.* 41.1. In Jewish thought the same tradition is expressed by Philo, e.g. *De somn.*, I.62–4; 182–8.

[4] An excellent study, Fowden, 'The pagan holy man', spotlights the philosopher's 'drift to marginality'.

[5] *Sermo* 337.2; cf. 336.1, etc. Tertullian, *De cor.* 9.2; Minucius Felix, *Oct.* 32.1–3.

[6] Cesarius of Arles, *Sermo* 229.2 (H); cf. 227.1, 228.1.

received no consecration other than by use. It housed the eucharistic community at its eucharistic worship, and it was by the first celebration of the eucharist within its walls that it was consecrated. The Christians' God was wholly present everywhere at once, allowing no site, no building or space any privileged share of holiness. True worship had no relation to any particular place. Until the fourth century Christians inhabited a spatial universe spiritually largely undifferentiated.

By contrast, the world in which Christianity established itself was full of holy places. The Roman town, which is where Christianity first took root, was itself a sacred enclosure, marked off from its environment by a foundation-rite which made the space enclosed by the town walls sacred, inviolable to defilement, equipped with gates for commerce with the outside world and for the elimination of pollution by the corpses of its dead. The urban space as such was sacred: its site determined by sacred ritual, its orientation and its boundaries defined a sacred space delimited from the 'outside', its whole area mirrored a celestial *templum* discerned by the augurs. The space within the walls bristled with sacred sites: the temples within their enclosures, and the public spaces organised around them. 'Your temples bring heaven near': so a pagan poet apostrophised Rome.[7] Nor were the temples the only sacred sites. The circus was an elaborate organisation of religious symbols – 'each of its monuments a temple', as Tertullian had said.[8] All public and much private life was channelled through a system of sacred spaces in the Roman town. Walls, temples, circuses, palaces defined the Late Antique town as a network of holy places.

A wealth of learning had been deployed by Christian chronographers and chroniclers to establish synchronisms between their own history and the history of the various nations or kingdoms of Antiquity. In that way they could relate their own sacred time-scheme to the chronologies of the world around. An analogous task had to be carried out for geography; but there was a difference. If their past was a forfeited inheritance, their space was a new acquisition. They had to plot the

[7] Rutilius Namatianus, *De red.* I.50.
[8] *De spect.* 8.3. On the symbolism of the circus and hippodrome, see Dagron, *Naissance d'une capitale*, 330–44.

biblical places on a map of the empire; but the territory of the Roman Empire was the spatial projection of an ancient culture and alien religions with their own pasts. To appropriate its space, Christians needed to take imaginative possession of it: to annex its space as they had to annex their own past (see ch. 6). But whereas that past had been their own, the topography of the Roman Empire was not. Their past they had to make their own like exiles returning to their homeland; the territory of the empire had to be colonised like a foreign land not long conquered. Like so many white settlers in Africa, they had to impose their own religious topography on a territory which they read as a blank surface, ignoring its previous religious landmarks and divisions.[9] By the end of the fourth century, however, the Christians had acquired their own sacred topography. It was a spatial projection of their sacred history. A place could become holy through some historical event, real or invented, the memory of a work of God done at a site at some particular moment of time. The primary holy sites were thus necessarily the places referred to in the scriptural narratives (see below, pp. 152–3); a small region on the eastern shores of the Mediterranean had a monopoly of these. Another category of sites that plainly qualified for holiness was that of the more ubiquitously distributed holy burials (it was these, rather than the actual sites of martyrdom that were venerated), the memorials of those who had borne faithful witness to the Lord and triumphed over death and the persecuting world. The martyrs' burials had the great further advantage of being capable – once the custom of transferring, and of dividing, relics had taken root – of being multiplied.

In the last chapter we considered the cult of the martyrs as the means whereby Christians bridged in their devotion and imagination the gulf which had come to divide their world from that of the persecuted Church. It also provided a means for turning the spatial world into a network of holy places. The catalyst of this development was the significance that came to be attached to the veneration not just of martyrs in general, but of the local martyr, if there was one, or of a local relic, if not.

---

[9] See Ranger, 'Taking hold of the land'. Christians did, of course, acknowledge the holiness of Jewish sacred sites.

Early in the fifth century a bishop of Turin preached to his congregation:[10]

Though we should celebrate, brothers, the anniversaries of all the martyrs with great devotion, yet we ought to put our whole veneration into observing the festivals especially of those who poured out their blood in our own home town [*domiciliis*]. Though all the saints are everywhere present and aid every one, those who suffered for us intervene for us especially. For when a martyr suffers, he suffers not only for himself, but for his fellow-citizens . . . So all the martyrs should be most devoutly honoured, yet specially those whose relics we possess here. For the former assist us with their prayer, but the latter also with their suffering. With these we have a sort of familiarity: they are always with us, they live among us.

What bishop Maximus spelled out to his congregation in Turin was the intimate link between the community and its own local martyr. The martyr should be no less a fellow-citizen of the local Christians in their town than he was their fellow-citizen in the City of heaven. Another author, writing in Gaul at much the same time about a group of martyrs, observed, almost in passing, that 'it is for the particular martyrs that they possess that particular places and particular towns are reputed illustrious'.[11] He could take for granted what, a generation before, was still a novelty. To understand how this came about, we can do no better than to begin with one of the most famous of early 'translations', that of the relics of Saints Gervasius and Protasius in Milan by Ambrose in 386.

Ambrose's own account of his actions provides many clues to its significance. Not long before he had dedicated a 'Roman basilica' with relics brought from elsewhere.[12] His congregation wanted the new church, the *basilica Ambrosiana*, to be dedicated in the same manner. Ambrose was willing: 'I will, if I find relics.'[13] He was acting in response to popular demand, perhaps well managed and orchestrated, but certainly revealing a single purpose shared by people and bishop. The relics duly turned up near the shrine of two already known Milanese martyrs and

[10] Maximus Taurin., *Sermo* 12.1–2.
[11] Eucherius, *Passio Agauniensium martyrum* 1 (*MGH SRM* 3.33). The appeal of *local* martyrs: 'Eusebius Gallicanus', *Hom.* LVI.4, XI. Beck, *The pastoral care*, 287–9 gives many Gallic examples of saints valued as local protectors of their 'own place' (esp. n. 7).
[12] On the relics, see Krautheimer, *Three Christian capitals*, 80 and n. 23.
[13] *Ep.* 22.1. Figures in brackets in the sequel refer to paragraphs of this letter.

were transferred, in the presence of 'an immense multitude' (2), to the Ambrosian basilica. Here a blind man was healed, and Ambrose preached two sermons. The discovery of the long-concealed martyrs gave 'the Church of Milan, hitherto barren of martyrs, the ability to rejoice in possession of the title and the example of her own sufferings' (*passionis propriae . . . et titulis et exemplis*) (7). The urge to find local martyrs plainly met a desire widely felt for the Milanese Church to have its own martyrs. They gave the Church new protectors and enhanced its ancient distinction (10). Ambrose appealed to the longing for solidarity with the generation of the martyrs which we have seen to be so characteristic of the post-Constantinian era (above, ch. 6, pp. 90–5). But he also made explicit an important further dimension which he and his flock thought crucial: they wanted to be the descendants, not of martyrs in general, but of their own martyrs. The relics of the Apostles did not satisfy this desire for their special, local patrons; the ancient distinction of their Church required possession of relics of the Milanese church's 'own sufferings'. The anomaly of a great Church without martyrs of its own was dissolved by this public 'resurrection of the martyrs' (9). Ambrose was speaking with almost legal precision: now his Church could trace its own descent, and consider itself the heir of its own martyrs.

This was not the first time relics had been used in dedicating a church. Ambrose himself had used relics of the Apostles – presumably objects that had been in contact with the bodies – when dedicating the Roman basilica. Nor was the Milanese Church's possession of local martyrs new or unique: the cemeteries surrounding the city were known to be full of martyrs' burials, and some old people seem to have been aware of reports about Gervasius and Protasius (12). What was the true significance of this recovery and translation of the relics? Legally, Ambrose's action could be construed as no more than the provision of a new and more fitting burial place for the dead.[14] It need not have been a breach of the old and recently re-affirmed prohibitions on interfering with burials, nor usurpation of the

---

[14] See Dassmann, 'Ambrosius und die Märtyrer', 57, n. 64, referring to *CJ* III.44.10, and assuming the permission envisaged in *CTh* IX.17.7. This paragraph owes much to this study.

imperial right to grant dispensation from the prohibition. Ambrose's action was far more revolutionary. Its novelty lay in the use he made of the relics. He placed them beneath the altar where he had intended to have himself buried, 'for it is fitting that the bishop should rest where he had been used to offer sacrifice; but', he said, 'I yield the ... position to the sacred victims ... He who suffered for all shall be upon the altar, those redeemed by His passion beneath it' (13). The relics of the saints were thus brought into association with the regular public worship of their own Church, no longer ignored, forgotten in their original anonymous resting place, or, like so many others, remembered in the suburban cemeteries as were deceased members of local families, with ancient rituals of family piety and, sometimes, wild and drunken abandon; but soberly, properly and publicly in their own church. The martyrs' cult would thus remain safely under clerical control; and, moreover, it would become embedded in the community's eucharistic worship.

This was the crucial step in the martyrs' entry into the mainstream of the Church's public, everyday, life. Hitherto their relics had been lying in the suburban cemeteries, in Milan as in Rome and elsewhere. The army of martyrs surrounded Rome – and other cities fortunate enough to have them – like a besieging force. From the second half of the fourth century sumptuous churches rose over their tombs and their refurbished burial chambers came to be adorned with finely chiselled inscriptions. The martyrs were not lacking honour and veneration. Some bishops went to great lengths to patronise and to enhance their burial places, and the multitudes flocked to them on the anniversaries. The City, Jerome wrote of Rome, would 'upheave itself', turning its back on the ancient temples and the civic monuments within the walls, to pay its respects to the martyrs beyond them.[15] Ambrose's new church in Milan was still outside the town walls, though it was a large church designed for congregational worship, and closer to the concentrations of population, not a memorial chapel in a cemetery. But before long, everywhere the martyrs were coming into the urban churches. Rightly has this been described as breaking the 'barriers that

---

[15] *Ep.* 107.1: *movetur Urbs sedibus suis.*

had existed in the back of the minds of Mediterranean men for a thousand years, and to join categories and places that had been usually meticulously contrasted'.[16] Early in the fifth century, the sight of a Christian body being brought into the city, thought to be a corpse, could still raise fears of pollution and rouse a pagan mob to fury.[17] Bringing the martyrs into the city, Christianity brought the dead back among the living. Not merely in thought and feeling, nor in strengthening the sense of their presence in time and in worship, but in their earthy reality, into the space of daily existence. The 'places of the saints'[18] scattered in the suburbs were brought into the town; the old gulf between the burial place and the urban churches was closed, and so was the gap between extramural anniversary celebrations and regular worship. In due course the prohibition of burial within the walls was further eroded.[19] The saints led the way; slowly, over the early medieval centuries, the bodies of the ordinary faithful were to follow them, from cemeteries on the edges of towns and villages into churches and church-yards closer to the heart of their communities,[20] 'not too far from the yew tree'.

Late Roman towns were thus becoming spatial reflections of the ancient Christian belief that the Church was a single community embracing all the saints, alive or dead. So it was in Rouen, not long before AD 400, when the citizens turned out, as if to welcome a visit from their emperor or a high imperial official, to greet the glorious arrival of a large collection of martyrs' relics. 'Look, what a throng of the heavenly army deigns to come to our city so that our habitation may be among the legion of saints and the great powers of the heavens', so their bishop addressed them; and, turning to the relics of the martyrs, 'You come from yourselves to yourselves; here you will find again the company you left behind, the saints ministering around the altar of the Lord Jesus Christ.'[21] The cement that most potently aggregated the community of the saints straddling heaven and earth was the martyrs' relics.

---

[16] Brown, *The cult*, 1–2.
[17] Mark the Deacon, *V. Porph.*, 23, 25 (eds. Grégoire and Kugener, 20, 22).
[18] Delehaye, '*Loca sanctorum*'.
[19] Kötting, *Der frühchristliche Reliquienkult*, 32–6.
[20] Bullough, 'Burial, community and belief'.
[21] Victricius of Rouen, *De laude sanct.* 1, 6.

Three steps can thus be distinguished in the process whereby
Roman towns – 'cities common to gods and men'[22] – were turned
into a network of Christian holy places. First, the huge momentum of the cult of the martyrs; second, the multiplication of
urban churches for public worship; and, third, the integration
of the two in the spreading custom of 'translating' relics into
urban churches. Taken separately, neither of the first two steps
would have been enough to create a new Christian sacred space.
In terms of topography, the cult of the martyrs at the *memoriae*
of their burial could be seen as a Christian perpetuation of the
care for the dead members of their families that the living were
expected to show towards them. Greatly intensified in the fourth
century for the reasons we have discussed, it deepened Christians' sense of the presence of their past, but did not change
their spatial world. The building of churches in growing numbers within towns, however, began a shift towards a new organisation of space: the ancient tissue of Roman sacred space was
being pulled out of shape by these new foci of the holy among
them. The church building proclaimed itself not as the successor
of the temple – for the Christian Church had no place for the
essential core of the ancient temple, the *cella* of the divinity;
what the church superseded was the temple enclosure and the
urban space organised around it, the spatial framework of the
worshippers' relation to the divinity. The church building united
under its roof the altar, the worshipping community – which
was in reality 'the temple of God' – and the cult-space.[23] The
physical appearance of the town could thus be greatly changed,
especially when, in due course, ancient shrines were destroyed,
allowed to decay or taken over and adapted for Christian use.[24]
More important, however, for our present discussion, was the
transformation of the spiritual townscape.

Crucial for this was the third and last of the fourth century's
innovations: the entry of the martyrs into the great urban churches. The deeply rooted notion that the dead did not belong
within the town, nor within the church building, was being
undermined. The Roman laws prohibiting burial within the

---

[22] See above, ch. 2, n. 7.
[23] Deichmann, 'Frühchristliche Kirchen', 114.
[24] *Ibid.* 109–10.

walls and the laws protecting the grave against disturbance had not been absolute prohibitions.[25] But the exceptions allowed by Roman law did not envisage the mass-invasion of towns which a law issued in 386[26] feared and tried to control. Legislation, however, could not stem the tide of relics flowing into the cities. Division of corpses, transportation of the fragments and eventually a lively trade in them made sure that even the unfortunate church that could not boast its own local martyr need not be deprived of the bodily presence of a celestial patron and protector. The relics of the first martyr, St Stephen, miraculously discovered in 415, spread over the Mediterranean world with astonishing speed. 'His body has brought light to the whole world', Augustine said in a sermon preached on one of his anniversaries.[27] The African Church had always tried to resist the cult of 'invented', unknown or fictitious martyrs and to curb the exuberance encouraged by the excesses of Donatist devotion to the martyrs. (See above, ch. 6, pp. 92–3.) It insisted that no shrine be erected in memory of any such alleged martyr, but only over the tombs of genuine martyrs.[28] This traditional restriction was being turned on its head and interpreted to enjoin the placing of martyrs' relics under or near to any altar, not, as originally intended, to prohibit the erection of altars over the burials of pseudo-martyrs. Instead of being forbidden to erect altars over the remains of false martyrs, Christians were now to place relics of martyrs, presumed to be real, not fictitious, beneath all altars.

Despite some resistance the cult of relics swept all before it. Around 400 Vigilantius, a priest with connections in Northern Spain, Southern Gaul and Italy, who also visited the Holy Land, incurred Jerome's wrath by voicing opposition:[29]

It is a pagan ritual we see brought into our churches when a mass of candles is lit in full daylight, and some bits of dust gathered into a

---

[25] Such as those that Ambrose may have taken the liberty to ignore: see above, n. 14, and Kötting, *Der frühchristliche Reliquienkult*, 21.

[26] *CTh* IX.17.7.

[27] *Sermo* 319.6.6.

[28] C. Carth. 401, *Reg. eccl. Carth.* 83 (*CC* 149.204–5). Note, however, that the merging of altar and tomb seems not to have generally taken place until the sixth century, and then only in the West: Deichmann, 'Märtyrerbasilika'.

[29] Jerome, *C. Vigilant.* 4. On Vigilantius, see Stancliffe, *St. Martin*, 301–11.

cloth and placed in a little container is kissed and adored by the faithful. Such people think they give great honour to the most holy martyrs by illuminating with vile candles those upon whom shines the full brightness of the Lamb's majesty, enthroned in their midst.

At this time it was still felt necessary to defend Ambrose's translation of the relics and their subsequent cult against detractors.[30] The Roman see, as often, remained reserved, at any rate about the dismemberment of corpses and broadcasting of the pieces, at least until the end of the sixth century.[31] In the end, outside pressures induced the popes to soften their hard line. The general change of mood is reflected in Augustine's own personal evolution between the years 401 and 422: earlier indifference and reserve changed into enthusiastic endorsement. It is not without significance that his thought on miracles and natural law also underwent change at this time. He had been edging towards an idea of nature, not unlike that found in some Stoic philosophers, as a complex of processes subject to their own natural law. This conception, however, dissolved in his mind as, towards the end of his life, he came to accept the prevalent belief in the everyday occurrence of miracles. 'The world itself is God's greatest miracle',[32] he wrote, defending God's freedom to work miracles; but doing so at the cost of dissolving the idea, barely embryonic, of a nature subject to its own laws in the freedom of the divine will. Now he was ready to see daily miracles wrought by the relics of Saint Stephen, recently discovered and brought to Africa, and to make use of them in his pastoral work among his congregations.

So the martyrs established new networks of holy places in Roman towns, where their presence was made spatially as immediate as it had to be temporally. 'Here', the actual spot, was 'the place' of the martyr's concrete immediacy in space as in time. Every church was a direct gateway to heaven; no longer, as it had been from the beginning, only a building to house the worshipping community, it became a shrine housing the holy

[30] Ps.-Jerome, *Ep.* 6.11 (*PL* 30.92).
[31] See McCulloch, 'From Antiquity to the Middle Ages'.
[32] *De civ. Dei* X.12; on natural law and its dissolution, Markus, 'Marius Victorinus and Augustine', 398–402. On Augustine's change of mind on relics, Saxer, *Morts, martyrs, reliques*, 240–5, 290–6; on his preaching, above, ch. 6, nn. 15–18.

relic. The sanctuary arch of St Martin's basilica at Tours bore the inscription: 'How awesome is this place! This is none other than the house of God, and this is the gate of heaven' (Gen. 28.17). What it proclaimed was true everywhere. Gateways to heaven were dotted over Roman towns as had been in former times the temples. 'The heavenly Jerusalem, its walls and buildings made in heaven', a sixth-century bishop preached, 'are transferred to this spot'.[33]

While the martyrs were invading, the urban tissue of the classical town was already weakening in many places, and was soon to do so in many more. From the fourth century onwards the public spaces in which ceremonial and social intercourse for pleasure and entertainment as well as for the display of political relationships were traditionally conducted were losing their focal importance in the life, and often in the topography, of the city. With the decline of public authority, public spaces were encroached on and privatised. Diminished and re-directed civic munificence created churches, chapels and monasteries instead of the traditional civic buildings. The retreat of the essential ingredients of the classical city – circus and baths, forum and porticoes, fountains and sewers, not to mention temples – assisted and at the same time was assisted by the transformation of life-styles and the conventions of social intercourse. The details, of course, vary from place to place and region to region, and no purpose would be served by an attempt to summarise here so large and so varied a scene, and one that is still only partially known. Happily it is not necessary to survey the variety of ways in which the urban environment, the visible townscape and the development of town plans underwent change.[34] Whether the dramatic rise in the number of churches, martyrs' shrines, baptistries and other ecclesiastical buildings caused a shift in the lay-out of a town or not, it always at least altered the

---

[33] Avitus, *Hom.* xxii.xxiii (*MGH AA* 6/2, 138.21–22) cf. *Hom.* xvii (*ibid.* 125.20–2).

[34] A sample: Ward-Perkins, *From classical antiquity*; Thébert, 'Vie privée'; Krautheimer, *Three Christian capitals*; for France, Février, 'Vetera et nova'; for northern and central Italy, Violante and Fonseca, 'Ubicazione e dedicazione' (I owe knowledge of this useful survey to the kindness of Maria Cesa). Bullough, 'Urban change'; Février, 'Permanence et héritage'; for comparison with Byzantium, Dagron, 'Le christianisme'. An outstanding study outside the scope of this book, but a model of the kind of work that is needed, Kennedy, 'From *polis* to *madina*'. The excellent survey by Barnish, 'The transformation of classical cities', reached me too late to use here.

spatial relations and the balance of importance of public spaces and buildings. At the extreme, a suburban shrine at the burial site of a martyr could act as a new focus around which new settlers would create the nucleus of a medieval town, leaving the old Roman town to crumble into a suburb. But even in the absence of so drastic a dislocation, the prominence and the density of Christian churches, chapels, hospices, clergy houses and monasteries, especially in towns whose older public spaces had shrunk or been virtually obliterated, is the symptom of a transformation no less dramatic for being drawn out over a century or more.

As Roman towns were becoming a network of Christian sacred sites, they were also taking their place in a larger geography of holy places. The town, surrounded by a ring of holy burials, was linked to others by sacred travel. Pilgrimage had been a well-established practice long before the elaboration of a Christian sacred geography. Visiting sacred sites was not unknown outside the Christian world; within it, it had long been common in the form of the relatively short journey – short in physical distance, though placing a vast psychological and sociological distance between the pilgrim and his home – between town and suburban burials and their *memoriae.* These visits to nearby shrines were, in principle, no different from the long pilgrimages across Europe or the Mediterranean. What mattered was the departure, the movement away from home, away from the established ties, stripped of one's role in society, of status and property. The pilgrim's way was a preparation for a new encounter: 'une prière marchée',[35] a marched prayer, a journey towards a place of holiness where power was present: power to transform the pilgrim's inner life, and, perhaps, miraculously, his outer, bodily existence; and, certainly, a power to transform, momentarily, the social constraints of normal living into a state of weightlessness and spontaneity which anticipated that community in which the pilgrim would, at the end, share in the full freedom of the life of the saints, beyond these 'social necessities'. The pilgrimage, along a particular route to a particular destination, was the reduced image and the symbol of the pilgrimage

---

[35] See Dupront, 'Pélérinage'. Cf. Brown, *The cult*, 42–5.

towards his final destination which the Christian's whole life was meant to be; and his arrival a foretaste of the final end of that journey.

The experience could easily be spatially and geographically extended. Pilgrimage sites were, characteristically, peripheral: on the edges of towns or outside their walls. These short pilgrimages radiating from towns to their suburbs came to form part of a larger nexus of routes, not unlike the 'hub and spoke' network of connecting airline routes in North America. The burials in the cemeteries continued to attract the devotion not only of the local town-dwellers, but of sacred tourists from further afield. Much space in the pilgrims' guides to Rome which survive from the early Middle Ages is devoted to the holy places surrounding the City.

It was no different with Jerusalem. Here, naturally, the sites, real, imagined, invented, but venerated and exploited, of the Lord's life and of the scriptural events, formed an extensive map of a region which would – though not until much later – become a 'holy land'.[36] Jerusalem and its environs, Palestine, Egypt and sometimes the Syrian hinterland were included in the pilgrims' itineraries. Pilgrims' tales, guidebooks, gazetteers, topographical dictionaries, maps and city-pictures in mosaic helped to familiarise Christians with a new sacred geography. Mementos brought back by returning pilgrims, souvenirs in various media, icons which combined representations of biblical events with specific elements of a holy site[37] or little pottery lamps treasured until swallowed by the soil where archaeologists have found them all over Europe, all must have contributed to a heightened awareness among Western Christians of the more distant corners in their sacred geography. In ways such as these the short outings to the extramural cemetery on a feast day interlocked with a vast network of longer routes which linked Europe with the religious centres of the Near East. The Roman *oikoumenē* became a set of holy places, unevenly distributed, but eclipsing for ever the sacred geography of the classical Greco-Roman world.

[36] On these see Wilken, 'Heiliges Land'; and Cardman, 'The rhetoric of holy places'. On maps of the Holy Land, see Tsafrir, 'The maps'.
[37] Weitzmann, 'Loca sancta', 55.

The new sacred geography replicated the history of salvation: it was the projection on the ground of the biblical events, with a thick overlay of the spots hallowed by the blood of the martyrs. Thus the pilgrim was persistently reminded of the history that gave the place its holiness. The appropriate passage of scripture (or, in Africa, the *passio* of the martyr) was read, the eucharistic sacrifice offered. One pilgrim to the Holy Land could take the routine of these occasions entirely for granted, and habitually remarked of the rites performed at each of her ports of call as carried out 'in the usual manner'. 'This is what I always desired above everything else: that wherever we came, that same place should always be read about from the Book'; 'this practice we always observed, following God's command, on arriving at our destinations'. Her reports on the holy sites of Sinai were intended to stimulate her sisters' interest in reading the things told in the books of 'holy Moses'.[38] For her, as for all pilgrims, the place enshrined a piece of sacred history and owed its holiness to the event.

A Christian topography had thus come into being from the fourth century on. But not without opposition, in part perhaps the outcome of instinctive distrust of holiness attached to places. The lingering antagonism to the cult of relics which we noted (above, p. 149) inevitably spilled over into distrust of pilgrimage. Thus Jerome, though himself one of the most dedicated of seekers-out of holy places, could also warn others against their attraction. 'What is praiseworthy is not to have been to Jerusalem, but to have lived well in Jerusalem', he wrote to his friend Paulinus; and he praised the hermit Hilarion, who only went to Jerusalem once, 'in order not to seem, on the one hand, to despise the holy places . . . nor, on the other, to seem to enclose the Lord in one place'.[39] And yet, Jerome shared the prevailing emotions: 'whenever we enter the Holy Sepulchre [in Jerusalem] we see the Lord lying in His winding sheet . . . and again we see the angel at the place of His feet, the cloth wrapped together at the head' (Jo. 20.7).[40] The ambivalence of his attitude reflects

---

[38] *Pereg. Eger.* 3.3; 10.7; 5.8. Reading of the *passio*: *C. Hippon.* (393), 5 (*CC* 149.21); *Brev. Hippon.* 36 (*ibid.* 186); *Reg. eccl. Carth.* 46 (*ibid.* 43).
[39] *Ep.* 58.2; cf. *Ep.* 129.
[40] *Ep.* 46.5; cf. *Ep.* 108. 8–14, on Paula's journey.

the heritage of reserve about holy places still powerful in the fourth century. But no such 'inconclusive theology of the holy places'[41] troubled visitors to St Martin's tomb only a few generations later. There, as an inscription assured the pilgrim, the saint 'presides from heaven over his tomb'; though his soul is in heaven, 'he is nevertheless here, whole and entire'.[42]

Christians had been more prepared to see places and buildings as the abode of demons than of saints, still less of God. While their instinctive resistance to the notion of a Christian holy place was being slowly eroded, and veneration of such places and pilgrimages to them gaining general acceptance, they still retained a vivid sense of the demonic power inhabiting pagan shrines and holy places. When Porphyry, the bishop of Gaza around 400, obtained the destruction of his city's great pagan sanctuary by imperial edict and with military assistance, Christian public opinion was divided between those who wished to burn it down, and those who were for saving labour by re-consecrating it to God. A divine revelation (in the form of a vision entrusted to a child) was required to resolve the doubt: the building was to be burnt to the ground, a new church, cruciform in plan, was to be built on the site of the old, round, sanctuary; its stones were made the paving around the church, where the trampling of Christian feet would proclaim Christ's victory over the heathen past.[43] Such hesitations persisted for centuries.[44] The bishop of Agrigentum in Sicily in the 590s[45] still thought it advisable to avert his gaze from the temple he would subsequently, having first exorcised the demons inhabiting it with prayer, turn into a beautiful church dedicated to SS Peter and

[41] The phrase is Sabine MacCormack's, '*Loca sancta*' (unpublished), where the classic case of Gregory of Nyssa's *Ep.* 2 (*PG* 46.1009–116) and the Reformation controversies around it are discussed. To her study I owe much.

[42] Nos. 15 and 13 in the Sylloge edited by L. Pietri, *La ville de Tours*, 809.

[43] Mark the Deacon, *V. Porph.* 66–79. For reservations about this work, see above, ch. 2, n. 5.

[44] For a full though inevitably incomplete list, see Deichmann, 'Frühchristliche Kirchen', 66–93, updated (very partially) in *RAC* 2.1228–41. An interesting variant, though in Greece, forms the subject of discussion in Gregory, 'The survival of paganism'. The first recorded take-over of a pagan temple for Christian worship, that of Caelestis in Carthage, seems, however, to have aroused no misgivings among Christians: Quodvultdeus, *Lib. prom.* III.38.44.

[45] If the romanticising *Life* written some ninety years later can be trusted: Leontius, *V. Greg. Agrig.* 90 (*PG* 98.709).

Paul. His contemporary, pope Gregory I, merely wanted the shrines of the pagan Anglo-Saxons to be sprinkled with holy water before being taken over for the worship of recently converted English Christians.[46]

The confident sense of the holiness of places gradually acquired by Christians was no simple substitution of a Christian for a pagan religious topography. Between the two lies a slow attrition of the Christian belief in the unholiness of pagan holy places, and the emergence, only slightly faster, of a readiness to envisage the possibility of holiness attached to particular spots. Such spots, invariably, were places with a history. It was the history that mattered.

---

[46] On the background of this, see Markus, 'Gregory the Great's Europe'.

11

City or Desert? Two models of community

In Part I we considered the uncertainties about the meaning of authentic Christianity in the decades around AD 400, and the varieties of response to them. In the course of these decades new images of the Christian life, personal and communal, came into being. The Roman matron Gregoria was hankering after the freedom of wealthy virgins in the seclusion of their family palaces; her spiritual mentor urged her to shoulder the responsibilities of a Christian wife and the mistress of an upper-class household.[1] Augustine's imprint on the development of the religious life in the West was making itself felt. It shows very clearly in a remarkable letter addressed by an unknown author to the virgin Demetrias. Demetrias was now no longer the young girl dedicating herself to the ascetic life whom Pelagius and Jerome had addressed (above, ch. 4, pp. 41–2), but a mature virgin of wide reputation and prestige. The author had learnt his lesson from Augustine well: his picture of the religious life as a life of peace and concord is full of echoes of Augustine's prescriptions for his monastic community.[2]

The prime object of the virtue of humility appears in the exercise of the communal duties by which divine mercy is propitiated and human society made cohesive. A great deal is done for the strengthening of love if, to quote the Apostle 'men outdo one another in showing honour' [Rom. 12.10], each holding the other in greater esteem, ready to serve those subject to them, not elated with pride if placed in a

---

[1] See above, ch. 5, p. 82, n. 71. For Augustine's advice to another married woman, see *Ep.* 262.
[2] *Ad Demetriadem*, 3 (*PL* 55.161–80).

position of authority; when the poor man does not hesitate to defer
to the rich, and the rich to hold the poor as his equal,

and so forth. In such happy and holy fellowship is 'Christian
liberty' achieved.[3] Riches are no bar to membership of such a
community;[4] what matters is humility. Concord, peace, sharing
as equals are the qualities that secure the life of the community.
Pride, especially the pride of refusing to acknowledge dependence on God's grace and claiming merit for what is His gift,
is the most destructive force.[5] In this thoroughly Augustinian
letter a mirror is held up to the noble Christian virgin: her
holiness resides not in her virginity, nor in her prestige and her
reputation, but in her humility; and humility, pride's antidote,
is ultimately identical with charity.[6]

The letter to Demetrias defines an ideal of Christian perfection
for an individual. The life of dedicated virginity had lost none
of its prestige; but it is not without interest that communal values,
the virtues of relationship with others, charity and humility above
all, should predominate in the personal ideal of Christian living
recommended here. These were the virtues central to Augustine's notion of the religious community, too; and that, too,
made its contribution to the history of Western spirituality. The
work of a generation of scholars has taught us that his views
marked a decisive shift towards the monastery conceived in
terms of concord, brotherhood and unity rather than the quest
of personal holiness through renunciation and ascetic living (ch.
5). The creation of a perfect community rather than the pursuit
of individual perfection came to be the keynote of his theology
of the monastic life. In this respect Augustine was not the first;
Basilian monasticism, particularly, had been moving in the same
direction. We have seen that this shift had much to do with
perplexities about the nature of the Christian life and its uncertain relationship to asceticism.

A question mark had come to hang over the ascetic ideal. It
had given a whole generation of Romans a means of defining
their Christian identity in a world now largely Christian. But

---

[3] *Ibid.* 4.
[4] *Ibid.* 5: was the author thinking of Sicilian Pelagian attacks on wealth here?
[5] *Ibid.* 8, 16.
[6] *Ibid.* 17, 18; and for the remarkable equation of humility and charity, 21.

now, especially since the clash between Jovinian and Jerome, asceticism seemed to threaten a dangerous gulf opening between an ascetic elite and the rest of the Christian community. Augustine, the ex-Manichee, was sensitive to such a dualism within the Christian community; and his opponents never allowed him to forget the hair's breadth that separated the ascetic ideal from a Manichaean denial of the flesh. He was ill at ease with Jerome's advocacy of virginity and asceticism; and at the very time that he sketched his theology of the monastic life for the monks of Carthage and depicted it as the anticipated heavenly City, he was also busy rehabilitating Christian marriage against Jerome. It was to take him years to develop a new understanding of sex, marriage and virginity; but while the outlines of that theology were forming in his mind, he already had at his disposal a vision of the truly human community. It enabled him to re-define the monastic life in terms which avoided the risk of dividing the Church into a spiritual elite and second-class Christians. Perfection had no more – and, of course, no less – to do with the monastic life than with that of the ordinary faithful. Its pursuit was equally required from all, equally beyond the powers of all, and equally dependent on God's freely given grace. Individually, the monk was subject to the call to perfection addressed to all Christians, just as he was not exempt from the universal stain upon the human condition. The monastery as a group, however, was anomalous in the wider community. In that anomaly resided its special function. (See above, ch. 5, pp. 80–1.)

Augustine's conception of monasticism thus lay at a parting of the ways. It did not, however, by any means supersede older traditions. Early monasticism was based on the conviction that Christian perfection could be achieved only by fighting the Devil in the Desert. The Egyptian hermits had wished only to lead the Christian life to the full. They were drawn into the Desert because it was not possible to live the Christian life in the City. For them self-abnegation was necessary to being Christian. This view of the ascetic life was re-inforced by the growth of a respectable, easy-going Christianity, and the despair it was liable to engender of the possibility of leading an authentic Christian life in the worldly Church of the Theodosian establishment. Here was the place of irredeemable mediocrity, of *tepor* –

lukewarmness – as Cassian was always saying. In the course of the fourth century the Church had become the world: it was not the place where Christian perfection could be found. The call of the Desert did not die away.

Augustine's re-definition of the monastery in terms which were essentially those of the City rather than the Desert thus brought a duality into Western monastic spirituality. The two images had a future in the monastic history of Europe extending far beyond the Middle Ages. Their interplay in the history of Western spirituality still awaits its historian.[7] My purpose here will not be to study different traditions of monastic spirituality except in so far as they implicitly provide a commentary on the form of the Christian life and the Christian community and their always problematic relation to the world, the flesh and the Devil.

Let us begin by contrasting Augustine's model of the monastery, built in the image of the City, with the alternative, constructed in the image of the Desert. Its finest Western statement is to be found in a little work *In praise of the Desert* addressed by Eucherius of Lyon to Hilary of Arles. Both men belonged to the first generation of monks settled on the island of Lerins in the community recently founded by Honoratus. Hilary was just returning to Lerins from Arles, where he had accompanied his kinsman and spiritual guide, Honoratus, when Honoratus became the bishop there in 426. Eucherius was another of Honoratus' early companions at Lerins. He hastened to welcome Hilary back to the island:

greater virtue brings you back to the Desert than first brought you there. For when you first arrived as a guest, you had your guide to conduct you and then to be your master in the heavenly *militia*; following him, leaving your parents, in him you found a parent. But now, having decided to follow him where his episcopal office took him, love has brought you back to the familiar retreat of the Desert.[8]

Hilary has 'longed for the place of solitude', as had Honoratus

---

[7] A start has been made by C. Leyser, in unpublished work in progress.
[8] *familiare secretum heremi*: *De laude heremi* 1 (*CSEL* 31.177). For the date of Honoratus' episcopate, see Additional Note at the end of the chapter.

and his brother before him.[9] This is the place, 'my Lerins', where holiness resides. It is here that Eucherius, and now Hilary too, must come to find it. To this place they must come to find the *interioria heremi instituta* – the inner life of the Desert; and like Moses, who had been commanded to loosen the straps of his sandals so as not to pollute the holy place, he who would come to the Desert must cut himself off from the cares of his former life and all previous ties.[10] This vocabulary of monastic conversion is saturated with the language of spatial separation: taking flight, seeking refuge, leaving behind, emigrating; and the language is meant to be literally understood.

Two striking features immediately contrast this image with Augustine's. The first is this central importance attached to place and to separation in space. Augustine's monk could have lived anywhere, provided it was in the community of his brothers, and the likeliest place to find that would have been in the precincts of the bishop's residence, within the city, rather than in remote islands.[11] Eucherius' spiritual paradise is located in a place: the Desert of Lerins. And 'the Desert' is no metaphor: it is 'God's unwalled temple'; God created it to people it with saints.[12] Eucherius' Desert is made holy by the people who have made it their home. Lerins, like other Deserts, deserves veneration on account of the pious men who have made it their retreat,[13] Honoratus before all. This was a theme dear to the early Lerinese writers, who had known and loved Honoratus. The island had been wild and inhospitable, avoided by all on account of 'its excessive squalor and the fear of poisonous animals'.[14] Honoratus' presence there has turned it into a 'camp of God' (Gen. 32.1–3), a site, as had been Jacob's resting place, 'resplendent with angelic ministrations'.[15] So Hilary is now returning to a Lerins transformed into a rich meadow flowing with streams, green with grass, bright with flowers, a delight to

[9] *Ibid.* 3 (178); Hilary, *Sermo* 10.3.
[10] *De laude heremi* 36 (189); cf. 31 (187) and 7 (180); *sepositi, quieti, silentes*: 31 (188) Cf. Vincent of Lerins, *Common.* I.1 (*PL* 50.639).
[11] See above, ch. 5.
[12] *De laude heremi* 3, 5 (178, 179).
[13] *Ibid.* 42: *piorum inluminatur secessu* (192).
[14] Hilary, *Sermo* 15.2; cf. *Reg. IV Patr.* 1.2.
[15] *Sermo* 16.1.

the senses of those who dwell in it: the joy of 'the inner man'. The body's Desert has become the garden of the soul.[16]

For the first generation at Lerins entry into the Desert was a liberation, an exodus from Egyptian captivity,[17] and the island they settled in a land of promise. Here was the bliss and repose of the angelic life, rather than a place of unceasing struggle with the Devil. Once Eucherius remarked[18] 'here is no place of safety': but this was not a dominant theme of his spirituality. Later monastic writers would lay more stress – as many had earlier – on the image of the Desert as the place of struggle with the demons, the place where the monk is stripped naked for the fight between salvation and damnation and the soul rendered transparent, its inmost, hidden, weakness exposed. Thus a later preacher, echoing Cassian, would address the monks of Lerins: 'we are here, but we are not secure . . . we have come to this place . . . not for quiet, not for security, but to join battle and to fight. This is a battlefield, we have come to wage war on vice.'[19] Whether an earthly paradise, as for the early Lerins writers, or a battlefield, as for others, the Desert is always a place. 'Here', in the monastic tradition of the Desert, is a refrain as regular as was 'to-day' in the preaching of Leo. (See above, ch. 9, p. 129.)

Place is immaterial on Augustine's view. But a second contrast is more far-reaching. Eucherius has nothing to say about the community; for Augustine it is central. The contrast can be epitomised in the way the two monastic traditions regard obedience. In his *Regulations for a monastery* Augustine considered obedience immediately after prohibiting any private possession and grumbling in the community. Similarly in the more detailed *Rule*, with equal deliberation, he dealt with obedience to the superior only in the penultimate chapter, after dealing with all the communal arrangements, and immediately following a chapter devoted to quarrels among the brethren

---

[16] *Ibid.* 39, 40 (191) and 42 (192). See also *Vita Hilarii* 7. Cf. Jerome, *Ep.* 14.10.
[17] Eucherius, *De laude* 44; Hilary, *Sermo* 17. Cf. 'Eusebius Gallicanus' *Hom.* 72 (=Faustus).13.
[18] *De contemptu mundi* (*PL* 50.723A).
[19] 'Eusebius Gallicanus', *Hom.* XL.6 (*CC* 101A, 480), 6.1 (*CC* 101B.861), alluding to *Inst.* IV.38; cf. XXXIX.2–3 (*CC* 101A.455–8). See Pricoco, *L'Isola dei santi*, 166–9, who stresses the comparative unimportance of this theme in the early Lerins tradition.

and their reconciling.[20] The importance assigned to the superior is modest: he is to distribute what is due to each member of the community – hardly the supreme importance assigned to him in an older monastic tradition.[21] A writer living under the Augustinian *Rule* has recently commented, 'for us obedience means solidarity with the community'.[22] Nothing could be further from the idea of obedience thus understood than the notion of a 'blind obedience': 'obedience only becomes perfect when the one who commands and the one who obeys come to share one mind . . . A totally obedient community would be one in which no one was ever compelled to do anything.' The role of the superior in such a community is to assist in forming and articulating the common mind, not imposing his will on his subjects. The subject's obedience is his coming to share in that common mind. To act obediently is to take part in building a community in which action will be free. This is a faithful transcription of Augustine's constant reiteration of the command to have 'one heart and one mind in God' (Acts 4.32).

Obedience here is 'horizontally' defined, in terms of communal relationships. For a 'vertical' concept we need go no further than John Cassian, the founder, probably around 415, of the monastery at Marseille, based on Egyptian models. In his *Institutes* Cassian gave examples of heroic obedience: of John, who conscientiously watered the dry stick given him by his master, twice daily, 'not mindful of the impossibility of the command', bringing water from two miles away, through wind and weather, through illness and health, and would have continued when, at the end of a year, his master tore up the stick to see if it had begun to sprout; or the monk who obediently steeled himself to feel no emotion at the sight of his little son neglected and maltreated: such examples, Cassian wrote, could not be passed over in silence, as 'the good of obedience . . . holds

---

[20] *Ordo monasterii* 4–6, and *Praeceptum* 6–7. The most convenient edition of the documents now is in Lawless, *Augustine*, 74–118, where they are given with a facing English translation.
[21] Augustine, *Praeceptum* 1.3. Cf. the classic statement by Jerome, *Ep.* 22.35: *prima apud eos* [coenobites] *confoederatio est obedire majoribus.* This letter was known to Cassian.
[22] McCabe, *God matters*, 231. The following quotations are from pp. 228–9.

the primacy among the other virtues'.[23] Augustine and Cassian both gave obedience supreme importance; but for quite different reasons. For Augustine, it constituted the unity of the community. For Cassian it was the monk's first step on the way to perfection: the acquisition of the monastic virtues through humility leading, eventually, to victory over the demons, over temptation, over himself, and the approach to the vision of God.

The same contrast is reflected in their different ideas of the bonds between members of the community. For Cassian, friendship could exist only between those of similar virtue. His treatise on friendship (*Conference* XVI) is soaked in classical ideas. When placed in the context of the monastic life, as it is here, it yields a remarkable and revealing conception of the love that is commended to the brothers. The love which unites the community is more than charity (*agapè*), the universal love which extends to enemies and friends alike; it is *diathesis*, 'the affection which embraces only a few, and only those linked by likeness in manners or in virtue'.[24] Love is a by-product, rather than a condition, of shared progress in perfection.[25] Pursuit of perfection was the highest value, justifying even a breach of loyalty to one's own community.[26] We need not dwell on the contrast with what Augustine regarded as the primary end of the monastic life. (See above, ch. 5, nn. 54–6.)

Cassian dedicated his second set of *Conferences* to Honoratus and Eucherius, and Lerins rapidly fell under his influence. The peculiar intellectual alchemy of the community managed to combine a veneration for Augustine[27] with a spirituality of markedly Cassianic stamp.[28] The imprint set by both on the *Rule* of St Benedict in the sixth century, diffused in the seventh and almost universally current in Western Europe from the early

---

[23] *Inst.* IV.30 (*CSEL* 17, 68). The discussion begins in ch. 23, the examples given are in chs. 24–9 (pp. 63–8). Cf. *Conl.* XVIII.3. Obedience and humility praised in later Lerins sermons: 'Eusebius Gallicanus', *Hom.* XXXVIII.2–3; XLII.1–2.

[24] *Conl.* XVI.14 (*CSEL* 13.448–9). Rousseau, *Ascetics*, 197 describes Cassian's *diathesis* thus: 'the penetrating, almost claustrophobic, intimacy of a tightly knit and isolated family'.

[25] *Conl.* XVI.3–6 (440–5).

[26] *Ibid.* XVII.1–30.

[27] Courcelle, 'Nouveaux aspects'.

[28] De Vogüé, *Les Règles des Saints Pères*, has studied the influence both of Augustine and of Cassian in the Lerinian Rules. His dating and identifications remain in doubt. On the contrasting views of obedience, see esp. pp. 80–8.

ninth, is now well known.[29] It is at present still very hard to estimate the respective importance of these cross-currents in monastic history, though we can be sure that their interplay long continued to determine much in Western spirituality. In a history of Christian spirituality, it would be a matter of some interest to investigate other aspects of the contrast between the types of outlook encouraged by the two types of monastic tradition. Similarly, in a history of monasticism, it would be important to trace the contributions respectively made by the two traditions of thought to the development of monastic institutions. But this is not the place to investigate the development of either monasticism or spirituality in Western Europe. For our present purpose the chief significance of the two concurrent models of the monastic community lies elsewhere: in the judgements they imply on the Church and the world around the monastery.

Cassian claimed to be following the monastic leaders of Egypt. But he had a far sharper awareness that the ascetic life was a vivid comment on the society from which the monk seceded. The immense silence of the Desert, the *heremi vastitas*,[30] constantly spoken of by the monastic writers, was the potent symbol of a break with the organised societies of Roman city-life. To enter the Desert was to assert one's freedom to extricate oneself from the suffocating bonds of that society, from the claims of property relationships, of power and domination, of marriage and family, and to re-create a life of primal freedom, whether in solitude or in an alternative and freely chosen social grouping. The social meaning of being thus set apart was sometimes made explicit. Cassian's eighteenth *Conference* contains such a statement, cast in the form of a summary of monastic history. The institution of communal monasticism he traced back to the Apostolic community. In the group described in Acts 4, Cassian saw the archetype of the truly Christian community:[31]

[29] De Vogüé, *La Règle de S. Benoît*, on all aspects of RB.

[30] E.g. Cassian, *Conl.* XIX.10. Cf. de Vogüé, *La Règle des Saints Pères*, 108, for a list; and Pricoco, *L'isola dei santi*, 135–7, 163. On the duality of the 'desert' as the place of silence and as the abode of demons see Guillaumont, 'Conception du désert'.

[31] *Conl.* XVIII.5.2–3 (510–11). I shall consider the distinction – important in itself, but irrelevant to the theme of this chapter – between the 'eremitic' and the 'coenobitic' forms of monastic life in the next chapter. Here the 'Desert' is intended to embrace both.

such, I say, was then the whole Church as now can be found with difficulty only in very few communities. But with the passing away of the apostles the multitude of believers began to lose their fervour [*tepescere coepisset*], and especially as crowds began to flock to faith in Christ from foreign nations of all sorts, from whom the apostles, mindful of their rudimentary faith and the tenacity of their pagan customs, required no more than that they should 'abstain from things sacrificed to idols and from fornication and from things strangled and from blood' [Acts 15.29]... and so the primitive rigour of the faith became attenuated, both among the people and its leaders. As their fervour cooled, many combined their confession of Christ with wealth; but those who kept the fervour of the apostles, recalling that former perfection, withdrew from their cities and from the society of those who thought this laxness of living permissible for themselves and for the Church, to spots on the edges of towns, or more remote places, and there practised privately and in their own groups the things which they remembered the apostles had instituted for the whole body of the Church.

Thus began the institutions of communal monasticism, among those of the faithful who 'segregated themselves from the spreading contagion'.

Like Jerome before him, and like many other ascetics, Cassian saw Christian history in terms of a decline from Apostolic perfection to corruption brought by wealth and respectability. It was only a short step to a vision of the monastic life as institutionalised protest, as a 'lived utopia'.[32] Primordially synonymous with Christianity, monasticism grew into a protest against a Church which had drifted away from its calling. In the ever growing *tepor*, the coolness, of the Church of the Roman establishment the only place for the fire of a real Christian life was outside its social framework, in the Desert. The monk's withdrawal into the Desert proclaimed visibly the Church's withdrawal from its true, original, and Apostolic identity. The monastic community would hold a mirror to the rest of the Church in which it could

[32] See above, ch. 5 (pp. 69–70, nn. 17–19). For a more sophisticated discussion, Séguy, 'Une sociologie', whose phrase *utopie pratiquée* I have borrowed in the text. De Vogüé, 'Monachisme', has described this use of Acts 4 as the genetic myth to account for the origins of coenobitism as 'la pièce maîtresse qui commande tout ce système' (214). He rightly gives much weight to the fact that this use of the Acts story (the 'Jerusalem' version of the myth) goes further than the 'Alexandrian' version (Philo's *De vita contemplativa* II.5.1, mediated through Eusebius, *HE* 11.17; cf. Jerome *De Vir. ill.* 8, 11) in adding the idea of secession from the Church to secession only from the (pagan) world (222–3).

see its own defection painfully reflected. Cassian was not greatly interested in pursuing the implications of this image for the Church at large, or for the world beyond it. He used his reconstruction of Christian history to define a spiritual itinerary. He was committed to a perfectionism of a kind for which the Christian norm could only be fully realised among an ascetic elite; and this implication Cassian, on the whole, was prepared to accept. 'Not even the words "And forgive us our trespasses" could bring down a monk to the level of other men.'[33] Seen in the panorama from the ascetic's mountain peak, the distance that separated the Church of the ordinary faithful from the faithless world dwindled to nothing. Looked at from the Desert, they merged into a single organised antithesis to its purity and freedom.

This is both tantalisingly like and unlike Augustine's image of the monastery in relation to the Church at large. The two accounts are alike in that they both present the monastery as a society which is a permanent challenge to the Church in the world. There the similarity ends. Cassian does not use Acts 4 very often, and when he does, it is generally as a myth of the genesis of *tepor*.[34] Augustine makes frequent use of it, but not in this sense. Nor does he make Acts 4 the beginning of a historical account of the emergence of monasticism. It was on the one hand a fact of the early Church's life, on the other a permanent ideal claiming the allegiance of all Christians. Though his favourite text, along with Psalm 132, for sketching the essentials of the monastic community, Acts 4.32–5, it has been observed, also remained his model for the Christian life as such: he cites the passage in whole or in part far more often in its application to the faithful in general.[35] Likeness to the Apostolic community is equally demanded of both Church and

[33] Rousseau, *Ascetics*, 204, referring to *Conl.* XXIII.18. See his carefully differentiated discussion of this theme, 200–5.
[34] See *Conl.* XXI.30, where an account is given, on the same lines, of the origin of the Lenten fast; *Inst.* II.5 and VII.17 use the text as *Conl.* XVIII.5, to account for decline into *tepor*; *Conl.* XII.2.5 to condemn avarice, XVI.6.4 to condemn quarrelling.
[35] Lawless, *Augustine*, 59, summarising Verheijen's work, says the ratio is roughly six to one. Frank, 'Vita apostolica', concludes from his survey of early Christian usage that the restriction of the 'apostolic life' to any group *within* the Church is an innovation not found before the fourth century. On Augustine's use of Acts 4, see Verheijen, 'Spiritualité'.

monastery, and cannot therefore be the basis of the distinction between them. The monastic group is not an elite in the Church. Augustine, as we have seen, was worried about allowing a split in the Church between an elite and the ordinary Christian. Nor, finally, is the separation between Church and monastery essentially a spatial one. Augustine has no interest in the Desert, and no need for it to hold a mirror up to a worldly Church or society. The cities of men are judged by reference to the City of God. Of that City the monastery was a dim anticipation, a shadowy representation, in so far as it was capable of representation on earth. The distance from which Augustine judges all human societies, Church and world alike, is the eschatological perspective in which he sees them; not from a group isolated, removed, spatially as well as spiritually maginalised. Cassian's monastery is the gathered community of the faithful set in the midst of – or, rather, set apart from – an apostate Church, as had been the early Church in – and from – a pagan world.

We shall have to return to Augustine's assessment of the Church and the world in the light of a fuller contrast with this, ascetic, alternative. Our most dramatic illustration of the latter can be found in the writings of Salvian. A refugee from the troubled north of Gaul, Salvian renounced his wife and family, adopted the religious life and maintained close links with Lerins. It is from the Desert he looks back on the world. While Cassian had sought to define a corner for the quest of perfection in a corrupt world, Salvian wished to transform the Church itself into an ascetic elite. If for Cassian the only true Christians were monks, for Salvian all true Christians had to approximate to monks. But in all essentials, Salvian and Cassian were agreed in their view of Christian existence.[36] In the manner characteristic of the Desert, Salvian conflates the Church and the world: the Romans he is denouncing, he is careful to tell us, 'exclude all the religious [i.e. monks and dedicated ascetics], and the handful of lay people like them'. He likes to stress the deep gulf between such men and the rest: in Africa, we are told, such lay people are lacking, and here the monks, 'that is to say, the saints of

---

[36] Leonardi, 'Alle origini', makes much of this contrast at the expense of the affinity between Cassian and Salvian.

God', were hated, ridiculed and cursed.[37] Salvian has sharply
divided the world: the utterly corrupt Roman world on the one
side, the few who have renounced it on the other. The division
of the world into the few – or very few, as he likes to add –
reverberates like a scarcely muffled drumbeat through Salvian's
pages. (The barbarians are not as bad as the Romans, and their
sins are excusable by their ignorance.) The Roman world is a
mass of perdition, excepting only a 'few, a very few' of the elect:
'apart from a tiny handful [*paucissimos*] who shun evil, what is
the whole assembly of Christians but a cesspool of vice?'[38] Salvian's Church is, in the last resort, the antithesis of two groups:
the near-perfect few, and the faithless, avaricious and corrupt
many. In Salvian's polemic the division between the few and
the many short-circuits the distinction between the 'religious'
and the lay Christian.

Salvian's picture of Christian history is identical with Cassian's,
but put to different use. Salvian was more interested in the
Church at large than in the 'very few'. He used the image of
the Church's pristine perfection not to account for the origins
of monastic life, but to condemn the Church which had betrayed
the purity of its origins. We are to learn from the example of
those who have gone before; we are to consider what was done
then – Salvian is referring to the renunciation of wealth – 'in a
full-blooded, not half-hearted way [*non mediocriter sed abundan-
ter*], by whole peoples, not by a very few . . . , things that are now
carried out by a few imitators of Christ'. The example he is
invoking is that of the Apostles reported in Acts 2 and 4, who
held all things in common and possessed nothing they called
their own. It was not the few, but the Christian people as a whole
that was then 'so perfect'.[39] His four books *To the Church* are
perhaps the most withering attack in Christian literature on the
possession of riches, far more savage in its uncompromising

---

[37] *De gub.* IV.13.62 (*CSEL* 8.87), VII.14.58 (173): the whole of Africa, 'except for a
very few servants of God, became a den of vice'. Hatred of ascetics: VIII.4.19 (197–8).
Cf. III.9.44 (57), VI.1.6 (125): *omnes aut paene omnes*; VII.3.14 (159), with a reference
to Paulinus of Nola. There are, of course, renegade monks, too: *De gub.* V.10.52–5
(118–20). *Ep.* 9.10 (219–20) speaks of 'such lack of faith among men and such weakness
in their faithless souls' and says 'this disease afflicts not only lay people, but also those
who usurp the name of religious'. It is to them that book II of *Ad eccles.* is addressed.
[38] *De gub.* III.9.44 (57).
[39] *Ad eccles.* III.10.41–3 (*CSEL* 8.282).

demands than any Christian attack on sexuality. The same force drives his fierce denunciation of contemporary Roman society in the apologia he addressed to his fellow believers to account for the disasters that a supposedly benevolent providence had allowed to afflict them: his eight books *On the government of God*:

> Woe to us and our iniquities, woe to us and our impurities! What hope is there for the Christian peoples in the sight of God when these evils cease in Roman towns only from the moment that they fall into the hands of barbarians? Viciousness and impurity are as it were congenital to Romans, their second nature and their quality of mind. Wherever Romans are there vice abounds.[40]

Historians of Late Roman society have found Salvian's work a goldmine of information about injustice towards and oppression of the poor and the exploitation of the lower classes by the rich and powerful. These are among the sins which Salvian diagnosed as the fatal flaw that sapped the Roman common-wealth. It is on their account that 'it is already dead, or drawing its last breath'.[41] In writing about the iniquities of the urban ruling classes, the tax system, the workings of rural patronage and the misery of the exploited, Salvian can be full and highly relevant, if sometimes one-sided. But his apologetic aim is not to condemn the Roman rich; it is to condemn the whole of Roman society, rich and poor alike, and thus to justify the dire fate it has met with at the hands of the barbarians. To do that, he needs to incriminate the poor no less than the rich. Having committed himself to condemning all Roman society in general terms (book III) and exposed the iniquities of the great, in specific and powerful detail (book V), he finds it necessary to backtrack in book VI: he is not attacking the faults of the few, he tells us; 'all, or, to speak rather less severely, nearly all, rush headlong into destruction'; and again, at the opening of the following book, 'the whole Roman world is wretched, and wallows in self-indulgence', and, significantly, he goes on to comment on the frivolity of the poor in the midst of troubles.[42] And so Salvian launches into his no less notorious, if very much less

---

[40] *De gub.* VI.8.40 (136).
[41] *Ibid.* IV.6.30 (73–4).
[42] *omnes enim admodum in perditionem ruunt aut certe, ut aliquid lenius dicam, paene omnes* – ibid. VI.1.3 (124); *totus Romanus orbis et miser et luxuriosus* – VII.1.6 (156).

informative, attack on Roman manners and morals in general, and on the shows and games (book VI) and on sexual aberration (book VII) in particular.

Historians understandably have refrained from taking these books seriously as evidence for the ubiquity of adultery (especially, it seems, in Aquitaine!), of sodomy (especially in Carthage!) and so forth. It is good polemic, and essential to the architecture of Salvian's argument. For the argument depends on a premise Augustine had repudiated – on a large scale in the *City of God* – that the sins of Christians can be measured by the severity of God's punishment. By contrast, Salvian thought God's reward for virtue and chastisement for sin were visible in worldly events. The troubles that afflict us are the proofs of our wickedness.[43] African sins had to be especially flagrant to account for the severity of divine punishment meted out there through the Vandals; Aquitaine and Septimania were, perhaps, singled out for special attention as areas in which aristocrats were known to have lost much land under Gothic occupation. What Salvian tells us, and what he allows to emerge between the lines, about the *spectacula*, though of little value as historical evidence, is nevertheless revealing. It will repay us to consider it briefly, not only because the comparison which it permits with Augustine's views (see above, ch. 8) is illuminating, but also on account of the insight it affords into the coherence of Salvian's intellectual universe.

As we read Salvian's fierce tirade, it becomes clear only gradually that we are in a different world from Augustine's. His denunciation follows well-worn tracks: the shows and games (*spectacula*) are scenes of all sorts of crime and vice; they excite the worst of human passions, the obscene delight in cruelty, they occasion vast expenditure to be incurred, and so forth.[44] It is only in the following chapter that we learn that he is speaking of things which 'are not happening all the time'. This concession to the rarity – or absence? – of gladiatorial games in the Gaul

[43] *Ibid.* IV.2.3 (66). Book III, however, begins with a statement more within the perspective of Augustinian agnosticism, quickly abandoned. Badot, 'L'utilisation de Salvien', 400, comments on Salvian's critique of Augustine.
[44] *De gub.* VI.2.10–12 (126–7). As in ch. 8, I do not discriminate here between shows, games, circus races and *spectacula* of various kinds.

of his day is made in order that he can go on plausibly to denounce what, by innuendo, are made to appear everyday occurrences: the shows in the amphitheatre, odeons, processions, pantomimes and their like. These are too disgusting to describe, even to know of; so he will keep to the 'impurities of the circus and the theatre', the representations of murder, adultery and sacrilege, too obscene to be publicly denounced. Omitting to comment on the circus games, Salvian then denounces the rest. The crimes perpetrated at the shows are the only crimes for which guilt is equally shared by actors and spectators. These are the things all, or nearly all, Romans do, and then complain of God's neglect of their well-being![45] In baptism, Christians have renounced the Devil, his *pompae* and his *spectacula*; so in the spectacles 'there is a certain apostasy from the faith and the creed itself, and deadly betrayal of the heavenly sacraments'. Worse still, public games are often held on festival days of the Church; and, like Augustine, Leo and others, Salvian notes that the churches are deserted for the circus.[46]

None of this is novel or very surprising, until the realisation dawns on the reader that Salvian is writing, in effect, about the past. 'To all this it may be replied', he allows, 'that these things don't happen in all Roman towns. True; and I will add, they no longer happen even where they used to happen.' In the cities of Roman Gaul and Spain fallen to the barbarians the spectacles have been destroyed along with the cities; elsewhere the poverty of the fisc prevents wealth being squandered on unprofitable obscenities. It does not really matter to Salvian whether these things are still done or not. He insists that Roman towns are still 'the sites and lurking-places of obscenity because they have formerly been the scene of all manner of impurity'. What this shows, he says, is what we would do if we had the opportunity.[47] The shows may have continued, at least occasionally, in some major centres such as Arles; but to go to the theatre or the circus, the provincial citizen, it seems, would now have to go to Rome

---

[45] *Ibid.* VI.3.15–19; 4.20 (128–30).
[46] *Ibid.* VI.6.31 (133); 7.37–8 (135); see above, ch. 8, n. 37.
[47] *Ibid.* VI. 8.39–44 (136–7). According to *Vita Hilarii* 20 (Cavallin, 97), the theatre at Arles had been plundered for building materials in the time of Hilary. On its existence in the sixth century, see ch. 13 below, at n. 32. Sidonius mentions a theatre at Narbonne, with evident approval, *Carmen* XXIII.40.

or Ravenna, where they are still functioning. That when in Rome or Ravenna they do as the Romans and the Ravennates do proves that the instincts of obscenity and profligacy have lost none of their power even in this time of trouble, insecurity and poverty. Laughing, the Roman people goes to its death.[48]

Salvian had a sharp sense of his contemporaries' frivolity in the face of disaster – such as others also detected, notably Severinus in the troubled frontier province of Noricum, and from which they attempted to rouse the local populations by their preaching. Eyes and minds could be closed to realities, even without the distractions provided by the great public shows. Salvian's preaching could, perhaps, be interpreted as an onslaught on widespread moral torpor and lack of seriousness and urgency. His comment on the request of the Trier nobles for the re-introduction of the games after the City's restoration seems intended in this sense, though it betrays a misunderstanding of impeccably patriotic motives.[49] But in fact his attack on the shows had no immediate target. The shows he was denouncing may not even have existed. They are not the real objects of his vitriol, but a convenient literary symbol.[50] Salvian was not wasting his breath condemning what he knew did not exist. He was using a fiction to state a view of Christian morality on which the shows would have to be condemned if they existed. And that was a morality far narrower in what it would permit than the morality of Gallic Christians in the fifth century.

For a comparison of Salvian's view with Augustine's it is crucial to bear in mind that Salvian is writing about the past. In Augustine's Africa the shows were still very much alive. Until April 399 (see above, ch. 8, pp. 110–12), Augustine was concerned with a traditional, secular pattern of living which, as he appreciated, still claimed varied loyalties and thus still had a place in the mixed society of a city such as Carthage. It could even promote civic cohesion; it was as well not to be too harsh to its

---

[48] *Ibid.* VI.9.49–52 (138–40); *moritur et ridet*: VII.1.6 (156).
[49] *De gub.* VI.15, and Ward-Perkins, *From classical antiquity*, 106, n. 51.
[50] Badewien, *Geschichtstheologie*, 93, notes that Salvian conceives the shows 'paradeigmatisch'. It may be that passages of Augustine, e.g. *De civ. Dei* 1.32, served Salvian as his source. None of the parallels suffice to prove dependence. The evidence for the dependence of *De gub.* VI.69 on Quodvultdeus, *Sermo* 10.1 (*De temp. barb.* 1), suggested by Courcelle, *Histoire littéraire*, 155, n. 1, is a little stronger.

devotees. We should not expect Salvian to have appreciated the value of the shows that had begun to change their role in Roman urban society even in Augustine's day and had, at any rate in large part, disappeared from Salvian's Gaul. Augustine's world was changing, as we observed, under his very eyes. Secular traditions were under pressure and attack, and not always by the leaders of the Church. Ancient customs, such as the games, were drawn into the confrontation of pagan and Christian, and incurred growing ecclesiastical censure. For Salvian they were bound up inextricably with a pagan and sacrilegious past. His abhorrence was akin to Augustine's indignation about the depravity he saw in them, and especially after 399, their tight association with pagan worship in the polemical pages of the *City of God.*[51] Nevertheless, it is important to notice the distance between the stand-points from which they judged the institutions and customs of their society. Salvian's norms were set by the ascetic's demand for perfection. Any falling short of this norm was a betrayal of the Christian name: 'It profits nothing to have a holy name without the morals that go with it ... Since we see hardly any section of the Christian people, hardly a corner of all the churches, that is not full of the filth and the stain of deadly sin, how can we flatter ourselves by calling ourselves Christians?'[52]

Measured against his standards, the pagan world and the Church, its primitive Apostolic purity lost, were fused into a single unredeemed mass. Only the ascetic elite, the 'few' he likes to make an exception to his blanket condemnations, could represent authentic Christianity. The Church could claim the name of 'Christian' only to the extent that it approximated to the condition of the perfect gathered in the Desert. The edge of the Desert marked the boundaries of the holy; all that lay beyond it, the impure world of the unregenerate and the apostate, the Church and the world of the city, were outside the range of the holy. In the perspective of the ascetic, there was a simple polarity: Christian perfection, faced with the profane, the worldly or the secular, the theatre and the circus.

[51] I.31–4; II.8, 13; IV.26.
[52] *De gub.* III.11.60 (62); cf. IV.1 (63–5); see above, n. 32.

This perspective holds the norm to be, in principle, attainable: it is in fact attained, or at least approached, by Salvian's 'very few'. The rest are condemned by reference to the standards embodied in their group. If we picture the world, the Church and the ascetic group as three concentric circles, the ascetic perspective would be the view from the smallest inner circle and would conflate the other two into one. By contrast, the perspective we might call 'eschatological' – Augustine's – holds the norm to be in principle unattainable, transcendent, and thus not directly applicable to any actual society. Augustine's scheme was less simple than Salvian's and had no place for the stark dichotomy between a spiritual elite and the rest. Augustine had rejected the concept of the monastic life conceived in terms of perfection and had set out to provide an alternative to the model of the Desert set over against the City. The Desert did not define an ideal to be aimed at. Groups could not be ranged on a scale according to the closeness with which they approached perfection. He rejected any possibility of a sociological separation of the holy from the unredeemed.[53] The holy could not be contained within the space of a sociologically defined milieu; any actual social group was always bound to comprise the holy and the worldly, the wicked, the depraved, 'inextricably intertwined'. It was in this perspective of the earthly and the heavenly Cities intermixed in the *saeculum* that he saw both the Church and the world. His Church could never, before its final purification, be a gathered community of the holy set in an alien world. And what the Church could not be in the world, that the monastery could not be in the Church. There was no place for a spiritual elite in the body of the faithful, any more than for a Christian elite in the Late Roman world. The monastery could not embody a utopia for the Church, or for Roman society, to aspire to: no social group could be that. The monastic community was not a model for other societies; rather, it was to represent to the Church its final calling. In Augustine's theology all human groups were irremediably tainted with sin and in the grip of the disorder consequent upon it. The monastery was no less

---

[53] This paragraph and the next summarise the central theme of Markus, *Saeculum*; see especially pp. 122–6, 166–86, and the Introduction to the second edition, pp. xiii–xvi. On Augustine's idea of the monastic community, see above, ch. 5, pp. 76–83.

subject to this necessity than any other society; but it was a permanent reminder of the eschatological City.

Sin placed all human institutions and groups irrevocably beyond the reach of any model of heavenly perfection. It made as deep a cut between the heavenly and the earthly Cities as it made into the human personality or into human societies. 'When will full peace come to a man? The time when an individual person is fully at peace, that is the time when peace will have come in its fullness to all the citizens of Jerusalem.'[54] The 'easy and concordant harmony' of flesh and spirit would be realised only in that 'miraculous peace' in which a fully human community would be, finally, achieved.[55] Here on earth harmony in the self and in society would always be elusive. The distance between the heavenly Jerusalem and any historical society was infinite. In the final analysis, there would be only two societies, the earthly and the heavenly Cities, with their radically opposed orientations: the one to self, the other to God. There could be no hierarchy of intermediate societies, and Augustine sharply rejected any notion that a human group could be modelled on the heavenly City, or reflect it as an image reflects its original. The heavenly City was the eschatological orientation, what the Church will be at the end, when it is purified of its chaff on God's threshing floor; but that is a purification that may not be anticipated. That City is not a model, but an anchor, a direction, the fixed point at the far end of the Church's unending pilgrimage. Augustine's sombre view of all human existence as wrenched out of its original wholeness gave it an unexpected autonomy in its own, fallen and irremediably sinful, state.

Still less, therefore, could the monastery serve as a model for the unredeemed world outside the Church. For that, as Augustine insisted, was necessarily a mixed society comprising people of divergent loyalties, groups with different and conflicting value-systems or ideologies. Secular society was required to keep a space in which they functioned. It could never be radically Christian, still less modelled on the society of the monastery. Secular society had its own sphere of action and its own, strictly limited, purpose. Its institutions served subordinate, but within

[54] *Enarr. in Ps.* 147.20.
[55] *Ep.* 6*.8. See above, ch. 4, n. 52.

their sphere, autonomous ends. For the simple dichotomy of monks and the rest, as seen in the ascetic's scheme, Augustine substituted a trichotomy of the world, the Church and the monastery. He looked at the world from a City, and the world he saw was one more subtly differentiated than the world as seen from the Desert.

It is not easy to assess the extent to which Augustine's influence deflected subsequent development of monastic life, institutions or spirituality. What is much clearer is the rapid disappearance from the minds of Western Christians of any trace of his eschatological perspective and the relative autonomy it assigned to secular society and its institutions. His three-part view of society was rapidly eclipsed behind the simpler ascetic scheme of two ideal types, in which the Church and the world were conflated. The contrast of Desert and City prevailed over the more complex tri-partite schema of the heavenly and earthly Cities, and a 'third something', the world of human groups in historical time, the *saeculum*, poised ambivalently between them. Secular society came to be looked at from the vantage point of the ascetic. How this came about must be considered in the next two chapters.

ADDITIONAL NOTE ON THE DATE OF CASSIAN'S THIRTEENTH *CONFERENCE*

I have adopted the generally accepted date for Honoratus' move from Lerins to Arles: 426. It depends on Cassian's dedication of the second set of his *Conferences* (XI–XVII) to Honoratus, at this time still abbot of a 'great monastery', and Eucherius. The traditional dating has been called in question by Sir Owen Chadwick in an important paper, 'Euladius of Arles', *JThS* 46 (1945), 200–5. The argument hinges on Prosper's request to Augustine (Augustine, *Ep.* 225.9) for reply to the doubts of 'Hilary, bishop of Arles' (an alternative reading has 'Euladius', or perhaps 'Heladius'). Cassian's thirteenth *Conference* is not mentioned in this letter, a fact which would be unaccountable for, so it is thought, if the letter had been written after this 'controversial piece of writing containing Cassian's famous opposition to Augustine' (Chadwick, 'Euladius', 201).

The generally held assumptions about Cassian's thirteenth *Conference* must, however, be subjected to critical scrutiny. If we discount the assumptions encouraged by centuries of received opinion and read the *Conference* with fresh minds, it is not at all obvious that it 'is essentially an act within the theological crisis', or indeed that it forms part of the controversy which has been labelled, since the seventeenth century, as the 'semi-Pelagian'. It has close links with the twelfth *Conference* (and to some extent with others in the set), and purports to be an attack on Pelagian views. The assumption that this is a disguise dictated by reluctance to attack Augustine openly is without foundation, imposed by a view of Gallic Christianity derived from an anachronistic perspective. It seems more natural to interpret the *Conference* in the context of the Pelagian views apparently held in Gaul which were condemned by legislation in 425 (*Const. Sirm.* 6, which seems to form part of a batch of similar legislation issued in the summer of 425: cf. *CTh* XVI.5.62, 63 and 64), as an attack not on Augustine's, but on Pelagian, views, albeit from a point of view more in line with a pre-Augustinian theological tradition than with Augustine's anti-Pelagian theology. We need not doubt that Cassian was conscious of departing from Augustine's views on Pelagianism in his own attack on its tenets; but it is not at all clear that Augustine's views had come under attack in Provence at the time this *Conference* was written. It seems to me likelier that the *Conference* was only subsequently drawn into the controversy. It is evident from Prosper's letter to Augustine (*Ep.* 225.2) that some anxiety, perhaps controversy, had preceded the arrival of the *De correptione et gratia* in Gaul. Cassian's *Conference* could well have been an early manifestation of such doubts. The crucial investigation that could settle this question still needs to be carried out: what works of Augustine's Cassian can be shown to have known, what use he made of his knowledge, and what the precise thrust of his argument was when he wrote this *Conference.* In the absence of such an investigation the impulse to read the *Conference* in the perspective of the 'semi-Pelagian' controversy – an assumption never seriously questioned (though Chadwick himself came closer to doing so than other scholars in his finely balanced account in *John Cassian*, ch. 4) – should be resisted. There may have been much less of this controversy outside the immediate circle of Prosper and his opponents in the years between 428 and 433 than is generally supposed, until the debate was revived in the changed political circumstances at the end of the fifth century. (For a survey of the question and recent discussion, see Markus, 'The legacy of Pelagius'.)

12

Desert and City: a blurring of frontiers

The fusion of Desert and City is one of the most momentous of the changes in the spiritual landscape of Late Antiquity. Cassian had warned his monks to keep away from women and from bishops. His influence on Lerins may have been considerable; but it did not prevent many of its monks, indeed its leaders, from taking on episcopal office.[1] The recruitment of a large section of the Gallic episcopate from the monastic circle of Lerins is only a facet of it. It eased the entry of ascetic ideas into the society and the minds of urban Christians, with still untold consequences for their view of themselves and the world around them. One scholar has written of this 'flow of talent from the monastic to the pastoral world' and concluded that the 'virtue of monks became less a text-book model of spiritual health for other men, and more of a transfusion into the blood-stream of the whole community'.[2] It would be unwise to press the 'less' and the 'more': the fact is that the influx of men and the nature of the model for spiritual health both had vast influence. For this reason it is important to plot the change that ascetic ideas themselves underwent.

Such a sketch must begin with Cassian himself, whose 'Desert' is in fact a more complex notion than the simple foil to the 'City' for which it has so far done duty here. To be sure, Cassian wished to maintain a division between his monastery and the world. To this extent this simplification may be acceptable as a transcription of his basic aim, to sketch an interior spiritual

[1] See Prinz, *Frühes Mönchtum*, 60–2. I deal with this theme more fully in chapter 13, below, pp. 191–201.
[2] Rousseau, 'In search of Sidonius', 366.

itinerary (in the *Conferences*) and an outline of the 'external mode of life' (in the *Institutes*) for monks,[3] that is to say, for those who wished to dedicate themselves to the pursuit of a perfection which could not be sought in the world. But for Cassian, the 'Desert' (*heremus*) stood not for the monastery, but for one form of the ascetic life: the solitary life of the hermit. It is a term of his regular vocabulary for the forms of monastic life. His abbot John, for example, had left his 'Desert' to subject himself in great humility to the life of the community (*coenobium*).[4]

Both the communal (coenobitic) and the solitary (anchoretic or eremitic) modes of monastic life had a respectable history behind them. Despite the more communal twist given to the monastic tradition by Basil and by Augustine, the solitary still generally enjoyed greater prestige. Cassian did not, at first, question, indeed, he instinctively followed, this fashion. The anchorites were the 'supreme' of the fathers, their profession was 'sublime'.[5] One reason for the superiority generally accorded to the solitary life was the tendency to equate it with the life of contemplation, unquestionably superior to the active life pursued by the coenobite living in his community. Cassian had himself accepted this equation when he began writing his *Conferences*.[6]

This superiority, however, is subtly but radically undermined in the course of the *Conferences*. In the final set it seems to vanish altogether. Cassian here speaks of the coenobites as not only the most ancient, but also the 'first in grace'; they are the 'perfect', the root from which was to spring the flower and the fruit of the anchorites. These latter desire loftier heights of perfection; the result of their effort, however, is described in a neutral, colourless, phrase as 'another kind of perfection'.[7] But Cassian reserves the drastic way he will demote the solitary life for the next *Conference*, and he does so by going out of his way to prepare his readers for a surprise. *Conference* XVIII ends with the

---

[3] *Conl., Praef.* I.5: the *Institutes* dealt with the *exterior ac visibilis monachorum cultus*, the *Conferences* with the *invisibilis interioris hominis habitus*.
[4] *Conl.* XIX.1, and the following chapters.
[5] *Ibid. Praef.* I.2, 4.
[6] *Ibid. Praef.* I.4.
[7] *Ibid.* XVIII.5.4–6.2.

confident expectation that we (along with Cassian and his companion) are to be initiated into the way of the anchorite, 'promoted from the infant school of the common life to the second grade, the anchoretic life'.[8] And so Cassian launches his readers on the devastating comment, placed in the mouth of the great abbot John, on the superiority conventionally accorded to the anchoretic life.

John had reached the heights of solitary contemplation but returned to the life of the 'junior school' of the community;[9] not only to show that the two forms of life are not mutually exclusive; but to commend the common life as more suited to all but the most exceptional of men even among ascetics. For, as John admits, the anchorite's life is, indeed, superior; but it exposes its practitioners to temptations and anxieties which are absent from the communal life. Thus, paradoxically, within the narrow compass of the community, in obedience and humility, in peace of mind and with tranquillity of heart, John found greater fulfilment than was possible amid the anxieties of the solitary life of the contemplative. The grounds traditionally given for the pursuit of the solitary life – total freedom from worldly care, total renunciation of all ties – are here turned round, to justify preference of the common to the solitary life. The Desert has become, by a powerful twist of irony, the place of coolness, where the fire of divine contemplation has been extinguished and carnal bonds have established their hold.[10] The perfection that monks may aspire to in either form of monastic life will be partial; few can hope to attain it in either, hardly any in both. Among those who did, Cassian (John) numbered the abbots Moses and Paphnutius:[11] significant choices – the exponents of the spiritual itinerary outlined in the first three *Conferences*. Cassian has removed the anchorite's ideal to a horizon so distant that it can no longer be the chosen object for monks to aim at. It leaves the coenobitic life as the only realistically available option. Abbot John's *Conference* is the warrant for Cassian's endorsement of the communal life as the

[8] *Ibid.* XVIII.16.15.
[9] *Ibid.* XIX.2.4; the sequel summarises chapters 3–9.
[10] *Ibid.* XIX.5.2.
[11] *Ibid.* XIX.8 and 9.1.

best practicable form for the attainment of the ascetic ideal, and the necessary comment on the optimism about spiritual progress implied in the early *Conferences.*

In the course of these two *Conferences* (XVIII and XIX) Cassian has come to abandon, subtly but decisively, the equation of the communal with the active and the solitary with the contemplative life. When he first expounded the Gospel story of Mary and Martha, Cassian unhesitatingly identified the 'better part' chosen by Mary with the life of contemplation, the inferior 'necessary and useful goods' represented by Martha with the active life; *theoria,* contemplation, being reserved for 'a few saints'. Whether the 'few saints' are to be identified as the great solitaries of the desert is left unstated, though nothing prevents the reader from assuming this, as indeed had Cassian in his Preface to this first set of *Conferences* (see above, p. 182).[12] Abbot John now offers his own definition of the communal and the solitary forms of monastic life, cast in terms which carefully avoid any use of the actual terminology of the 'active' and the 'contemplative' lives: the end of the coenobite's life consists in 'having all his desires mortified and crucified, taking no thought, according to that command of evangelical perfection, for the morrow'; the hermit's – described in oddly similar terms – in 'having a mind freed from all earthly things and thus united, as far as human weakness permits, with Christ'.[13] Gone is the implicit identification of the communal with the active, of the eremitical with the contemplative life.

This shift in Cassian's view of the contemplative life seems to be well on the way in a *Conference* in the second set, written at some time between the first ten and the last seven. This *Conference* (XIV) is devoted to the active (*praktike*) and the contemplative (*theoretike*) lives. Cast in what is to all appearances a traditional mould, Cassian's argument is nevertheless truly revolutionary. In using the language of the 'active' and the

[12] *Ibid.* I.8. I consider *Conl.* XXIII.3, below, p. 187, n. 21. The temptation to interpret the first in the light of the second of these passages should be resisted. Some scholars, giving insufficient weight to the chronological gap that separates them, have sometimes fallen into this trap. For a notable exception, see Olphe-Galliard, 'Vie contemplative', esp. 273–80, who, however, gives Cassian insufficient credit for independence of his sources and originality.

[13] *Conl.* XIX.8.3–4.

'contemplative' life he was drawing on a venerable usage, going back to the Greek philosophers and a respectable chain of Christian (and indeed Jewish) writers.[14] But his own re-definition gave the terms quite a new application. Origen, the fountain-head of Christian thought on this as on so many subjects, had made the old philosophical conception of the 'practical' (or 'active') life stand for the moral discipline preparatory to the second stage on the way to salvation, which he identified with the 'theoretical' (or 'contemplative'). They were to be combined in the lives of Christians. Later Christian writers separated the two forms of life, assigning each to different groups of people, engaged in different activities, in a manner more reminiscent of the Greek philosophers. Around the end of the fourth century the terms had become appropriated to distinguish the monastic from the secular mode of life: the monk's was the contemplative, the worldly Christian's the active life. The distinction had become highly topical in monastic circles in Cassian's time and was much discussed among the Egyptian ascetics he had visited. Cassian's own monastic outlook had been influenced by one of these ascetic teachers, Evagrius.[15] For the widely current identification of 'monastic' with 'contemplative' and 'secular' with 'active', Evagrius substituted a usage in which both 'active' (*praktike*) and 'contemplative' (*theoretike*) applied to monks; but for him they were successive stages on the way to the perfection aimed at by the anchorite.

Evagrius had drawn the distinction between the active life and the contemplative very sharply; Cassian set out to blur it. Having minimised the superiority of the solitary to the communal life, Cassian also made room for both the active and the contemplative lives in the only practicable form of monasticism he could recommend, the communal. For him, they were not so much forms of life adopted by different kinds of monk, as stages on a journey; moreover, even within an individual's ascent on the ladder of

[14] The best summary is Guillaumont and Guillaumont, *Evagre le Pontique*, 38–53, on which my account is based. See further n. 20 below.
[15] On Cassian and Evagrius, see Chadwick, *John Cassian*, 25–30; on *praktike* and *theoretike* 86–94, see Rousseau, *Ascetics*, 177–82, and 'Cassian, contemplation and the coenobitic life'. The relation between Cassian and Evagrius has been studied by Marsili, *Giovanni Cassiano*. On their definitions of *praktike* and *theoretike*, see pp. 106–15. Some of his conclusions will need revision in the light of work in progress by Elizabeth Clark.

perfection, the two stages overlapped. Abbot Paphnutius, in Cassian's first set of *Conferences* (III) had been the model of the ascetic's journey through self-denial and the cultivation of the virtues to solitary contemplation. The ascetic theory founded on his example – a sequence of renunciations and training in virtue leading to contemplation – mapped a straight progression towards perfection. Contemplation was the summit of perfection; the active life was the exercise of virtue, the struggle with sin and the Devil, and the achievement of passionlessness. It was presupposed by and necessary for the advance to contemplation.[16] But with the dethronement of the solitary life, Paphnutius' progression could no longer be the model for a monastic itinerary. Its successive stages had to be telescoped. Hence in Cassian's mind the two lives were 'entangled beyond hope of unravelling'.[17]

With their telescoping, the very nature of contemplation also underwent a profound change at Cassian's hands. Cassian sets out from a distinction formulated in a very traditional way: *praktike* is concerned with the discipline of purifying life of vice and the acquisition of virtue, *theoretike* with the understanding of divine things and their meanings.[18] The former is distributed among all the various forms of the monastic profession – the hermit's no less than the coenobite's.[19] It is with his exposition of *theoretike*, however, that Cassian sets out on a path of his own.

Cassian re-thought the content of the idea of 'contemplation'. What those who were actually engaged in the 'contemplative life' were doing was something significantly different from what this life was traditionally understood to involve; and 'contemplation' as traditionally understood was quietly removed from the sphere of what was achievable here on earth. In this second respect Cassian's re-working of this theme rejoins a tradition of thought of which Augustine was the outstanding representative. In Augustine's exposition the story of Mary and Martha (or of Leah and Rachel, or of Peter and John) had also been a statement of the superiority of the contemplative over the active life. But

---

[16] This is the view still asserted in *Conl.* XIV.2 and 9.
[17] Chadwick, *John Cassian*, 93.
[18] *Conl.* XIV.1.3.
[19] *Ibid.* XIV.4.

for him the contemplative life was 'the eternal life of delight in the contemplation of God', whereas all human life here on earth was, like Leah's and Martha's, a life of 'laborious necessity', uncertain of the outcome of our works, a life in which we see but as in a glass, darkly; a life of labour, not rest; of need, not fulfilment.[20] The best that could be had in this mortal life was 'an incipient [*inchoata*] contemplation', to be completed when Christ returns in glory to gather his faithful from the corners of the earth. Mary in the Gospel story lived this fragmentary anticipation of the contemplative life; by living it, her life was a sign which pointed to its eschatological fulfilment. Cassian's mind did not move as easily and as instinctively as Augustine's in the dimension of temporal signs as pointers to an eschatological realisation. But in his penultimate *Conference* Cassian appears to be thinking of the contemplative life in a similarly 'eschatologised' perspective. The pearl of great price, by comparison with which precious stones lose their lustre, is the 'life of that world to come where there shall be no change of the good, no fear of loss of true blessedness'; that is the life Mary does not possess, but – just as for Augustine – which her life points to as an anticipatory sign.[21]

In *Conference* XIV Cassian does not speak of the contemplative life in this eschatological perspective. But contemplation, understood as some kind of experience or vision in this life, is in fact absent from his discussion here. It may be that he was already beginning to think of contemplation in this sense as unattainable in this life, and therefore confined himself to the nearest he thought one could get to it here. However that may be, it is remarkable that in this *Conference* 'contemplation' is quite simply identified with the study and understanding of the scriptures, in their literal and their spiritual senses.[22] Bible-reading and meditation on it had long been an integral part of monastic routine. Saint Martin was said never to have rested from reading

---

[20] The quotations are from Augustine, *C. Faust.* XXII.52 and *In Ioh. Ev. Tr.* XXI.5. A fine and full account is given by La Bonnardière, 'Marthe et Marie', to which I owe more than to the sketch by Csányi, *Optima pars*, 65–74. References to Augustinian passages are given by both. See also O'Daly and Verheijen, '*Actio – contemplatio*', and Cayré, *La contemplation augustinienne*, 30–51.
[21] *Conl.* XXIII.3.
[22] *Ibid.* XIV.8.

and to have excelled in expounding the scriptures;[23] and bibles were available to Egyptian monks. Cassian's simple identification of contemplation with biblical knowledge is, nevertheless, striking. Scriptural understanding has become the object of monastic discipline and the summit of the monk's spiritual progress. There is a hint in the way he expounds this that a primary purpose of gaining a true understanding of scripture is to 'comprehend in its entirety the discipline of the active life',[24] thus implying even a subordination of *theoretike* to *praktike*! The understanding of scripture seems to round back on itself, returning to feed, not contemplation, but the life of action. Cassian has modified the traditional ladder of monastic perfection so profoundly that it has, in effect, ceased to be the itinerary for spiritual progress from the active to the contemplative life. The monastic life emerges as a cyclical discipline of *askesis* preparatory to the understanding of scripture, which in turn is intended to nourish the ascetic discipline required for an understanding of scripture.

The final chapters of this *Conference* suggest a reason. The aim here appears to be to prepare the monk to teach others. Whether Cassian had in mind the migration of monks to bishoprics must remain in doubt. He leaves no doubt, however, that among those to whom the spiritual programme outlined here is addressed are preachers. The spiritual knowledge achieved through the preparatory purification of the heart will not be 'barren or inert, but a living and fruitful teaching [*doctrina*]; and rich showers of the Holy Spirit will fertilise the seed of the word of salvation which you will have sowed in the hearts of your hearers'.[25] The discipline of monastic life serves to equip the monk to be a preacher, for without that discipline the word must remain sterile. Teaching is worthless unless it proceeds from experience.[26]

Cassian must be reckoned among the most important and influential of the writers who reinforced the momentum that communal monasticism was acquiring. He did so with the aid

---

[23] Sulpicius Severus, *Vita Mart.* 25, 26.
[24] *Conl.* XIV.9.2: *festinate actualem, id est ethicam, quam primum ad integrum comprehendere disciplinam.*
[25] *Ibid.* XIV.16.9. Note the strongly active sense of *doctrina* as the act, rather than the content, of teaching.
[26] *Ibid.* XIV.9.6; cf. 14; and especially, XIII.18.

of turning traditional notions of the contemplative life to new uses. In doing so, he helped to define a monastic observance in which 'active' and 'contemplative' were closely intertwined. The monastic ideal was thus opened up for imitation in wider circles, notably by secular clergy; and, as we shall see, the two forms of living and their respective spiritualities tended to converge.

Cassian's conflation of the contemplative ideal with the active life brought contemplation, understood in the sense he gave it, within range of the clerical life. Contemplation equalled spiritual knowledge, and this was nothing other than the study and understanding of scripture. Priests and bishops could pursue this almost as well as monks. Another path leading to the same destination was explored by an obscure writer around AD 500, Julianus Pomerius. A refugee in Provence of African origin, Julian was, like many Africans, well acquainted with Augustine's writings.[27] An unknown bishop, also called Julianus, perhaps an *alter ego*, put a series of questions to him. He began with a request to have the nature of the contemplative and the active life expounded to him, and went on to ask whether someone with pastoral care in the Church might be able to share in the contemplative life. Julian's answer was constructed in what is unmistakably an Augustinian perspective. It had the same practical effect as Cassian's, and shared with his the reluctance to allow that contemplation in its old and full-blooded sense could be had in this life. Julian kept to the definition of contemplation as seeing God, and concluded, in a paragraph impeccably Augustinian in substance and in flavour, that it is not to be had here. It will be the reward of those no longer engaged in fighting, who have triumphed in battle. Here, in this 'laborious pilgrimage', the Christian soldier's fight will cease only with death. Then, his nature restored and his infirmity healed, he shall be made capable of the contemplative life and rewarded 'inexplicably' with joy in the sight of the Author of his blessedness.[28]

Not until this transcendence of the contemplative life has been firmly established in the first five chapters does Julian begin to

---

[27] Dependence on Augustine has been demonstrated by Plumpe, 'Pomeriana'; see also Solignac, 'Julien Pomère', 21; and on the questions of grace Tibiletti, 'La teologia della grazia' has shown Julian's strongly Augustinian sympathies. Much remains to be done in exploring the relationship. That between Julian and Cassian has remained, so far as I know, unexplored.

[28] *De vita cont.* I.1.1–2.

raise the very possibility of a 'contemplative life' here on earth. Even now, however, the contemplative life is not something to be had here, only 'approached', 'to be carried towards', yearned for, by surrender of earthly wealth, honour and transient delights. The fullness of what can be glimpsed here dimly shall finally be revealed to those who even here love the contemplative life.[29] Only then does Julian concede that some form of the contemplative life can be had here, where the Christian walks in faith, in some fragmentary anticipation.[30] Having made this concession in passing, he straightaway returns to speak as if he had not; and goes on to advise those who love and seek the contemplative life on how they must conduct themselves to attain it. The advice turns out to be, not surprisingly, in line with Cassian's – and many others': pursue the 'active' life of purging the vices and cultivating the Christian virtues, detachment and renunciation.[31] And so he returns to his eschatological – and very Augustinian – starting-point: 'The active life is the journey, the contemplative is arrival at the summit; the one makes a man holy, the other perfect.'[32]

Bishop Julianus, whose questions Julian claims to be answering, might have consoled himself with the thought that what is not available to a busy shepherd of men is available to nobody else either. But Julian does not stop on this note of spiritual sour grapes. He carefully begins his answer to the second question put to him by pointing out the inescapable implication of what has been said about the contemplative life: of course, he says, 'princes of the Church can and must pursue it'.[33] But then he recounts four meanings which others have given to the 'contemplative life': knowledge of future and hidden things; freedom from entanglement in worldly cares; the study of the sacred scripture; or, finally, more perfect than any of these, the vision of God. The first and the last will elude bishops – as everyone else – except in the most fragmentary anticipation of what they will be in their fullness. But bishops can have the

[29] *Ibid.* I.5.
[30] *Ibid.* I.6; cf. 10.
[31] *Ibid.* I.7–8.
[32] *Ibid.* I.12.1.
[33] *Ibid.* I.13: *vitae contemplativae posse et debere fieri sectatores* (the repeated use of this word here is striking).

middle two: detachment from secular cares (which turns out not to mean being liberated from worries about matters such as church property, but dealing with them in the right frame of mind, in a spirit of detachment) and scriptural study. And now Julian is ready to carry out the rest of his design, which is, in effect, a handbook for the life and teaching of a good bishop. Subtly, the pursuit of the contemplative life has been re-interpreted as trying to be a good pastor, and a treatise on the contemplative life turned into a handbook for bishops. Once, towards the end of his book, Julian returns to compare the two professions: he asks 'we must consider whether they act justly who, having cut themselves off from all busy-ness [*occupationibus*], devoting themselves to spiritual pursuits, do nothing for the good of human society, and putting their own desires before the profit of all, despise the common good for the sake of the freedom [*vacationis*] which they have chosen for themselves'.[34] The very terms in which the question is put – rhetorically? – weights the scales against the contemplative life understood in any conventional sense. In the comparison that follows Julian is careful to avoid using the term and the reader is left to draw his own conclusion. He blandly equates – carefully avoiding the formal terminology of the 'contemplative' and the 'active' lives – the life of those who receive the 'ineffable sweetness of heavenly wisdom' in a life free from worldly care, with the life of those whose 'spiritual occupation' with holy labours for the good of human society brings them manifold fruit.[35]

Julianus Pomerius, like Cassian some seventy years before him, has drastically modified the ascetic ideal. Both, in their different ways, turned it into something that could be appropriated more easily by the pastoral clergy; both have made a scriptural spirituality its summit. Cassian seems to have expected that some of his monks, properly trained in the school of the monastic life, would end up as bishops; Julian went so far as to place the pastoral life on a level with the contemplative, at times even hinting that it might be a higher calling for those 'who, on account of the merit of their behaviour or their learning, have

[34] *Ibid.* III.28.1.
[35] *Ibid.* III.28.2.

191

been chosen'; for them it would amount to a betrayal of the demands of justice 'to prefer leisured study [*otiosum studium*] to the fruitful service of the common good in ruling the many'.[36] Cassian had not gone as far as this, and he did not compare the worth and dignity of the monastic with the pastoral calling. As we have seen, he seems to have envisaged a 'leakage' from the monastery into the world outside: monastically schooled bishops would teach their flocks the virtues of Christian living and the truths of the scriptures. But there was a further hint in Cassian's writing that the monastery was to be not only a seminary of individual bishops; as a community, it would also have the function of being a model for the Christian society around it.

From the earliest days the Provençal monastic foundations had close links with urban churches. Cassian founded his monastery in Marseille under the patronage of the city's bishop, Proculus. As we have seen, his fourteenth *Conference* appears to have been written partly with the teaching duties of bishops in mind. Cassian gives us occasional hints that his Desert had never been meant to be very far removed from the City. The last *Conference* is, in effect, an apologia for Cassian's work in Gaul. Cassian and his companion wanted to return to Gaul, to live a monastic life in close proximity to their fellows, perhaps promoting the conversion of many people. Here, abbot Abraham is made to voice the old ascetic objection to their plan with a rebarbative insistence on the gulf that must at all costs be maintained: even if they are close to their kinsmen, they must be as if dead to them, so that they will not be 'relaxed' by either receiving assistance from them or assisting them in their needs.[37] With this rebuff as a firm reminder of the tradition on which Cassian was turning his back, Abraham is gently steered in his closing remarks, notwithstanding what he had said, into something not far short of an endorsement of Cassian's notion of the monastic community's place in society:[38]

Finally, to conclude this discussion, is it not true, I ask you, that those who serve Christ faithfully evidently receive a hundred-fold favour in

---

[36] *Ibid.* III.28.1.
[37] *Conl.* XXIV.5 (cf. 1).
[38] *Ibid.* XXIV.26.

that they are honoured for His name's sake by the greatest rulers? and that while they do not seek renown among men, they receive the veneration of judges and the powerful, even in the trials of persecution? Their lowliness might have led to their being despised even by people of middling status, on account of the obscurity of their birth or servile condition, had they remained in the lay state; but on account of the nobility of their *militia* of Christ nobody would dare to disparage the lowness of their rank or the obscurity of their birth. Rather, the servants of Christ are gloriously ennobled by the very calumnies that often embarrass those of lowly status

– and so abbot Abraham concludes his discourse with a significant reference back to the abbot John who had returned to his monastery from the heights of solitary contemplation. Though of lowly origin, he was now venerated by the great, 'who hold the reins of power and empire and are feared by the kings of the earth, who seek his advice from distant regions and entrust the crown of empire, its well-being and the fortunes of war to his prayers and his merits'.

This is the answer to Cassian's desire, expressed at the beginning of the *Conference*, to 'gain great good from the conversion of many',[39] the plan that had met so rough a reception from abbot Abraham. Abraham's quiet conversion is a masterstroke in the artistry and the subtlety of argument that characterise the *Conferences*. It sanctioned Cassian's appeal to the legacy of Egyptian monasticism in order to establish the credentials of his own, Gallic, version. This was to be altogether closer to the lay world, helping it to its 'conversion'. The monastery was to become a community which articulated the values that animated, in a diffuse and inchoate form, the wider lay world. It was to inspire, guide and canalise the aspirations and some of the wealth and energies of Christian lay people. The charisma of the representative holy man was passing to the holy community.

In his final remarks abbot Abraham applied the prophetic promise to the monks: 'then shalt thou delight in the Lord, and I shall raise thee above the high places of the earth and feed thee with the heritage of Jacob thy father' (Isa. 58.14). He had also used (c. 18) the image of the city set upon a hill that cannot

---

[39] *Ibid.* XXIV.1. *Conversatio* is a well-attested alternative reading to *conversio*.

be hidden, or the light not hidden under a bushel but set on a candlestick (Matt. 5.15): they were images held in great favour by writers within the Lerins circle.[40] A later abbot of Lerins, become a bishop, preached a sermon in praise of his predecessor, Maximus, likewise an abbot of Lerins become bishop. He made use of the same image: Maximus, the monk, could not hide his light from the world around him. His episcopal city was, in every sense, 'close to the desert', the Desert of Lerins.[41] This *rapprochement* came about chiefly through the practice of filling vacant bishoprics with monks, indeed abbots, of the monastery. As monasteries found themselves exploited for their products, as their monks or abbots were being taken to minister as bishops to neighbouring churches, teaching came to be seen as central to the link between monastery and the outside world. Monastic contemplation was the process of acquiring what would be imparted to others in the active life of teaching outside.

Lerins was the foremost source of the great teachers of Southern Gaul from the start. Its founder, Honoratus, became bishop of Arles; Hilary, his companion at Lerins, succeeded Honoratus as bishop of his see. Praising his predecessor, Hilary spoke in his sermon of his teacher: Honoratus had trained him (*erudivit*) with immense care and solicitude, for them, the congregation he now inherited from his predecessor.[42] Hilary himself was said by his biographer to have 'put into action by teaching what he had learnt' at Lerins.[43] Maximus had been taught at Lerins so that he might teach at Riez.[44] The idea of the monastery as preparation for the ministry was a recurrent theme in the biographies of Lerinese monk–bishops. Caesarius reminded a congregation of monks that with God's help they learn by reading what they are to impart to others.[45] The conception of the

---

[40] E.g. Hilary, *Sermo* 10; *Vita Hilarii* 31; 'Eusebius Gallicanus', *Hom.* LXXII.1 (*In depositione sancti Honorati episcopi*, *CC* 101A.775). Rousseau, 'In search of Sidonius', 366, n. 64, also draws attention to Eucherius, *De laude* 36, and remarks that the imagery can be traced from here 'in a progressive development'.

[41] 'Eusebius Gallicanus', *Hom.* XXXV.8 (*CC* 101.407). The sermon is almost certainly the work of Faustus of Riez.

[42] *Sermo* 36. See Vessey, 'Ideas of Christian writing'. This paragraph and the next owe much to this outstanding study, especially pp. 108–37.

[43] *Vita Hilarii* 10.

[44] 'Eusebius Gallicanus' *Hom.* XXXV.5 (*CC* 101.404).

[45] *Sermo* 238.1 (*CC* 104.949).

monastery as the source of sound teaching became very firmly established in Provence. When Faustus, the ex-abbot of Lerins, received a doctrinal statement from a wandering ascetic which he found unsatisfactory, he sent him back to school: read before you write, he was told, read the approved authors, subject yourself to the discipline of an abbot and you will not go astray.[46] Reading and teaching – especially the Bible – came to be attached to the idea of the monastic life, exemplifying its contemplative and active aspects; and reading and teaching integrated the monastic with the clerical ideal. What was expected from the priest or bishop engaged in the secular ministry in late fifth-century Gaul was not very different from what was expected of monks: those who are to carry out the ministry must be trained 'in the word of God'.[47]

In Faustus' letter to Graecus the ancient ideal of the ascetic life is almost turned on its head. Graecus, the unattached ascetic of dubious orthodoxy, was told to moderate the 'intemperate rigour of his abstinence' which, Faustus thought, 'leads to infirmity of mind, and the presumption of writing'. Graecus was thus bidden 'to return to the royal road': the sensible and orderly life of the monastery would restore the soundness of his mind. Faustus thought of the monastery no longer as the 'Desert' of ascetic renunciation; it had become the generator of the spiritual power to be dispensed by those who had received proper religious formation under its discipline. Caesarius gave a poignant expression to the complex emotions aroused by a request to preach to the monks of Lerins, the community in which he had received his own training: how could he give them what was asked for, droplets from his little stream, to nourish them, who are the fountains of Christ's living waters? As a bishop, he has been thrust from the repose of the harbour into the exhausting struggle with the world's tempests; he has entered the arid world of *tepor*: how is he to address the fervent? Their prayers

---

[46] *Ep.* 7 (*CSEL* 21.207): *magis imitanda legas quam legenda conscribas.* The incident has been carefully studied by Vessey, 'Ideas of Christian writing', 337–46. In his letter to Ruricius, *Ep.* 8, Faustus similarly recommends preparation in the 'school of a great monastery', preferably that of the *insulana angelica congregatio.*

[47] *Statuta eccl. ant.*, 79 (*CC* 148, 179): they are also to work (like monks: cf. Cassian, *Conl.* XXIV.12, and Augustine, *De op. mon.*, above, ch. 5, p. 73, n. 39), for their living! The collection has been plausibly attributed to Gennadius.

and his humility will combine to keep in being the solidarity threatened by his separation from them; he prepares the receptacle of his heart for the inflow of divine water through them, to irrigate the dry land, to fill the hungry, refresh the weary.[48] Their own special alumnus is kept united to the community by the tightest bonds, unbroken by his ministry in and to the city.

Thus the life of the monastic community was opening out to that of the larger Christian community in the world. While monks began to see their 'Desert' merging into the 'City', so also the emphasis in the way the monastic life itself was conceived was changing; and it was changing in a direction which allowed the monastic community to serve as a model for the Christian community at large. We have already observed (above, ch. 5) a shift from primarily ascetic to primarily communal patterning in the monastic ideal, culminating, especially, in Augustine's monastic Rules. This shift has also been discerned in the development of the Lerins community, as reflected in successive versions of its Rule.[49] Here and there monastic founders encouraged a form of monasticism in which the ascetic quest for perfection was supreme. But the importance attached to the communal life grew from strength to strength, even in the Jura communities, which have rightly been seen in terms of such a reaction. Saint Eugendus, the last of the Jura fathers, was expressly said by his biographer to have rejected the example of the Eastern archimandrites in his decision to adopt a wholly common life for his monks; and he made a special point of appealing to Cassian as the inspiration for a pattern of monastic observance particularly suitable for Gaul.[50] Finally, the *Rule* of Saint Benedict, though reflecting much previous monastic teaching, including especially Augustine's and Cassian's,[51] was also a work of true originality. It, too, stands in this line of development. It is significant that the *Rule* could serve a recent writer as a guide, quite simply, to the fully Christian life, not only within the religious community,

---

[48] *Sermo* 236.1–2 (*CC* 104.940–2).
[49] De Vogüé, *Les Règles des Saints Pères*, esp. pp. 27–37. Whether the community had a written Rule in its earliest years must remain uncertain.
[50] *Vita Eugendi* 170, 174 (ed. Martine, SC 142). The whole of this section lays a strong and deliberate stress on the growing communal orientation of the Jura observance. On the Jura monasteries as ascetic revival, see König, *Amt und Askese*, 228–33.
[51] See ch. 11, n. 29.

but in the lay world;[52] and that a modern philosopher could see it as a pointer to the 'construction of new forms of community within which the moral life could be sustained so that both morality and civility might survive the coming ages of barbarism and darkness'.[53]

In a double way, therefore, the boundary between Desert and City was being blurred, and the distance between the monastic life and the life of the parishes diminished. The image of the monastic community was becoming adapted to serving as a model for the Christian community in the world, while the ascetic ideal it proposed to its members was becoming adapted to serve as the model for bishops and clergymen. The stage was set for the wholesale invasion of the Gallic Church by ascetics and of the Christian view of the world, the flesh and the Devil by their ideas.

[52] De Waal, *Seeking God*, esp. 28–35.
[53] MacIntyre, *After virtue*, 244–5.

13

The ascetic invasion

Monks were becoming part of the daily experience of a great many town-dwellers in fifth- and sixth-century Gaul. Bishops, especially if they had themselves been monks, often founded monasteries and nunneries, and monks served the suburban sanctuaries of local saints. Monks were present in towns and in their close neighbourhood, and could influence – just by being there? by example? – lay people, such as the young Honoratus and his brother.[1] Monastic practices were becoming familiar in ever widening circles. In the last chapter we observed some of the ways in which the boundaries that divided the Desert from the City were being blurred in the ascetic spirituality of Gallic monasteries as that developed in the fifth century. We now turn to consider how the impact of this spirituality made itself felt in the larger world of the Gallic Church; how the values upheld for the Desert found a foothold in the City.

Above all else, and especially in Gaul, the invasion of the City by the Desert was achieved through the confluence of aristocratic and ascetic traditions in its episcopate. Men of standing in lay society, with wealth, prestige and secular *savoir faire*, were in great demand to fill clerical offices and vacant bishoprics. The practice of electing such men became especially common in fifth-century Gaul, during a time when secular administration was weakening in many Western cities, and bishops were taking over the leadership of their communities. Caesarius, the bishop of Arles in the first decades of the sixth century, addressing his fellow-bishops, could speak of their duties to the 'city or the

---

[1] Hilary of Arles, *Sermo* 12.1.

church committed to our care', without thought of distinguishing between church and city.[2] The cultured aristocrats who flocked to the monasteries of Gaul would have provided a rich reservoir of *episcopabiles*, men highly eligible to fill the office of widening importance in urban society. The community of Lerins (not uniquely, but more than any other) was able to satisfy some of the demand for high-born ascetics; and its reputation was spread rapidly through the episcopate by its alumni scattered among the bishops. But it was not only their wealth and aristocratic background, their connections, their prestige and their literary culture that made such men desirable in troubled times. The ascetic tradition represented, especially, by Lerins and the spirituality of its members was coming to be valued for itself. Its appeal reached far beyond the cloister. Already around 430 pope Celestine I was worried about the extent of the monastic take-over in the Gallic Church, and warned Gallic bishops not to allow a 'new college' to emerge as a source of future bishops.[3] Sidonius Apollinaris, himself a member of the charmed circle of the Gallo-Roman nobility, a holder of high secular office and soaked in the literary culture of his class, was, as were others like him, touched by the ripples spreading from Lerins. The friends with whom he corresponded included several bishops whose spiritual roots lay in the island monastery; and Sidonius was not blind to their significance. As a bishop in later life, he felt himself to be moving on the fringe of the 'Senate of Lerinese ascetics' scattered as bishops in Gallic cities.[4] 'The angelic community of the island', as its ex-abbot Faustus, bishop of Riez, referred to it in a letter to another aristocrat–bishop,[5] hovered on a horizon not too distant to the majority of Gallic bishops until the early sixth century.

Gaul in the fifth and sixth centuries is the area where the continuity of a dominant class of Late Roman society can be traced through the comparatively small number of families, often related among themselves, with a shared culture and background, who had a near-monopoly of episcopal office.

---

[2] *Sermo* 1.8 (*CC* 103, 6).
[3] Celestine, *Ep.* 4.iv.7 (*PL* 50.433); for Tours, see Sulpicius Severus, *Vita Mart.* 10.8–9.
[4] *Ep.* IX.3.4. See also *Carmen* XVI.104–28 and *Ep.* VII.13.1.
[5] Faustus, *Ep.* 8 (*CSEL* 21.210; also in *CC* 64.407).

Among them asceticism came to blend with, even to give additional support to, the traditional ideology and prestige of the Gallo-Roman elite class. There can hardly be a more significant expression of this appreciation than a remark that rolled from the pen of Sidonius in a letter to an ex-praetorian prefect when he described him as 'more fittingly numbered among the perfect of Christ than the prefects of Valentinian'.[6] In line with Sidonius' verdict on Ferreolus is the general opinion, as it is reflected in the epitaphs of bishops.[7] Generally they give details of a nobleman's family and his career, as traditional inscriptions recording the *cursus honorum* of a senatorial career would have enumerated them. The tenure of a bishopric is their high point: it is presented as the culmination of a career of worldly success, marked by the same public virtues of justice, generosity, accessibility and kindness, and effectiveness in protecting the community assigned to the late bishop's care. The 'eloquence' often referred to in such epitaphs combines tribute to the traditional elite culture with praise of its 'bishop-specific' application: his preaching and teaching (239). Most significant for our present purpose, however, is the addition to the standard forms of the epitaphs, current from the fifth century, of some mention of the late bishop's renunciation or self-denial. In the conclusion of their most thorough investigator, 'there is hardly a single biography, hardly a single funerary inscription of an aristocratic lay person or bishop, which does not show at least some trace of an ascetic colouring ("stylisation ascétique")'(235).

Such were the qualities bishops liked to be remembered for. What their communities admired in them is also what their biographers liked to dwell on. The image of the holy bishop was coming to merge with that of the ascetic; personal sanctity was harnessed to the life of the Church.[8] The charisma of the ascetic flowed into pastoral channels; spiritual power enhanced episcopal authority, while subtly changing the models to which

[6] *Ep.* VII.12.4. Rousseau very justly remarks that 'he [Sidonius] felt ready to welcome a reinterpretation of the rights and obligations that attended wealth in Gallic society' ('In search of Sidonius', 366). I owe much to his perceptive study, esp. 366–71.

[7] The epitaphs have been studied by Heinzelmann, *Bischofsherrschaft*, 191–211. The quotations in the sequel are from the pages indicated in brackets.

[8] Rousseau, 'The spiritual authority', has studied this hagiographical development in the context of its Eastern background.

the bishop was expected to conform. Thus when Caesarius left Lerins to join the clergy of Arles, he was described by his biographers in terms of the hagiographical stereotype frequently applied to clergy taken from among the monks: 'by rank and office a cleric, yet in humility, charity, courtesy and through the cross, he remained a monk'.[9] Not all bishops succeeded in combining the life of a pastoral apostolate with their monastic and ascetic spirituality; but the appeal of the ideal was undiminished by their failure.[10]

Through its monk–bishop the people was linked to a source of spiritual life with a distinctly ascetic tinge; and the model for the life of the Christian community came, naturally, to be infected by the model for the monastic life. Influence of this sort must have had a deep and subtle effect on congregations exposed to it, though the extent to which it deflected the development of either urban or rural churches is very hard to judge. Augustine's biographer, for instance, had spoken of the daily growth of true brotherhood in the Church (Acts 12.24), of the unity and peace spreading through it, as the crowning reward of Augustine's work.[11] Augustine, and probably his biographer, too, would have recognised here the ideal of the monastic community as Augustine conceived it (see above, ch. 5, pp. 77–8). But in this respect the monastic community only summed up, and anticipated, what the whole Christian community was called to be. Specifically monastic and ascetic values are less easy to detect in pastoral work and preaching.

Caesarius' pastoral activity is richly documented by a series of over two hundred sermons, as well as by scantier reports given by his biographers. It has been well described more than once, and cannot be surveyed again here.[12] Some of its features, however, deserve notice, if only as a notable example of monastic spirituality in episcopal action. Most significant among the

---

[9] *Vita S. Caesarii* I.11; cf. 45–6; 53; II.5. A different, though no less ascetic, episcopal style is hinted at by the biographer of Germanus of Auxerre, who continued as bishop to wear military apparel: *Vita Germani* 4.

[10] Fulgentius' career offers a paradoxical example of a monk–bishop who, unlike Augustine, failed to integrate the monastic and the clerical life in his own spirituality. See below, ch. 14, n. 3.

[11] Possidius, *Vita Aug.* 13.1.

[12] Beck, *The pastoral care, passim*, though dated, contains the material.

practices that had come to be widely followed in monasteries (as well as, of course, among the clergy) which Caesarius wished to encourage among his lay flock, was reading the Bible.[13] In wealthy and aristocratic households this was no novelty, but part of the gradual expansion of a Late Roman aristocrat's literary culture to include the Christian scriptures. What is striking, however, about Caesarius' repeated admonitions to his congregations is the width of the circles in which he evidently thought they could be obeyed. Bible-reading was to replace heavy drinking protracted into the night, scurrilous gossip and dirty jokes. To the literate he recommended spending the long winter evenings reading the Bible; those who could not read, should employ – as do illiterate merchants – some poor literate person to read to them; and, out of church, his congregations were to mull over the bishop's sermons.[14] Caesarius could assume that direct access to the Bible, either at first or at second hand through literate poor men, was widely available to his audiences. His sermons may contain an incidental warning to modern scholars not to underestimate the extent of some sort of literacy in Christian circles around AD 500.

Caesarius seems to have aimed at extending the use of reading and meditation as 'instruments of perfection'[15] far beyond monastic, and even beyond clerical, circles. The Christian community was to live in constant confrontation with its sacred text; the Bible was to mark out the boundaries of a new community of discourse. In other ways, too, Caesarius tried to introduce customs that his clerical and lay congregations would share with the monks. To these belongs his introduction of offices of the monastic liturgy, in this case for the secular clergy serving in the cathedral, but for the benefit of lay people.[16] Nothing, Caesarius once said, gave him so much joy as hearing his people join in these services; on dark winter mornings, he would have liked them to rise for matins.[17] Through his participation in the

---

[13] On its centrality in the monastic tradition, see Pricoco, *L'isola dei santi*, 98–100. See also Van Dam, *Leadership and community*, 63.
[14] *Sermo* 6.2, 8; 8.1–2 (*CC* 103.31–2; 41–3); cf. 7.3 (38–9); 198.5; 196 (*CC* 104.801–2; 792–4): especially in Lent.
[15] The phrase is Vessey's: see 'Ideas of Christian writing', 90.
[16] *Vita S. Caesarii* I.15; Caesarius, *Sermo* 196.2.
[17] *Sermo* 75.1; 72.1.

bishop's cathedral worship, as well as in the pattern of his fasting and the times when he abstained from sexual relationships, the urban Christian would be drawn into a liturgical rhythm shared by the communities of monks and nuns in and around Arles.

Caesarius' world view was the ascetic's (above, ch. 11), marked by the tendency to conflate norms of conduct that apply to monks, to clergy, to lay Christians. In the true manner of the ascetic, Caesarius was apt to obliterate the lines which divide the ascetic from the clergy, the clergy from the laity, and the Christian from the non-Christian, substituting for a differentiated value system a simpler division between good and wicked, holy and reprobate. 'There are only two things, and nothing between them': Caesarius discovered in a dream, heaven and hell.[18] The ascetic's world is one in which 'but these two tell, each off the other'. In his scheme, the world and the flesh will always tend to fall into the Devil's domain. Standards upheld to the lay world or the secular clergy will appear as imperfect approximations to the ascetic's standards, concessions to the weak, rather than as norms appropriate to the several forms of the Christian vocation. It would be unrewarding to catalogue the items in the repertory of the demands Caesarius made on his people to foster the severe moral discipline he wished to impose on them. The thrust of his ascetic morality is more easily visible by comparing his views with Augustine's at some key points.

From the beginning, Caesarius' name has been linked with Augustine's. His predilection for the sermons of Hilary, Ambrose and especially Augustine, and his insistence on his clergy using his own sermons, often adapted from Augustine's preaching, to edify their flocks is well known;[19] his biographers represented his death as a long-awaited reunion with Augustine.[20] But on several matters concerned with lay Christian life and society the contrast between his views and Augustine's is revealing. Caesarius, though clearly highly educated, shared the ascetic's age-old distrust of secular learning. His biographers credited him with rejecting the 'fictions of human learning'

[18] *Vita S. Caesarii* II.6.
[19] *Sermo* 1.15; 2, etc.; *Vita S. Caesarii* I.54.
[20] *Vita S. Caesarii* II.46, 48.

which his learned African teacher, Julianus Pomerius, offered him, and suggest that he slept through his lessons.[21] Though, in fact, Julianus' influence on Caesarius' mind was by no means negligible, and his library and his memory were praised as well stocked,[22] Caesarius professed the ascetic's contempt for worldly learning. He liked to compare the seven plagues with which God afflicted Egypt to the components of secular culture: the frogs stood for the verses of the poets, the gnats for the cunning of the philosophers.[23] Such ideas had been commonplaces in popular preaching, and, indeed, Caesarius borrowed them from Origen and Augustine. What, however, there is no trace of in his mind is Origen's and Augustine's insistence that it was right to 'spoil the Egyptians' by taking from them their treasures and devoting them to God's service: using secular learning to understand and expound the Gospel. Reading works of secular literature had recently been prohibited in a Gallic collection of canon law;[24] the time was no longer propitious to secular thought and letters.

It is also to his ascetic mentality that we should attribute the strict limits he set to what is allowable within the range of Christian behaviour. Like Salvian (above, ch. 11), he laid down exacting requirements of would-be Christians. 'We must know that it is not enough for us to have received the name of Christian if we do not do the deeds of a Christian', he said in one of the sermons he required his clergy to preach in his parishes.[25] This is one of the most frequent themes of his preaching. Baptism brings obligations which must be faithfully kept: 'avoid drunkenness like the pit of hell, fear pride, envy, vanity, like the sword of the Devil ..., do not commit theft or fraud, come often to church, love and honour the clergy, give tithes even from your poverty and alms as much as you can'.[26] His frequent portraits of the good Christian are not, however, limited to upholding

---

[21] *Ibid.* I.9.
[22] *Ibid.* I.16.
[23] *Sermo* 99.2; cf. 100.3, 163.1 (from Augustine, *Q. evang.* II.33).
[24] *Statuta eccl. ant.* 5 (*CC* 148.167). On date and authorship, see above, ch. 12, n. 47.
[25] *Sermo* 13.1; cf. 12, 14, 15, 16, 19, 157.6.
[26] *Sermo* 171.3. Cf. 19.3, which, interestingly, includes commands to give just judgements and prohibits the taking of bribes.

the central Christian values and commending the conduct expected of a loyal member of the Christian community. 'He who is baptised must avoid all manner of profanity', for by such things 'the sacrament of baptism is forfeited'.[27] The profanity Caesarius was so often denouncing was not just failure to live up to the exacting standards of Christian morality. He was referring to a reluctance to abandon old ways of thought and action, patterns of behaviour embedded in a society that was older than Christianity. Caesarius tried to shape the routines which would create a new kind of Christian society. That effort involved displacing habits which often proved to be tenacious.

In the countryside this society reached far back beyond the changes brought by Roman influence. The dissolution of ancient patterns of ritual and conduct under the influence of Christianity was 'a belated and largely unwitting triumph of romanisation'.[28] What Caesarius was attacking here was the remnants of a culture which maintained its grip in areas little touched by Roman, now Christian, influence. Caesarius could only use the simple criteria of a Christian ascetic culture to judge it; and to him it was necessarily pagan, its practices the condemned 'profanities' which he saw as incompatible with the profession of the Christian faith. His sermons have been ransacked by scholars of pre-Roman and Roman religion, and they do indeed provide a large catalogue of practices that he regarded as pagan, superstitious or sacrilegious, evidently still current in remote places. But it is dangerous to assume that customs traditional in a peasant society necessarily bore the heavy charge of religious significance which the bishop of the neighbouring Christian town would attribute to them. To accept them indiscriminately at Caesarius' valuation as 'pagan' would be to fall into the trap of conflating in the most arbitrary manner what falls within 'religion' and what is no more than part of the pattern of traditional behaviour. It would be to sidestep the necessity, for example, of discriminating between alternative forms of medical practice: the folk-medicine practised in areas remote from towns and the more sophisticated

[27] *Sermo* 19.4; 13.5, 53.1.
[28] Brown, *The cult*, 121.

and more expensive forms of healing that might be available there. For both, Caesarius would substitute a blessing by the priests or anointing by the bishop.[29] His norms provided no criterion for discriminating within complex parts of a pre-Christian pattern of behaviour, and they required him to condemn them indiscriminately as 'profane', and therefore incompatible with the profession of Christianity. They functioned, rather, to define the identity of the group, the Christian community united with its bishop under a shared loyalty and a shared value-system. For a long time to come this would remain a fragile consensus, which bishops would need every available device and determination to foster. Much of Caesarius' extensive pastoral activity was aimed at spreading the devotional and spiritual life of his cathedral and the urban monasteries throughout the area of his, and his neighbouring bishops', dioceses.

Caesarius was no less concerned to see his uncompromising Christian standards established in the life of his urban congregations. Here the traditions of behaviour had been shaped by centuries of exposure to Roman influence. But to Caesarius the problem they posed was the same as he saw in rural paganism: they fell outside the boundaries of the ascetic code of Christian conduct. His denunciation of 'furious, bloody or shameful spectacles' as the 'pomp of the Devil', and as such comprehended in what Christians renounced at their baptism,[30] is reminiscent of Salvian's (see above, ch. 11). Those who resort to the circus, the theatre or the hunt to dispel sadness or anxiety are bidden to turn inward for true divine consolation. Let the soul be cleansed daily, so that it can be kept free of the major pollution that would cost, like the cleansing of a long-neglected stable or house, revulsion and despair.[31] There is a ring of genuine pleading in Caesarius' attempt to dissuade his congregation from consoling themselves with such tawdry pastimes. It may be that some of the shows were still held in Arles in his time. If this is the case, it is at present uncertain whether they had survived continuously, or had been re-introduced only very recently,

[29] *Sermo* 50.1; 52.5; 19.5; 184.4–5.
[30] *Sermo* 12.4; 89.5; 134.1; 150.3.
[31] *Sermo* 61.3.

perhaps in the last years of Caesarius' episcopate.[32] If they were held there in the 530s, as appears to be the case, then unlike Salvian, Caesarius would have been preaching against something that could still be seen in his own city. But his objection sprang from the same roots as Salvian's: the shows fell outside the boundaries of the radically Christian morality which left no room for a secular sphere between 'Christian' and 'pagan'.

The extent of Caesarius' success in imposing his ascetically conceived Christian pattern of life in his own churches cannot be gauged. It is hard to know whether other bishops, though some of them no doubt shared Caesarius' ascetic life-style, also shared his zeal for imparting something of it to their congregations. At any rate, it is evident from a careful survey of the evidence that no sustained attempt was made to displace the older patterns for nearly another two hundred years. The last council Caesarius is known to have attended was held in 533. His preoccupation with the traditional customs which he interpreted as pagan played hardly any part in the deliberations of the Gallic Church until around 740, the time of Boniface's missionary activities in the Frankish fringe-territories.[33] During this time the centre of gravity of the Church in Gaul shifted northwards, into the lands now settled by Franks. The problems of adjustment to a Germanic social environment grew in urgency. Combing through the acts of Gallic councils one finds, not unexpectedly, much anxiety among the bishops, concerning marriage, about the relations between clergy and a warrior aristocracy, about problems raised by royal influence and control, especially in matters of property rights, and about the discipline, independence from outside interference as well as

---

[32] Procopius, *Gothic War* III.33.5. The formulaic character of Caesarius' phrase, identically repeated in the sermons referred to in n. 30 above, and the derivation of 134.1 from Augustine's *Enarr. in Ps.* 50.1, where Christians' attendance at the circus is mentioned, raises doubts. Caesarius mentions visits to the circus or the theatre – along with the gaming-tables and hunting – among the things which make him anxious about the spiritual well-being of his flock: *Sermo* 61.3. Circus games at Arles are attested by Sidonius Apollinaris (*Ep.* I.11), and may have been sporadically held, perhaps at times of affluence or important visits. Current excavations in the circus may shed light on when the circus was in use. I am grateful to Hagith Sivan for information concerning these, and for showing me the summary report in *Revue d'Arles* 1 (1987), 57–60. On the theatre, see above, ch. 11, n. 47. On Italy, below, ch. 14, p. 217.

[33] On this theme, see Markus, 'From Caesarius to Boniface', where details are given.

the proper supervision, of communities of monks and nuns.[34]
It is hardly likely that the bishops would have found less of the
suspect usages, analogous to those Caesarius regarded as 'pagan',
in these less Roman areas, had they chosen to look. But, compared with Caesarius' determination to stamp them out, they
showed remarkably little interest in them. Occasional complaints,
even in royal enactments, about drunken vigils, scurrility, ribald
singing and country-dancing, especially on Sundays and festival
days, or about the widespread and almost venerable practice of
using the sacred books for purposes of divination, unseemly
behaviour in churches, just about exhaust the repertory of popular usages that gave anxiety. The only indications of a pagan,
or half-pagan, world lying beyond the respectable bounds of
urban Christianity occur in the acts of a council held at Tours
in 567 and another at much the same time at Auxerre. What
incurred the bishops' disapproval here were two things: celebration of the Kalends of January, which seemed to them clinging
'to bits of paganism' and incompatible with a genuine profession
of Christianity; and the resorting to stones, trees and springs in
remote spots held sacred by pagans, customs which 'do not
belong to the nature of the Church'.[35]

Only at this point do we reach the threshold of a darker world,
in which real pagan devilry may have been at work. Even so,
we have seen (above, ch. 7, esp. at n. 21) that episcopal worries
about New Year celebrations go back a long way, and are hardly
evidence for 'pagan survivals' among their flocks. What the New
Year celebration was not in Roman towns, that it need not have
been in Germanic countrysides; it is hard to tell. But stones,
trees and springs are another matter. They certainly do bring
us within range of the kind of practices that had also worried
(along with the New Year celebrations, too) Caesarius. What is
striking, however, is that such things should show up so little in
the conciliar records, and that when they do, they are dealt with
in so summary and general a fashion. By Caesarius' standards,
the Gallic bishops were perfunctory in the extreme. There is no
record in Gaul – as there is in the writings of Martin of Braga
in the Iberian peninsula – of detailed and specific condemnations

---

[34] For a fine survey, see Wallace-Hadrill, *The Frankish Church*, 94–109.
[35] Tours, 567, c. 23; cf. Auxerre (561/605), canons 1, 3, 5.

such as Caesarius' had been. The unconcern of councils is reflected by such other evidence as we have. The *Lives* of saints, among them of missionaries active in Northern Gaul and further afield, tell the same story; with one exception, and that a significant one.

The one exception is a chapter in the *Life* of St Eligius of Noyon, one of a group of missionary saints at work in the seventh century.[36] Here we find long lists of customs condemned; and not only do they bear a strong family likeness to those condemned by Caesarius and by Martin of Braga somewhat later in Spain, but Eligius is made to condemn them in words for the most part actually borrowed from their writings. In fact, however, even Eligius was no exception to the general pattern. As is widely agreed, his biography was extensively re-worked in the eighth century, and it now seems that the part especially subjected to re-working begins precisely with this chapter. It is about the same time – the middle decades of the eighth century – that other documents began to appear which display similar interest in 'country matters', the details of 'paganisms' (*paganiae*). Some of them clearly spring from the milieu of Boniface's missionary activities and reflect his concerns. We must conclude that it is with Boniface rather than with Caesarius that the Frankish Church entered on a new era of its history. Caesarius' norms had to wait two centuries to be imposed on a Church which was, on the whole, content to do its best in trying to follow ancient patterns of Christian living. Even the games and shows went uncensured by any Gallic bishop after Caesarius. At much the same time as John of Ephesus described a circus built for the entertainment of the people of Antioch as a 'Church of Satan',[37] Gregory of Tours poured scorn on king Chilperic's absurd pretensions in building circuses in Soissons and Paris; but he did so not from any sense of their diabolic purpose, but to illustrate the frivolity of the king's character at a moment when more strenuous action was required.[38] Even the programme of the ascetic reformers of Provence had condemned

---

[36] *Vita Eligii* II.16; for discussion, see the study mentioned above, n. 33, and M. Banniard's examination of the *Vita Eligii* in the same volume.
[37] *HE.* III.v.17 (ed. E. W. Brooks, 202–3).
[38] *Hist. Franc.* V.17; see also VIII.36 on games at Metz.

only those who missed church services on feast days in order to attend the spectacles.[39]

Boniface's work in Gaul was more than an attempt to restore a moral and canonical discipline in the Gallic Church that had been eclipsed in the course of the political upheavals of the preceding half century. It inaugurated a new conception – akin to Caesarius' – of what being a Christian involved. It was brought to the Frankish Church by an outsider, one who had less contact with its ancient traditions than earlier missionaries, and no urge to work within them. Boniface's reform in the Gallic Church is all of a piece with the one intervention he attempted in the affairs of the Roman Church:[40] when he wanted the pope to stamp out the 'paganisms' that had continued unchecked in Rome, what he was asking for was the abolition of customs the Roman Church had long ago come to terms with. They turn out to be nothing more than the rumbustious celebration of the New Year and the wearing of bracelets by women. In Rome, as in Gaul, his conception of what Christian living in the world meant required a sharp break with the past. In Gaul, the ascetic ideology publicised by Cassian, Salvian, by Lerinese ascetics and bishops, and, finally, Caesarius, could now become adopted by kings and councils for their people. But Italy and Africa were a different matter.

---

[39] *Statuta eccl. ant.* 33.
[40] *Ep.* 50 (Tangl, 84–5).

14

Within sight of the end: retrospect and prospect

The transformation of Gallic society may have been very influential in shaping medieval Christendom; but it was untypical of what was going on elsewhere in Western Europe, notably in Italy, and in North Africa, in the fifth and sixth centuries. To appreciate the contrast, we may begin by returning once more to Eucherius, monk of Lerins and bishop of Lyon (see above, ch. 11). For all his dedication to the life of renunciation and his love of the Desert, Eucherius was not out of line with Cassian, or his colleagues and successors at Lerins, in giving the ascetic ideal a profoundly social bearing. His treatise, *On the contempt of the world,* can be read as a plea for the spiritual renewal of the leading classes of Roman Gaul; and his pamphlet on the martyrs of the Theban legion is a *tour de force,* uniting apparent contraries in a single image: the martyrs are turned into champions of the empire that persecuted them.[1] The work is a startling endorsement of the imperial establishment by an ascetic turned bishop. Eucherius' Desert was from the start intended to make its mark on Gallic society.

This presents a vivid contrast with a monastic tradition such as that of the Jura monasteries. There a different ascetic ideal was being kept alive. We catch a glimpse of it in the story told of abbot Lupicinus' encounter with the *patricius* Chilperic, a story designed to commend the holy man's *parrhesia,* his independence of mind in confrontation with the authorities, and his apparent readiness to denounce them, to prophesy the

---

[1] On this see Pricoco, *L'isola dei santi,* 227–42. There is a significant parallel in *De contemptu, PL* 50.722A to the imperial ideology to be found in *De laude* 2 and 4.

demise of the empire and to predict the imminent ruin of the province.[2] This story comes from a milieu which had set itself up in reaction against the direction mainstream Christianity was taking in Gaul. It remained a protest in the margin of the history of Gallic Christianity. In the course of the century from Eucherius to Caesarius the ascetic ideal was transformed; and so was its relation to the Christianity preached to their churches by aristocratic bishops with ascetic sympathies. The ascetic ideology had moved from the fringes of society to its centre. From institutionalised alienation the monastery had turned into focused representation of the community's social ideal.

This did not happen in Italy or Africa. The reasons are many, and different in the two cases. Two things, however, they had in common. One was the absence of a monastic culture as rich as that of Gaul. The other was the absence in their episcopates of such a heavy preponderance of aristocratic bishops; of aristocratic bishops, moreover, many of whom shared a monastic background, monastic sympathies and a monastic outlook. Neither the African nor the Italian churches experienced the take-over by ascetics that came to set the tone of Gallic Christianity – even if it could not be carried through even there until the eighth century (see above, ch. 13).

Augustine's death in 430 coincided with the occupation of the Roman heartland of Africa by the Arian Vandals. Monastic life did not die out during the century of Vandal occupation; but it did not determine the style and the tone of African Christianity in the manner we observed in Gaul.[3] Other anxieties preoccupied African Christians and their clergy. 'The Ark of the Lord has fallen into enemy hands',[4] a bishop of Carthage said, echoing the woes of colleagues who saw their churches taken over by Arians, their property confiscated, their faith at times under fierce attack. 'The whole choir of your martyred predecessors

---

[2] *Vita Lupicini* 92–3; on the Jura monasteries as ascetic reaction, see above, ch. 12, n. 50.
[3] The *Life* of Fulgentius provides the best evidence. On the failure of Fulgentius to integrate the monastic with the episcopal career – though he is described as *magister utriusque professionis* (Ferrandus, *Vita S. Fulgentii* 17) – see König, *Amt und Askese*, 167–87, who suggests that *Vita S. Fulgentii* 2 is an attempt to disguise the gulf between his failure and Augustine's success.
[4] Quodvultdeus, *Lib. prom.* II.24.50.

is with you':[5] the admonition to steadfast fidelity brought the example of the martyrs back to life with a brutal literalness of meaning which had long ago slipped into a remote past. 'Pray for the liberation of this land'[6] was a prayer that had an urgency which could easily acquire apocalyptic overtones. It is no wonder that even a disciple of Augustine managed to forget, or to ignore, Augustine's warning against reading the Book of Revelations historically. As bishop of Carthage Quodvultdeus, a correspondent of Augustine's while a deacon, wrote a major work some twenty years after Augustine's death,

which systematically enumerated all the signs of the Apocalypse and labelled them fulfilled, occurring and to be fulfilled. The present fell in the 'half time of the Antichrist'. In one passage he identified the Vandals and the Goths with Gog and Magog and adduced in support Augustine's prohibition against such an exegesis by dropping the crucial negative. If so highly placed a theologian could not maintain Augustine's eschatological teachings, one might suspect that lesser clergy fared still worse.[7]

In Gaul Augustine's eschatological view-point on temporal things was eclipsed by an ascetic perspective; in Africa it was wiped out by the carefully maintained sense of apocalyptic doom under Vandal domination. In sermon after sermon the bishop of Carthage called his people to repentance 'amid the distress and anxiety of this time';[8] 'amid such slaughter, amid ruin, captivity and death' – 'where now is Africa, that was once the world's garden of delights? Where so many provinces, where so many of its most splendid towns?'[9] The distractions of circus and theatre flourished in this troubled province; so did their denunciation by the bishop. Like Tertullian and like Salvian, he saw them as the epitome of the Devil's 'pomp'. Addressing the catechumens and those recently baptised, he liked to remind them that this was what they were required to renounce. By

[5] Honoratus Antoninus, *Ep. cons.* Victor of Vita makes persecution the pervasive background of his history: see e.g. *Hist. pers.* III.21.
[6] Quodvultdeus, *Sermo* 8.7 (*De ult. iv feria*). I follow the numbering of the sermons given by R. Braun in his *CC* edition, p. 518. I also give their traditional titles for clarity.
[7] Landes, 'Lest the millennium be fulfilled', 158. The reference is to *Lib. prom.* IV.13.22. For the comparison with Augustine, see Fredriksen, 'Tyconius', 67–8, and n. 43.
[8] *Sermo* 1.1 (*C. Iud.*).
[9] *Ibid.* 13.1, 2, 5, 6 (*De temp. barb.* 2).

going to the shows, 'you will be exposed, O Christian, your cover will be blown, when you profess one thing and do another . . .; not keeping faith with your profession: now entering the church to pray, next shamelessly applauding the actors in the shows'.[10] This present time of God's wrath calls for repentance: and yet, 'even in these hard times, when the whole province is faced with its end, the shows are daily frequented. Human blood is daily shed in the world around us, while madmen's voices still echo round the circus!'[11] It sounds like Salvian; but the bishop's urgency, unlike Salvian's, springs from a sense of impending doom. The end is near; it calls the baptised Christian not to give up his fight with the Devil, whose works he has renounced.[12] African cities could maintain the civilised amenities of traditional urban living; but African Christians had no business to enjoy them. Roman men of letters patronised at the Vandal court might continue to write polite verse in the best literary fashion; but the Catholic clergy could not tolerate such light-hearted luxuries.

The doom-laden air of North Africa lightened only in the last years of Vandal rule, the decades just preceding the Roman re-conquest of the province in the 530s. The experience of Italian Christians in the later fifth century and the sixth was, in most ways, just the contrary of that of their African brethren. Here the rule of barbarian kings did not weigh heavily on their Roman subjects. Aristocrats, sometimes of the ancient families of the ruling elite, continued to serve them in the administration of Roman society, as they had previously served the emperors, and could safeguard the continuity of the established routines of government. Roman civil servants under king Theodoric went on consulting the records of their predecessors in office;[13] Boethius as consul could work in his spare time on a commentary on Aristotle's *Categories*;[14] a Christian prefect of the City could restore a statue of Minerva damaged in a recent riot.[15] Until

[10] *Ibid.* 5.1 (*De symb.* 3); cf. 1.2, 4 (*C. Iud.*); 3.2 (*De symb.* 1); 4.1 (*De symb.* 2); 10.1, 3 (*De temp. barb.* 1); 11.3, 5 (*De acc. ad grat.* 1); 13.2 (*De temp. barb.* 2). Quodvultdeus' sermons strongly suggest that the shows still flourished in Africa.
[11] *Ibid.* 10.1 (*De temp. barb.* 1).
[12] *Ibid.* 9.2 (*De catacl.*).
[13] Cassiodorus, *Variae* I.26.2.
[14] Boethius, *In Cat.* II. *Praef.* (*PL* 64.201B). The best summary I know of this continuity is Chadwick, *Boethius*, esp. 6–16.
[15] *CIL* VI.526 (=1664),

the last strained years of Theodoric's reign (d. 526) traditions of civility and of secular culture kept a reassuring solidity in Ostrogothic Italy.

The Ostrogothic government put much effort and resources into the maintenance of the old order. Officials continued to look after the public entertainments; circuses and theatres were restored, kings and consuls continued to spend lavishly on public displays.[16] In the end, it was not ecclesiastical displeasure that brought about their eclipse, but the diversion – under Christian influence, to be sure – of the resources that had gone into their financing into ecclesiastical building and charitable works. Even this change in the direction of civic munificence was, however, insufficient to destroy the games. They were a source of prestige to their patrons great enough to be highly valued; and clerical opposition was less than half-hearted.[17] As long as consuls continued to be appointed in Italy (until 534), and in towns such as Ravenna and in Byzantine Sicily, where games may have been held much longer, the old traditions of aristocratic munificence continued to thrive and ensured the survival of public entertainments. Only the shrinking of aristocratic patronage, in the course of the damage inflicted on the senatorial class by the Gothic wars, and the exodus of aristocrats to the East, seem finally to have sapped the strength of the foundations on which the old secular traditions of urban living no less than of literary culture rested.

Secular education and letters remained, as they always had been, the prerogative of an elite; but all the signs point to their survival with a vitality not notably diminished in the course of the fifth century. It is significant that when Cassiodorus conceived his plan to found, in collaboration with the learned pope Agapetus, a Christian university in Rome in 535, his vision had been to match the flourishing state of secular studies with a corresponding institution for sacred letters.[18] This secular culture was still deeply embedded in Italian society in the first

---

[16] A sane survey is given by Ward-Perkins, *From classical antiquity*, 99–118.

[17] I know of no clerical condemnation (apart from Leo I's remarks on the Apollinarian games, cf. above, ch. 9, n. 16) after the passing and somewhat routine remarks of Peter Chrysologus, *Sermo* 71.5.

[18] *Inst.* I, *Praef.* This testimony is confirmed by Facundus, *Pro def.* XII.4.12 (I owe this reference to Barnish, 'The work of Cassiodorus', n. 138). On the fate of pope Agapetus' library, Marrou, 'Autour de la bibliothèque'.

decades of the sixth century. Even the conflicts of the 520s, which culminated in the judicial murder of Boethius and his father-in-law Symmachus, were no permanent check to the continuity of Roman secular culture and education, and of administrative and social stability. The philosophical culture such as that which Boethius could turn to, or a literary tradition which found expression in the elegies of Maximian or the correspondence of Ennodius, could still be taken for granted. The 530s, however, were the last moment when they could be so taken for granted. This was the age of hope. Justinian's constitution, *Deo auctore*, issued in 530 to set in motion the construction of the *Digest*, was a solemn and public proclamation of his faith in the great enterprise of which his legal codification was to form a part: the restoration of the empire in its territorial integrity, its juridical institutions as its connective tissue, embodying a vision of a unified orthodox Christian society.[19] In the 530s, with the opportunities for re-conquest, the dream became a hope. The Vandal war seemed to set the seal of divine approval on Justinian's grand design with its speedy and decisive victory 'which exceeds all the wonderful works God has wrought in the world'.[20] The great hope 'escalated, briefly, into unlimited expectation'.[21]

The hope and the expectation collapsed very quickly. The long drawn-out war of re-conquest in Italy undermined the old social order more drastically than the half-century of rule by barbarian kings;[22] the pacification of Italy was achieved little more than nominally, and only fleetingly, in 554; and the second Council of Constantinople (553–4), far from securing religious unity, released only further divisions. The government's inability to secure lasting peace in North Africa, the sufferings of a war-torn Italy, ravaged repeatedly after 543 by plague, renewed threat from Persia, the emergence of a monophysite Church in the East and schism in the West, combined to disappoint the hopes of the 530s. Of Justinian's great vision only the codified law survived as an isolated fragment. The second half of the sixth century was not only a time of lost hopes. The world of

[19] *CJ* I.17.2. On this and what follows, see Markus, 'La politica'.
[20] *CJ* I.27.1.
[21] Honoré, *Tribonian*, 1 .
[22] On this, see Brown, *Gentlemen*.

the 530s had vanished for ever. Justinian's plans for unification produced, paradoxically, an empire more divided, a society more localised and regional, a culture vastly impoverished by the collapse of secular institutions and secular learning, and by the virtual disappearance of the aristocratic elites on which it largely depended in Italy.

Cassiodorus, the former minister of Gothic kings, was uncommonly well placed to take the measure of the change that had come over the world. When the partnership of Goth and Roman, which he had devoted all his working life to fostering, became finally impossible, Cassiodorus took refuge in Constantinople. On his return to Italy in 554 he retired to the monastic community and library he had founded on his property in southern Italy. Here he had been settled for nearly thirty years when, around 580, in his ninety-third year, he sat down to write his last work, a book on spelling for his monks. Justinian had been dead for ten or more years, Lombard invaders were raiding in northern and central Italy and had established themselves in the plains and cities of the north; the Italian Church was divided by schism; his own desire to found an institution for Christian higher learning was frustrated by the upheavals of war and its sequel. The old order was gone, its remnants transferred to Constantinople, with his senatorial friends who had migrated there. Italy was a new world indeed, what Cassiodorus called 'modern'.[23] Nowhere can this novelty be so poignantly experienced by the modern reader as in this, Cassiodorus' last work. That it was to be his last he knew; proudly he catalogued his previous writings in his Preface. It was written at the request of his monks, who complained that knowledge of what the ancients had written was not much use to them if they could neither write down their thoughts nor decipher what they read. Cassiodorus knew his monks, and he knew what they needed. It was not the education he had received, still less that of Boethius, and of their generation: 'My purpose is to plait together into one braid what ancient tradition has made available for proper use by modern custom, and to make it quickly and easily accessible. It is right to omit in this enterprise what is of

---

[23] Cassiodorus appears to be the first writer to use *modernus* regularly to refer to his own age: Freund, *Modernus*, cited by O'Donnell, *Cassiodorus*, 235, n. 9.

merely antiquarian interest, so as to avoid requiring unnecessary and anachronistic labour, useless in the present age.'[24]

Cassiodorus was writing for men of a new age, and said as much in his Preface. The last words of this little book contain a hint – it is no more – of an upheaval in his expectations of them:[25]

> Farewell, brethren, and please remember me in your prayers. I have taught you, among other things, in a summary manner, the importance of correct spelling and punctuation, universally acknowledged to be a precious thing; I have prepared a full course of reading to assist you in the understanding of the holy scripture. Just as I have striven to separate you from the mass of the unlearned, so may the heavenly power not allow us to be swallowed with the wicked in the community of punishment.

To read these last words Cassiodorus addressed to his monks is to become conscious of the gulf that had opened between the hopes of the 530s and what had taken their place fifty years later. The final sentence of Cassiodorus' treatise brings home the full pathos of the moment: the community for which he was writing was to be an elite in its world; but not an elite distinguished from the masses by access to the intellectual and literary resources that Cassiodorus himself and his contemporaries had been able to draw upon. The tinge of literary frivolity carried by the conventions of a classicising culture, over which Ennodius, for example, sometimes betrayed a sense of guilt[26] (a sense of guilt that a modern reader may be tempted to find rather well founded) would be as inconceivable in the last decades of the sixth century as the towering intellectual accomplishment of a Boethius. The literary and philosophical culture which made these possible, or the relics of religious traditions which could still, in the time of the Gothic wars, rally some Romans in a genuine pagan revival,[27] no longer provided options available in the 580s.

---

[24] *De Orth., Praef.* (*PL* 70.1241D).

[25] *Ibid. Concl.* (*ibid.* 1270B). We should, however, heed the warning against overstating the ignorance of the monks of Vivarium given by Barnish, 'The work of Cassiodorus'.

[26] E.g. *Opera*, 438 (Vogel, 300–4); 39 (38); 422 (292); 431 (297); 442 (305) – despite his assurance that Rome had been wholly purged of its ancient pagan error: 49.128f. (66).

[27] Procopius, *Gothic War* I.24.28f.; 25.18f.

The intellectual elite which Cassiodorus expected his community to be differed from that of Boethius, or Ennodius and his pupils, not only in the intellectual equipment it could be assumed to be in a position to possess. It was also expected to mobilise these intellectual resources, exclusively, in the study of the scriptures. We should not allow ourselves to be misled by the similarity between this programme of study, outlined in his *Institutes* (and referred to in the paragraph quoted above), and Augustine's *On Christian teaching*. Cassiodorus was undoubtedly following Augustine's recipe for the utilisation of secular disciplines.[28] But more than a century and a half lay between the composition of the two works, and the interval had transformed the nature of the task the two men were faced with. Augustine's sketch for a Christian culture and an educational programme to achieve it had been born of a confrontation with pagan claims to sole rights in a heritage to which they would have liked to see Christians as alien usurpers. Augustine rejected the claim, and wrote to assert Christian rights to borrow and to integrate in a new synthesis, based on a scriptural foundation, what could be useful in the construction of a Christian wisdom. By the time Cassiodorus began work on the *Institutes*, most probably in 562, Augustine's hostility to pagan culture had no relevance. There was no pagan culture now. Christians had made it thoroughly their own. Even the minority culture that classical learning had been was rapidly becoming a thing of the past. The recipe remained the same; but the conditions for its application had changed beyond recognition.

In the Middle Ages the *Institutes* was read as an educational handbook. For Cassiodorus it defined the central task of his community: 'it seems to have taken the place of a formal *Regula*; it is clearly the founder's apologia for his enterprise and exhortation and guide for those to come after him'.[29] By a different route, Cassiodorus arrived at a destination akin to Cassian's, and Julianus Pomerius' (above, ch. 12): a conception of monastic spirituality centred on scriptural study. His route, and, in some measure, its final outcome, certainly bore from the outset a more distinctly intellectual stamp. We cannot imagine that he could

---

[28] For an excellent interpretation of the *Institutiones*, see O'Donnell, *Cassiodorus*, 202–14.
[29] *Ibid.* 202.

have recommended – as had Cassian[30] – techniques for forgetting classical literature imbibed in youth. Cassian's way had been the ascetic's, re-interpreted and given a more scriptural and more pastoral twist. Cassiodorus was brought to a similar view of the community's task, but from a sharp sense of the paucity of the intellectual resources available. A culture essentially scriptural in substance was the aim of both; for Cassian through an ascetic rejection of secular culture, for Cassiodorus through his awareness of the impoverishment of the available secular culture.

In these different ways – through scriptural reading being turned into an instrument of perfection in the ascetic ideology as interpreted by Cassian and propagated by ex-monks of Lerins, diffused in Gallic society and adopted by bishops such as Caesarius of Arles as a model for the whole Christian people in their care (above, chs. 11–13), as well as through the weakening of the fabric of secular interests and education – a much more thoroughly biblical orientation came to mark monastic culture. This ascetic culture came to set the tone for Christians in general, and Christian living came to be conceived as a life lived in permanent confrontation with a canonical text (together with a number of secondary texts, mainly of the Christian Fathers, which tended to become quasi-canonical). The community of discourse was shaped by the scriptures. In the intentions of churchmen such as Caesarius, the linguistic community was, ideally, to be co-extensive with the Christian community, the boundaries of the one defining the extent of the other.

In Western Europe[31] the late sixth century marks a real break with the world of antiquity, closed off access to much of its intellectual culture, and even more drastically, to its ways of looking at, understanding and speaking about that world. We have been taught to appreciate the importance of thriving urban institutions in Augustine's Africa, and their part in shaping social and intellectual intercourse.[32] We cannot read, for instance,

---

[30] *Conl.* XIV.12–13.

[31] Averil Cameron has suggested that at much the same time a similar process of cultural and religious re-adjustment took place in the Byzantine world: see her 'Images of authority', and her contribution to the symposium *The seventh century: change and continuity*, ed. J. Fontaine and J. N. Hillgarth (forthcoming).

[32] See especially Lepelley, 'Saint Augustin et la cité', esp. p. 37; and Eck, 'Das Episkopat'. For a general dicussion of this theme, see Markus, 'The sacred and the secular'.

Augustine's correspondence with Maximus, the pagan professor of Madaura, or with Nectarius, pagan citizen of Calama, without becoming conscious of the powerful threads that bound together traditional Roman religion and intellectual culture within a flourishing municipal life. In Africa, and elsewhere around the Mediterranean, this symbiosis of old and new, of pagan and Christian, furnished the conditions for a sustained debate, an unceasing need for Christians to take the measure of forms of thought and expression, of ways of feeling, a culture older than their religion. The Christian Church still felt itself to be on the edge of an old-established order. Augustine sometimes thought bishops had little 'clout' with the authorities; the two orders, the Church's and the secular world's, ran alongside each other, the secular still carrying a weight and a momentum with which Christians had to reckon seriously.

In two ways this relationship changed profoundly in the later sixth century. Growing ecclesiastical 'clout' eclipsed secular power and brought about extensive re-drawing of the contours of society. The concomitant change, however, is of more direct interest to us here. These decades following the 540s also mark the displacement of an older tradition of thought concerning the nature of the Christian community in Late Antique society: a tradition which Augustine had been unique to articulate, but one which continued a precarious existence in a diffuse manner for a century or more after him. At about the time that Cassiodorus wrote his last book, another descendant of an aristocratic family, one of the few left in Italy, the former prefect of the City (this is most probably the office he held in 573), Gregory, like Cassiodorus, founded monastic communities in some of his family properties, and retired to one of them, in Rome. Unlike Cassiodorus, Gregory had only a short spell of public office behind him. His active life was only just about to begin: in 578 or 579 he was called by the pope to act as his representative and agent at the court in Constantinople. On his return from there, after another short interval of monastic retirement, in 590 he was to become pope to succeed his predecessor, a victim of the plague, in a City flooded by the Tiber, exhausted by plague and by famine. In the very years that Cassiodorus was writing about spelling, Gregory was engaged in expounding the Book of Job

223

for the 'brethren' who accompanied him to Constantinople. In one of these discourses he spoke of the work for the man of God: 'in the midst of the unsteady flow of time he knows how to keep steady the steps of his mind'.[33] Gregory could not have known the security and confidence of the world Cassiodorus had been born into and which Cassiodorus spent much of his energies in promoting as long as he could. Gregory grew up in that 'modern' world which Cassiodorus had watched come into being before his eyes. We could try to understand Gregory's work as a search for security and permanence amid the uncertainties of his world. This it undoubtedly was on one level; but to keep to this level would be to miss the extent to which it also represents a re-definition of knowledge itself, a cultural and spiritual integration at a time when the old meanings, the old certainties and the shape of knowledge and discourse were breaking or had broken down.

We should not, however, misunderstand the nature of these shifts. Some of the important developments in the intellectual and cultural history of Europe have their roots in what, in the sphere of traditions of intellectual enquiry and interpretation, Alasdair MacIntyre has called 'epistemological crises'.[34] Such a crisis occurs when established traditions have become sterile and are seen to lead intellectually to a dead end; when the use of hitherto accepted ways of thought 'begins to have the effect of increasingly disclosing new inadequacies, hitherto unrecognised incoherences, and new problems for the solution of which there seem to be insufficient or no resources within the established fabric of belief' (362). Such a crisis is resolved by the adoption of a 'new and conceptually enriched scheme', which can simultaneously deal with the sterility or incoherence produced by its predecessor, account for the previous difficulty in doing so, and carry out these tasks 'in a way which exhibits some fundamental continuity of the new conceptual and theoretical structures with the shared beliefs in terms of which the tradition of enquiry had been defined up to that point' (362).

---

[33] *Mor.* XXXI.28.55.
[34] I take my summary from his *Whose justice?*, 361ff. Figures in parentheses indicate page numbers from which I have quoted.

What we have been dealing with is the reverse of such an epistemological crisis. The elimination – except for its most basic constituents such as orthography, grammar and the like – from Christian discourse of a whole sphere which we may call 'secular' is something in the nature, rather, of what we might call an 'epistemological excision'. The new interpretative scheme in this kind of case is not one that has been conceptually enriched, and it does not displace one which has revealed itself as lacking the resources to meet the demands made upon it. The shift to a radically and almost exclusively scriptural culture and the adoption of a framework for thought formulated within scriptural horizons was a shift of this latter kind. Its ways of thinking were, indeed, profoundly continuous with an already ancient tradition of thought. It did not solve problems previously insoluble, or answer questions previously unanswerable; rather, losing certain kinds of interest, it by-passed or suppressed them. The shift amounted to a constriction in what was comprised within the sphere of Christian discourse, a self-limitation to one of the constituents of what had once been a richer variety, and an exuberant development of thought within this newly defined world of discourse. To explore this development would be to enter the spiritual and intellectual world of early medieval Christianity.

It is important to be clear that such a constriction of discourse is not quite the same thing as an impoverishment of literary and intellectual culture, though the two things may go together. It is possible to imagine a good deal of secular learning being put to good use within a scripturally defined perspective. It is possible to find examples of such use – by Gregory the Great, by Isidore of Seville and a host of later writers – without secular learning thereby raising any questions that were incapable of being answered in scriptural terms and thus without pressing against, expanding or breaking through the boundaries of discourse. Christian culture in the early medieval centuries became essentially and radically biblical in a way it had not been before. The heterogeneity that had characterised it, at any rate, from Augustine to Boethius, and provided it with a fruitful play of internal tensions for its enrichment and growth, was gone; but a good deal of secular learning could, and sometimes did, continue to play an important part within it.

We have observed how a number of things converged to encourage the emergence of a biblical culture. This has been an important thread in the book's argument. But the argument has been on two fronts. I have tried to sketch a shift in the way that Late Antique Christians saw and represented to themselves their religion and its relation to the secular world around them. This project (as I argued in chapter 1) involves on the one hand an enquiry into their conception of what constitutes their religion, where its boundaries are drawn, and by implication, its relation to what lies outside those boundaries, the 'secular world'. The shift in the location of these boundaries is explained, in part, by the shift in the nature of Christian discourse, its adoption of a thoroughly biblical framework of interpretation, and the consequent liability of what falls outside such a framework to be excluded from discourse. But only in part; for the boundary between what is seen as 'sacred' and 'secular' is a product not only of thought- and speech-habits, its shifting position defined not only by shifts in the perspectives of thought, imagination and language.

It is also determined by what there is. A drainage of secularity, in other words, is determined from two sides: produced by minds which see as 'sacred' (or its contrary, 'profane') what had earlier counted as 'secular', which see meanings more extensively defined in a sacred, biblical perspective; or by the disappearance from the world of that which had been seen as 'secular'. Both these shifts took place during these two centuries. As Christian discourse shrank to scriptural, so the world of which it spoke shrank to the sacred. The secular became marginalised, merged in or absorbed by the sacred, both in discourse and in the social structure and institutions. Corresponding to the 'epistemological excision' of the secular from Christian discourse a 'de-secularisation' of its society (see ch. 1, p. 16) took place on a variety of levels. I have traced this process in some of what seemed to me the most revealing areas in which secular institutions and practices were engulfed within a sacred sphere, and investigated the pressures which brought this about. How secular Roman time was transformed into Christian liturgical time; how the geography of the Roman Empire received a thick overlay of sacred topography; how popular entertainments and customs were modified, or resisted modification, under the pressure of the sacred – or, if not the sacred, the clergy. In all this, we observed a convergence towards a society defined by contours largely religious in nature. The pressures behind this de-secularisation also turned out to have a variety of sources. Foremost among them was the growing appeal of ascetic ideals, and their wide diffusion in Christian circles beyond monastic communities. The enduring unease about what constituted an authentic Christian identity in a largely christianised world reinforced this appeal, while also raising troubling questions about the Christian Church's present in relation to its past. And in a society in which older traditions of civil authority and secular administration were greatly weakened, clerical power naturally assumed growing dominance, and in doing so, contributed to the eclipse of secular traditions.

Thus the Christian community to which Gregory belonged was, in the first place, the new community of discourse whose emergence over the preceding two hundred years we have been following in this book. The mental world he and his contemporaries inhabited was the outcome of a huge shift in the intellectual and imaginative horizons of Western Christians since the time of Augustine. But it was also a world in which the configurations of society were irretrievably changed. It had been possible imaginatively to dismantle the outward forms of ancient civilised society long before Gregory's time. John Chrysostom had done just this in sermons preached at Antioch in 387. The imperial statues had been destroyed in riots. The emperor, to punish the population, closed the theatre and the hippodrome. John Chrysostom, preaching in the aftermath of the troubles, welcomed the punitive measures:

for what is there that is harsh about them? that the emperor has shut the orchestra and forbidden the hippodrome – that he has stopped up these founts of iniquity? . . . or the baths, those intolerable places, whose closing has driven the citizens from dissolute self-indulgence to philosophy?

The emperor had taken the first steps to turn Antioch into a Christian city; it was now up to the citizens to complete the work:

learn what the true dignity of the city is ... It is not the suburban amenities of Daphne, not its many and large fountains, not the size of its population or its leisured strolling in the forum till late at night, nor the plentiful goods in its shops ... Virtue, meekness, almsgiving, vigils, prayers, sobriety, true wisdom of soul – these are the things a city should be praised for.[35]

Chrysostom has neatly turned the traditional idea of what makes a city inside out. What was the very essence of a classical city, the forum, the baths, the theatres and circuses, made it a diabolical parody of a Christian city. But in the 380s that parody was still a present reality: Antioch. Gregory's Rome, and similarly most Western cities, had lost most of what had made Antioch so good a target for Chrysostom's preaching. This is the difference that gave Gregory's social ideal a foothold in the reality around him. The massive secularity of John Chrysostom's and of Augustine's world had drained out of Gregory's. There was little room for the secular in it. The Devil was close, always ready to swallow up the world and the flesh.

[35] *Hom. ad pop. Ant.* XVII (*PG* 49.176, 179). On the polemical and ascetic background of John's preaching, see now Hunter, *A comparison*, 3–66, and Brown, *The body*, 306–19.

Sources referred to

Names of editors, place and date of publication are given only for editions not in *PG, PL, PLS, CC, CSEL, GCS, MGH*, SC. Works of the authors listed below are usually referred to in their customary abbreviated forms. Isolated texts to which full reference is given in the notes are not included.

Ad amicum aegrotum (Ps. Jerome) (*PL* 30)
AMBROSE
   Epistolae (*PL* 16)
   Explanatio super psalmos xii (*CSEL* 64)
   Expositio in psalmum cxviii (*CSEL* 62)
AMBROSIASTER
   Quaestiones veteris et novi testamenti (*CSEL* 50)
ARNOBIUS IUNIOR
   Liber ad Gregoriam (*PLS* 3)
ATHANASIUS
   Vita Antonii (*PG* 26)
AUGUSTINE
   Confessiones (*CC* 27)
   Contra duas epistulas Pelagianorum (*CSEL* 60)
   Contra Faustum Manichaeum (*CSEL* 25)
   Contra Fortunatum Manichaeum (*CSEL* 25)
   Contra Gaudentium (*CSEL* 53)
   Contra litteras Petiliani (*CSEL* 52)
   De beata vita (*On the blessed life*) (*CC* 29)
   De bono coniugali (*On the good of marriage*) (*CSEL* 41)
   De catechizandis rudibus (*CC* 46)
   De civitate Dei (*City of God*) (*CC* 47–8)
   De consensu evangelistarum (*CSEL* 43)
   De diversis quaestionibus ad Simplicianum (*CC* 44)
   De doctrina christiana (*Of Christian teaching*) (*CC* 32)

Sources

De dono perseverantiae (*PL* 45)
De Genesi ad litteram (*CSEL* 28)
De Genesi contra Manichaeos (*PL* 34)
De gestis Pelagii (*CSEL* 42)
De gratia Christi et de peccato originali (*CSEL* 42)
De gratia et libero arbitrio (*PL* 44)
De moribus ecclesiae catholicae et de moribus Manichaeorum (*PL* 32)
De natura et gratia (*CSEL* 40)
De nuptiis et concupiscentia (*CSEL* 42)
De opere monachorum (*On the work of monks*) (*CSEL* 41)
De ordine (*CC* 29)
De peccatorum meritis et remissione (*CSEL* 60)
De perfectione iustitiae hominis (*CSEL* 42)
De praedestinatione sanctorum (*PL* 44)
De sancta virginitate (*On holy virginity*) (*CSEL* 41)
De sermone Domini in monte (*CC* 35)
De Trinitate (*CC* 50–50A)
De vera religione (*CC* 32)
Enarrationes in Psalmos (*CC* 38–40)
Epistolae (*CSEL* 34, 44, 57, 58, 88)
Epistolae ad Romanos inchoata expositio. Augustine on Romans, ed. and trans. Landes, *q.v.* under 'Secondary literature referred to' under 'Fredriksen'
In Iohannis evangelium tractatus (*CC* 36)
Opus imperfectum contra Iulianum (*PL* 45)
Ordo monasterii and *Praeceptum*, ed. Lawless, *q.v.* under 'Secondary literature referred to'
Retractationes (*CC* 57)
Sermones (*PL* 38–9; *PLS* 2; 1–50: *CC* 41)
Soliloquia (*PL* 32)

AVITUS OF VIENNE
Homiliae (*MGH AA* 6/2)

BOETHIUS
In Categorias Aristotelis (*PL* 64)

BONIFACE
Epistolae ed. M. Tangl (*MGH Epp. selectae*, 1. Berlin, 1955)

CAESARIUS OF ARLES
Sermones (*CC* 103–4)

CASSIAN
Conlationes (*Conferences*) (*CSEL* 13)
Institutiones coenobiorum (*CSEL* 17)

CASSIODORUS
De orthographia (*PL* 70)
Institutiones, ed. R. A. B. Mynors (Oxford, 1937; 1961)
Variae (*MGH AA* 12)

Codex Theodosianus, ed. T. Mommsen and P. Meyer (Berlin, 1905)
Concilia Africae (*CC* 149)
Concilia Galliae (*CC* 148–148A)
CONSTANTIUS OF LYON
   Vita Germani episcopi Autissiodorensis (*MGH SRM* 7)
Corpus Iuris civilis, ed. T. Mommsen, P. Krueger, R. Schoell and G.
   Kroll (Berlin, 1869–95)
CYPRIAN
   Epistolae (*CSEL* 3)
De divitiis (*PLS* 1)
De vita christiana (*PLS* 1)
ENNODIUS
   Opera (*MGH AA* 7)
Epistola ad Demetriadem (Anon.) (*PL* 55)
Epistula ad adolescentem (*PLS* 1)
EUCHERIUS OF LYON
   De contemptu mundi (*On the contempt of the world*) (*PL* 50)
   De laude heremi (*In praise of the Desert*) (*CSEL* 31)
   Passio Acaunensium martyrum (*MGH SRM* 3)
EUSEBIUS OF CAESAREA
   Demonstratio evangelica (*GCS* 23)
   Commentarii in Psalmos (*PG* 23)
   Historia ecclesiastica (*Ecclesiastical history*) (*GCS* 9)
   Vita Constantini, ed. F. Winkelman (*GCS*, 1975)
'EUSEBIUS GALLICANUS'
   Homiliae (*CC* 101, 101A, 101B)
FACUNDUS OF HERMIANE
   Pro defensione trium capitulorum (*CC* 90A)
FAUSTUS OF RIEZ
   Epistolae (*CC* 64)
   Sermones (*CSEL* 21)
FERRANDUS
   Vita S. Fulgentii, ed. G. Lapeyre (Paris, 1929)
GELASIUS I (FELIX III)
   Epistolae, Tractatus, ed. A. Thiel (*Epistolae Romanorum pontificum*.
   Braunsberg, 1868)
GENNADIUS
   De viris illustribus, ed. E. C. Richardson (TU 14/1. Berlin, 1896)
Gesta conlationis Carthaginensis a. 411 (*CC* 149A)
GREGORY I
   Dialogorum libri IV (*SC* 251, 260, 265)
   Homiliae in Evangelia (*PL* 76)
   Homiliae in Hiezechielem (*CC* 142)
   Moralia (*CC* 143, 143A, 143B)
   Registrum epistolarum (*CC* 140–140A)

Sources

GREGORY NAZIANZEN
Orationes (*PG* 35)
GREGORY OF TOURS
Historiarum libri X (*Hist. Franc.*) (*MGH SRM* 1.1)
Liber in gloria martyrum (*MGH SRM* 1.1)
HILARY OF ARLES
Sermo de Vita Honorati (SC 235)
HONORATUS ANTONINUS
Epistola consolatoria ad Arcadium (*PL* 50)
ISIDORE OF SEVILLE
Etymologiae, ed. W. M. Lindsay (Oxford, 1911)
JEROME
Adversus Iovinianum (*PL* 23)
Contra Vigilantium (*PL* 23)
De viris illustribus, ed. E. C. Richardson (TU 14/1. Berlin, 1896)
Epistolae (*CSEL* 54–6)
JOHN CHRYSOSTOM
Contra oppugnatores vitae monasticae (*PG* 47)
Hom. contra ludos et theatra (*PG* 56)
Hom. in Kalendas (*PG* 48)
Hom. ad populum Antiochensem (*De statuis*) (*PG* 49)
JULIANUS POMERIUS
De vita contemplativa (*PL* 59)
LEO I
Epistolae (*PL* 54)
Tractatus (*CC* 138–138A)
LEONTIUS
Vita Gregorii Agrigentensis (*PG* 98)
LIBANIUS
Orationes, ed. R. Foerster (Berlin 1909–27)
MARK THE DEACON
Vita Porphyrii. Marc le Diacre, Vie de Porphyre, ed. and trans. H. Grégoire and M. A. Kugener (Paris, 1930)
The martyrdom of Polycarp, ed. J. B. Lightfoot (London, 1898)
MAXIMUS OF TURIN
Sermones (*CC* 23)
MINUCIUS FELIX
Octavius (*CSEL* 2)
NOVATIAN
De spectaculis (*CSEL* 3)
OROSIUS
Adversum paganos (*Historiarum*) *libri VII* (*CSEL* 5)
Passio Sancti Leodegarii (*MGH SRM* 5)
PAULINUS OF NOLA
Epistolae (*CSEL* 29)
Carmina (*CSEL* 30)

PELAGIUS
  Epistola ad Demetriadem (*PL* 30)
  Epistola ad Celantiam (*CSEL* 56)
Peregrinatio Egeriae (*CC* 175)
PETER CHRYSOLOGUS
  Sermones (*CC* 24, 24A, 24B)
POSSIDIUS
  Vita Augustini (*PL* 32)
PROBA, FALTONIA BETITIA
  Cento (*CSEL* 16)
PROCOPIUS
  Wars, ed. and trans. H. B. Dewing (Cambridge, Mass. and London, 1914–40)
PROSPER
  Chronicon (*MGH AA* 9)
PRUDENTIUS
  Peristephanon (*CSEL* 61)
QUODVULTDEUS
  Liber promissionum (*CC* 60)
  Sermones (*CC* 60)
Regula Benedicti (SC 181–6)
Regula Magistri (SC 105–7)
Regulae sanctorum patrum (SC 97–8)
RUTILIUS NAMATIANUS
  De reditu suo, ed. Doblehoffer, *q.v.* under 'Secondary literature referred to'
SALVIAN
  Ad ecclesiam (*To the Church*) (*CSEL* 8)
  De gubernatione Dei (*On the government of God*) (*CSEL* 8)
  Epistolae (*CSEL* 8)
SIDONIUS APOLLINARIS
  Carmina (*MGH AA* 8)
  Epistolae (*MGH AA* 8)
SOCRATES
  Historia ecclesiastica, ed. W. Bright (Oxford, 1978)
SOZOMEN
  Historia ecclesiastica (*GCS* 50)
Statuta ecclesiae antiqua (*CC* 148)
SULPICIUS SEVERUS
  Dialogorum libri II (SC 133–5)
  Epistolae (SC 133–5)
  Vita Martini (SC 133–5)
SYMMACHUS, QUINTUS AURELIUS
  Relationes (*MGH AA* 6/1)

TERTULLIAN
   De corona (*CC* 2)
   De idololatria (*CC* 2)
   De praescriptione haereticorum (*CC* 1)
   De spectaculis (*CC* 1)
THEODORE OF MOPSUESTIA
   In epistolam ad Galatas, ed. H. B. Swete (Cambridge, 1880–2)
THEODORET
   Historia ecclesiastica (*GCS* 44)
   Historia religiosa (SC 234, 257)
VICTOR OF VITA
   Historia persecutionis Africanae provinciae (*CSEL* 7)
VICTRICIUS OF ROUEN
   De laude sanctorum (*CC* 64)
VINCENT OF LERINS
   Commonitorium (*CC* 64)
Vita Audoini (*MGH SRM* 6)
Vita Eligii (*MGH SRM* 4)
Vita Hilarii Arelatensis, ed. S. Cavallin (Lund, 1952)
Vita S. Caesarii (*MGH SRM* 4)
Vitae patrum Iurensium (SC 142)

Secondary literature referred to

Andresen, C., 'Altchristliche Kritik am Tanz – ein Ausschnitt aus dem Kampf der alten Kirche gegen heidnische Sitte', *Kirchengeschichte als Missionsgeschichte*, 344–76

Angenendt, A., *Kaiserherrschaft und Königstaufe* (Berlin, 1984)

Armstrong, A. H., 'Gnosis and Greek philosophy', in *Gnosis. Festschrift für Hans Jonas*, ed. B. Aland and U. Bianchi (Göttingen, 1978), 87–124; repr. in his *Plotinian and Christian studies*, XXI

'Man in the cosmos. A study of some differences between pagan Neoplatonism and Christianity', in *Romanitas et Christianitas*, ed. W. van den Boer (Amsterdam, 1973), 5–14; repr. in his *Plotinian and Christian studies*, XXII

'Neoplatonic valuations of nature, body and intellect', *Augustinian Studies* 3 (1972), 35–59

Plotinian and Christian studies (Collected studies. London, 1979)

'Plotinus', in his *Cambridge history*, 195–268

'The self-definition of Christianity in relation to Platonism', in Sanders, ed., *Jewish and Christian self-definition*, 74–99

(ed.), *Cambridge history of later Greek and early medieval philosophy* (Cambridge, 1967)

Babcock, W. S., 'MacMullen on conversion: a response', *The Second Century* 5 (1985/6), 82–9

Badewien, J., *Geschichtstheologie und Sozialkritik im Werk Salvians von Marseille* (Göttingen, 1980)

Badot, P., 'L'utilisation de Salvien et de la *Vitae Patrum Iurensium* comme source historique', *Revue de l'Université de Bruxelles* 54 (1976), 391–405

Barnes, T. D., *Constantine and Eusebius* (Cambridge, Mass., 1981)

'The Constantinian reformation', in *The Crake lectures, 1984*, ed. M. Fancy and I. Cohen (Sackville, New Brunswick, 1986), 39–57

'The editions of Eusebius' *Ecclesiastical history*', *GRBS* 21 (1980), 191–201

Tertullian (Oxford, 1971; 2nd edn 1985)

Secondary literature

Barnish, S. J. B., 'The transformation of classical cities and the Pirenne debate', *Journal of Roman Archaeology* 2 (1989), 385–400

'The work of Cassiodorus after his conversion', *Latomus* 48 (1989), 157–87

Baus, K., *Der Kranz in Antike und Christentum. Eine religionsgeschichtliche Untersuchung mit besonderer Berücksichtingung Tertullians* (Theophaneia, 2. Bonn, 1940)

Baynes, N. H., 'The thought-world of East Rome', in *Byzantine studies and other essays* (London, 1955), 24–46

Beatrice, P. F., *Tradux peccati: alle fonti della dottrina agostiniana del peccato originale* (Studia patristica mediolanensia, 8. Milan, 1978)

Beck, H. G. J., *The pastoral care of souls in south-east France during the sixth century* (Rome, 1950)

Berrouard, M. F., 'Les lettres 6* et 19* de Saint Augustin. Leur date et les renseignements qu'elles apportent sur l'évolution de la crise "pélagienne"', *REAug* 27 (1981), 264–77

Bieler, L., *Theios aner: das Bild des "göttlichen Menschen" in Spätantike und Frühchristentum* (Vienna, 1935–6)

Bohlin, T., *Die Theologie des Pelagius und ihre Genesis* (Uppsala Universitets årskrift 9, 1957)

Bonner, G., *Augustine and modern research on Pelagianism* (Villanova, 1972; repr. in his *God's decree*, XI)

'The extinction of paganism and the Church historian', *JEH* 35 (1984), 339–57

God's decree and man's destiny (Collected studies. London, 1987)

'*Libido* and *concupiscentia* in St Augustine', *StPatr* 6 (TU 81. Berlin, 1962), 303–14; repr. in his *God's decree*, IX

'Some remarks on Letters 4* and 6*', in *Les lettres de saint Augustin découvertes par Johannes Divjak*, 155–64; repr. in his *God's decree*, XII

St Augustine of Hippo: Life and controversies (London, 1963)

Bowersock, G.W., 'Symmachus and Ausonius', in *Symmaque*, ed. F. Paschoud (Paris, 1986), 1–15

Brown, P., 'Art and society in Late Antiquity', in *Age of spirituality: a symposium*, ed. F. Weitzmann (New York, 1980), 17–37

'Aspects of the christianisation of the Roman aristocracy', *JRS* 51 (1961), 1–11; repr. in his *Religion and society*, 161–82

Augustine of Hippo: a biography (London, 1967)

The body and society. Men, women and sexual renunciation in early Christianity (New York, 1988)

The cult of the saints. Its rise and function in Latin Christianity (Chicago and London, 1981)

The making of Late Antiquity (Cambridge, Mass., 1978)

'The patrons of Pelagius: the Roman aristocracy between East and West', *JThS* n.s. 21 (1970), 56–72; repr. in his *Religion and society*, 208–26

'Pelagius and his supporters: aims and environment', *JThS* n.s. 19 (1968), 93–114; repr. in his *Religion and society*, 183–207

Religion and society in the age of Saint Augustine (London, 1972)

'The saint as exemplar in Late Antiquity', *Representations* 2 (1983), 1–25 (the substance of which appears in a truncated form in *Persons in groups*, ed. R. C. Trexler (Binghampton, N.Y., 1985), 183–94)

'Sexuality and society in the fifth century A.D.: Julian of Eclanum', in *Tria corda: scritti in onore di Arnaldo Momigliano*, ed. E. Gabba (Como, 1983), 49–70

Brown, T. S., *Gentlemen and officers. Imperial administration and aristocratic power in Byzantine Italy* (Rome, 1984)

Bullough, D. A., 'Burial, community and belief in the early medieval West', in *Ideal and reality in Frankish and Anglo-Saxon society*, ed. P. Wormald (Oxford, 1983), 177–201

'Urban change in early medieval Italy: the example of Pavia', *Papers of the British School in Rome* 34 (n.s. 21) (1966), 47–115

Cameron, Alan, *Circus factions* (Oxford, 1976)

Claudian. Poetry and propaganda at the court of Honorius (Oxford, 1970)

Porphyrius the charioteer (Oxford, 1973)

Cameron, Averil, 'Images of authority: elites and icons in sixth-century Byzantium', *Past and Present* 84 (1979), 3–35

Campenhausen, H. von, *Die Idee des Martyriums in der alten Kirche*, 2nd edn (Göttingen, 1964)

Cardman, F., 'The rhetoric of holy places', *StPatr* 17 (1982), 18–25

Cayré, F., *La contemplation augustinienne* (Paris, 1954)

Chadwick, H., 'The ascetic ideal in the history of the Church', *SCH* 22 (1985), 1–23

'Augustine on pagans and Christians', in *History, society and the churches. Essays in honour of Owen Chadwick*, ed. D. Beales and G. Best (Cambridge, 1985), 9–27

Boethius. The consolations of music, logic, theology and philosophy (Oxford, 1981)

'Enkrateia', *RAC* 5 (1962), 343–65

Priscillian of Avila (Oxford, 1976)

Chadwick, O., *John Cassian*, 2nd edn (Cambridge, 1968)

Chéné, J., 'Les origines de la controverse semi-pélagienne', *Année théologique augustinienne* 13 (1953), 56–109

Clark, E. A., *Ascetic piety and women's faith. Essays in Late Ancient Christianity* (Lewiston, N.Y.; Queenston, Ont.; Lampeter, 1986)

'Heresy, asceticism, Adam and Eve: Interpretations of Genesis 1–3 in the later Latin Fathers', in her *Ascetic piety*, 353–85

La conversione al cristianesimo nell'Europa dell'alto medioevo, Settimane 12 (1966)

Secondary literature

Courcelle, P., *Histoire littéraire des grandes invasions germaniques*, 3rd edn (Paris, 1964)

'Nouveaux aspects de la culture lérinienne', *REL* 46 (1968), 379–409

Recherches sur les Confessions de Saint Augustin (Paris, 1950)

Cranz, F. E., 'The development of Augustine's ideas on society before the Donatist controversy' *HThR* 47 (1954), 255–316; repr. in *Augustine: a collection of critical essays*, ed. R. A. Markus (New York, 1972), pp. 336–406

Cristianizzazione ed organizzazione ecclesiastica delle campagne nell'alto medioevo, Settimane 28 (1982)

Csányi, D. A., *Optima pars. Die Auslegung von Lk. 10.30–42* (Studia monastica, 2. Montserrat, 1960)

Cullmann, O., *Christ and time* (London, 1951) (English trans. of *Christus und die Zeit*)

Dagron, G., 'Le christianisme dans la ville byzantine', *DOP* 31 (1977), 1–26

Naissance d'une capitale (Paris, 1974)

Dassmann, E., 'Ambrosius und die Märtyrer', *JAC* 18 (1975), 49–68

Daut, W., 'Die "halben Christen" unter den Konvertiten und Gebildeten des 4. und 5. Jahrhunderts', *ZMR* 55 (1971), 171–88

Deichmann, F. W., 'Frühchristliche Kirchen in antiken Heiligtümern', *Jahrbuch des deutschen archäologischen Instituts* 54 (1939), 105–36; repr. in his *Rom, Ravenna*, 56–94. References given to original

'Märtyrerbasilika, Martyrion, Memoria und Altargrab', *Römische Mitteilungen* 77 (1970), 144–69, repr. in his *Rom, Ravenna*, 375–400

Rom, Ravenna, Konstantinopel, Naher Osten (Wiesbaden, 1982)

Delehaye, H., 'Loca sanctorum', *Analecta Bollandiana* 48 (1930), 5–64

Les origines du culte des martyrs (Subsidia hagiographica, 20. Brussels, 1933)

Sanctus. Essai sur le culte des saints dans l'Antiquité (Brussels, 1927)

De Waal, E., *Seeking God. The way of St Benedict* (London, 1984)

Dihle, A., 'Zur spätantiken Kultfrömmigkeit', in *Pietas: Festschrift für Bernhard Kötting* (*JAC* Erg. Bd. 8 (1980), 39–54)

Doblehoffer, E. R., *R. Cl. Namatianus. De reditu suo*, herausgegeben von E. R. Doblehoffer (Heidelberg, 1972)

Dodds, E. R., *Pagan and Christian in an age of anxiety* (Cambridge, 1965)

Dölger, F. J., *Sol salutis. Gebet und Gesang im christlichen Altertum, mit besonderer Rücksicht auf die Ostung in Gebet und Liturgie* (Münster, 1925)

'Das Sonnengleichnis in einer Weinachtspredigt des Bischof Zeno von Verona. Christus als wahre und ewige Sonne', *Antike und Christentum* 6 (1950), 1–26

Dupront, A., 'Pélérinage et lieux sacrés', in *Méthodologies de l'histoire et des sciences humaines. Mélanges en l'honneur de Fernand Braudel*, vol. II (Toulouse, 1973), 189–206

Durán, D., *Book of the gods and rites* and *The ancient calendar,* by Fray Diego Durán, trans. and ed. by F. Horcasitas and D. Heyden (Norman, Okla., 1971)

Duval, Y. M., 'Des Lupercales de Constantinople aux Lupercales de Rome', *REL* 55 (1977), 222–70

'Pélage est-il le censeur inconnu de l'*Adversus Iovinianum* à Rome en 393? ou: du "portrait-robot" de l'hérétique chez S. Jérome', *RHE* 75 (1980), 525–57

'Saint Cyprien et le roi de Ninivé dans l'*In Ionam* de Jérôme', in *Epektasis,* 551–70

Eck, W., 'Das Episkopat im spätantiken Africa', *HZ* 236 (1983), 265–95

Emery, P. Y., *L'unité des croyants au ciel et la terre* (Paris, 1962; English trans. 1966)

Epektasis, ed. J. Fontaine and C. Kannengiesser (Paris, 1972)

Erdt, W., *Christentum und heidnisch-antike Bildung bei Paulin von Nola* (Beiträge zur klassischen Philologie, 82. Meisenheim, 1976)

Evans, R. F., *One and holy* (London, 1972)

'Pelagius, Fastidius, and the pseudo-Augustinian *De vita christiana*', *JThS* n.s. 13 (1962), 72–98

Pelagius: inquiries and reappraisals (London, 1968)

La fête, pratique et discours (Annales littéraires de l'Université de Besançon, 262. 1981)

Février, P. A., 'Approches de fêtes chrétiennes (fin du IVe et Ve s.)', in *La fête, pratique et discours,* 149–64

'Permanence et héritage de l'antiquité dans la topographie des villes de l'Occident durant le Haut Moyen Age', *Settimane* 21 (1971), 41–138

'La tombe chrétienne et l'au delà', in *Le temps chrétien,* 163–83

'Vetera et nova: le poids du passé, les germes de l'avenir, iiie–ive siècle', in *La ville antique,* ed. G. Duby, *Histoire de la France urbaine,* vol. I (Paris, 1981), 399–493

Fontaine, J., 'Valeurs antiques et valeurs chrétiennes dans la spiritualité des grands propriétaires terriens à la fin du IVe siècle occidental', *Epektasis,* 571–95

(ed. and trans.), *Sulpice Sévère, Vie de Saint Martin* 3 vols. (Paris, 1967–9)

Foucault, M., *L'usage des plaisirs* (*Histoire de la sexualité,* vol. II. Paris, 1984)

Fowden, G., 'Bishops and temples in the eastern Roman Empire, A.D. 320–435', *JThS* n.s. 29 (1978), 53–78

'The pagan holy man in late antique society', *JHS* 102 (1982), 33–59

Fox, R. L., *Pagans and Christians* (Harmondsworh, 1986)

Frank, K. S., 'Vita apostolica: Ansätze zur apostolischen Lebensform in der alten Kirche', *ZKG* 82 (1971), 145–66

Secondary literature

Fredriksen, P., *Augustine on Romans. Propositions from the Epistle to the Romans; Unfinished commentary on the Epistle to the Romans*, ed. and trans. Paula Fredriksen Landes (Texts and Translations, 23. Chico, Calif., 1982)

'Beyond the body–soul dichotomy: Augustine on Paul against the Manichees and the Pelagians', *RechAug* 23 (1988), 87–114

'Paul and Augustine: conversion narratives, orthodox traditions and the retrospective self', *JThS* n.s. 37 (1986), 3–34

'Tyconius and the end of the world', *REAug* 28 (1982), 59–75

Frend, W. H. C., 'Paulinus of Nola and the last century of the Western Empire', *JRS* 59 (1969), 1–11

Freund, W. *Modernus und andere Zeitbegriffe des Mittelalters* (Neue Münstersche Beiträge zur Geschichtsforschung, 4. Cologne and Graz, 1957)

Geertz, C., 'Religion as a cultural system', in his *The interpretation of cultures* (New York, 1973), 87–125

'Ritual and social change: a Javanese example', in his *The interpretation of cultures*, 142–69

Geffcken, J., *The last days of Greco-Roman paganism*, trans. S. MacCormack (Amsterdam, 1978)

Goodman, N., *Ways of worldmaking* (Hassocks, 1978)

Gregory, T. E., 'The survival of paganism in Christian Greece', *AJP* 107 (1986), 229–42

Greshake, G., *Gnade als konkrete Freiheit: eine Untersuchung zur Gnadenlehre des Pelagius* (Mainz, 1972)

Gross, J. *Entstehungsgeschichte des Erbsündendogmas*, vol. I (Munich and Basle, 1960)

Guignebert, C., 'Les demi-chrétiens et leur place dans l'Eglise antique', *RHR* 83 (1923), 65–102

Guillaumont, A., 'La conception du désert chez les moines d'Egypte', *RHR* 188 (1975), 3–21

Guillaumont, A. and C. Guillaumont, *Evagre le Pontique, Traité pratique ou le moine* 2 vols. (SC 170–1. Paris, 1963)

Hadot, P., *Marius Victorinus. Recherches sur sa vie et ses oeuvres* (Paris, 1971)

Haight, R., *The experience and language of grace* (Dublin, 1979)

Haller, W., *Iovinianus* (TU 17/2. Berlin, 1897)

Halporn, J. W., 'Saint Augustine Sermon 104 and the epulae venerales', *JAC* 19 (1976), 82–108

Harl, M., 'La dénonciation des festivités profanes dans le discours episcopal et monastique en Orient chrétien à la fin du IVe siècle', in *La fête, pratique et discours*, 123–47

Harnack, A. von, *History of dogma*, vol. III (English trans., London, 1897)

Militia Christi (Tübingen, 1905)

Das Mönchtum: *seine Idee und seine Geschichte* (Giessen, 1881)

Heinzelmann, M., *Bischofsherrschaft in Gallien* (Beihefte der Francia, 5. Munich, 1976)

Heussi, K., *Der Ursprung des Mönchtums* (Tübingen, 1936)

Honoré, T., *Tribonian* (London, 1978)

Hunt, E. D., *Holy Land pilgrimage in the Later Roman Empire*, *A.D.* 312–460 (Oxford, 1982)

Hunter, D. G., 'Resistance to the virginal ideal in late fourth century Rome: the case of Jovinian', *TS* 48 (1987), 45–64

(ed. and trans.), *A comparison between a king and a monk/Against the opponents of the monastic life. Two treatises by John Chrysostom* (Lewiston, N.Y.; Queenstown, Ont.; Lampeter, 1989)

Huskinson, J. M., *Concordia apostolorum: Christian propaganda at Rome in the fourth and fifth centuries* (BAR Int. ser., 148. Oxford, 1982)

Judge, E. A., 'The earliest use of the word "monachos" for monk (P. Coll. Youtie 77)', *JAC* 20 (1977), 72–89

Jürgens, H., *Pompa diaboli. Die lateinischen Kirchenväter und das antike Theater* (Tübinger Beiträge zur Altertumswissenschaft, 46. Stuttgart, 1972)

Kahl, H.-D., 'Die ersten Jahrhunderte des Missionsgeschichtlichen Mittelalters', *Kirchengeschichte als Missionsgeschichte*, vol. II/1, 11–76

Kantorowicz, E. H., '*Puer exoriens*: On the Hypapante mosaics of S. Maria Maggiore', in *Perennitas: Beiträge zur christlichen Archäologie und Kunst, P. Th. Michels zum 70. Geburtstag*, ed. H. Rahner and E. von Severus (Münster, 1963), 118–35; repr. in his *Selected studies* (New York, 1955), 25–36

Kelly, J. N. D., *Jerome: his life, writings and controversies* (London, 1975).

Kennedy, H., 'From *polis* to *madina*: urban change in Late Antique and early Islamic Syria', *Past and Present* 106 (1985), 3–27

Kirchengeschichte als Missionsgeschichte, vol. I, ed. H. Frohnes and U. W. Knorr (Munich, 1974); vol. II/1, ed. K. Schäferdiek (Munich, 1978)

Klauser, T., 'Der Festkalender der alten Kirche im Spannungsfeld jüdischer Tradition, christlicher Glaubensvorstellungen und missionarischen Anpassungswillens', *Kirchengeschichte als Missionsgeschichte*, vol. I, 377–88

König, D., *Amt und Askese: Priesteramt und Mönchtum bei den lateinischen Kirchenvätern in vorbenediktinischer Zeit* (Regulae Benedicti Studia, Supplementa, 12. St Ottilien, 1985)

Kötting, B., *Der frühchristliche Reliquienkult und die Bestattung im Kirchengebäude* (Arbeitsgemeinschaft für Forschung des Landes Nordrhein-Westfalen, Geisteswissenschaften, 123. Cologne and Opladen, 1965)

Secondary literature

'Reliquienverehrung, ihre Entstehung und ihre Formen', *Trierer theologische Zeitschrift*, 67 (1958), 321–35

Krautheimer, R., 'The architecture of Sixtus III: a fifth century renaissance?' in *De artibus opuscula XL*, ed. M. Meiss (Princeton, N.J., 1961), 291–302; repr. in his *Studies in early Christian, medieval and Renaissance art* (New York, 1969), 181–96

Rome: profile of a city (Princeton, N.J., 1980)

Three Christian capitals: topography and politics (Berkeley, Calif., 1983)

Kuhn, H., 'Das Fortleben des germanischen Heidentums nach der Christianisierung', *Settimane* 12 (1966), 743–57; 787–91

La Bonnardière, A.-M., 'Les "Enarrationes in Psalmos" prêchées par saint Augustin à Carthage en décembre 409', *RechAug* 11 (1976), 52–90

'Marthe et Marie figures de l'Eglise d'après saint Augustin', *Vie spirituelle* 86 (1952), 404–27

Lamirande, E., 'La signification de "christianus" dans la théologie de saint Augustin et la tradition ancienne', *REAug* 9 (1963), 221–34

Landes, R., 'Lest the millennium be fulfilled: apocalyptic expectations and the pattern of Western chronography 100–800 CE', in *The use and abuse of eschatology in the Middle Ages* (Leuven, 1988), 137–211

Lawless, G., *Augustine of Hippo and his monastic rule* (Oxford, 1987)

Le Goff, J., 'Culture cléricale et traditions folkloriques dans la civilisation mérovingienne', *Annales économies, sociétés, cultures* 22 (1967), 780–91; English trans. in his *Time, work and culture in medieval Europe* (Chicago, 1980), 153–8

Leipoldt, J., 'Griechische Philosophie und früchristliche Askese' (Berichte über die Verhandlungen der sächsischen Akademie der Wissenschaften, Leipzig; Philosophische–Historische Klasse, 106/4. Berlin, 1961)

Leonardi, C., 'Alle origini della cristianità medievale: Giovanni Cassiano e Salviano di Massiglia', *Studi medievali* 18 (1977), 491–608

Lepelley, C., *Les cités de l'Afrique romaine au Bas-Empire*, vol. I (Paris, 1979)

'Léon le Grand et la cité romaine', *RevSR* 35 (1962), 130–50

'Saint Augustin et la cité romano-africaine', in *Jean Chrysostome et Augustin*, ed. C. Kannengiesser (Paris, 1975), 13–39

Les lettres de saint Augustin découvertes par Johannes Divjak (Paris, 1983)

Liebeschuetz, W., 'Pelagian evidence on the last period of Roman Britain', *Latomus* 26 (1967), 436–47

Lienhard, J. T., *Paulinus of Nola and early Western monasticism* (Theophaneia, 28. Cologne and Bonn, 1977)

Lieu, S. N. C., *Manichaeism in the later Roman Empire and medieval China: a historical survey* (Manchester, 1985)

Lods, M., *Confesseurs et martyrs* (Cahiers théologiques. Neuchâtel and Paris, 1958)

Lorenz, R., 'Die Anfänge des abendländischen Mönchtums im 4. Jahrhundert', *ZKG* 77 (1966), 1–61

McCabe, H., *God matters* (London, 1987)

McCulloch, J. M., 'From Antiquity to the Middle Ages: continuity and change in papal relic policy from the sixth to the eighth century', in *Pietas: Festschrift für Bernhard Kötting* (*JAC* Erg. Bd. 8 (1980), 313–24)

MacIntyre, A., *After virtue: a study in moral theory* (London, 1981)
Whose justice? Which rationality? (London, 1988)

MacMullen, R., *Christianizing the Roman Empire* (New Haven, 1984)
'Conversion: a historian's view', *The Second Century* 5 (1985/6), 67–81
Paganism in the Roman Empire (New Haven, 1981)
'What difference did Christianity make?' *Historia* 35 (1986), 322–43

McShane, P. A., *La romanitas et le pape Léon le Grand* (Tournai and Montreal, 1979)

Madec, G., *Saint Ambroise et la philosophie* (Paris, 1974)

Malone, E. A., *The monk and the martyr* (Catholic University of America, Studies in Christian Antiquity, 12. Washington, 1950)

Mandouze, A., *Saint Augustin. L'aventure de la raison et de la grâce* (Paris, 1968)

Markus, R. A., 'Alienatio: philosophy and eschatology in the development of an Augustinian idea', *StPatr* 9 (TU 94. Berlin, 1966) 431–50
Christianity in the Roman world (London, 1974)
'Church history and the early Church historians', *SCH* 11 (1975), 1–17; repr. in Markus, *From Augustine to Gregory the Great*, II
Conversion and disenchantment in Augustine's spiritual career (Villanova, Pa., 1989)
From Augustine to Gregory the Great: history and Christianity in Late Antiquity (Collected studies. London, 1983)
'From Caesarius to Boniface: Christianity and paganism in Gaul', in *The seventh century: change and continuity*, ed. J. Fontaine and J. N. Hillgarth. Forthcoming.
'Gregory the Great's Europe', *Transactions of the Royal Historical Society*, 5th ser. 31 (1981), 21–36; repr. in Markus, *From Augustine to Gregory the Great*, XV
'The legacy of Pelagius: orthodoxy, heresy and conciliation', in *The making of orthodoxy*, ed. R. D. Williams (Cambridge, 1989), 214–34
'La politica ecclesiastica di Giustiniano e la chiesa d'Occidente', in *Il mondo del diritto nell'epoca giustinianea: caratteri e problematiche*, ed. G. G. Archi (Ravenna, 1985), 113–24

'Manicheism revisited: Augustine's *Confessions* and the controversy with Julian'. *Collectanea Augustiana: Mélanges T. J. Van Bavel* (Leuven, 1990), 913–25

'Marius Victorinus and Augustine', Pt V of *Cambridge history of later Greek and early medieval philosophy*, ed. A. H. Armstrong (Cambridge, 1967), 331–421

'Paganism, Christianity and the Latin classics', in *Latin literature of the fourth century*, ed. J. W. Binns (London, 1974), 1–21; repr. in Markus, *From Augustine to Gregory the Great*, V

'The problem of self-definition: from sect to Church', in *Jewish and Christian self-definition*, vol. I, ed. E. P. Sanders (London, 1980), 1–15; 217–19; repr. in Markus, *From Augustine to Gregory the Great*, I

'The sacred and the secular: from Augustine to Gregory the Great', *JThS* n.s. 36 (1985), 84–96

Saeculum: History and society in the theology of saint Augustine (Cambridge, 1970; 2nd edn 1989)

Marrou, H.-I., 'Les attaches orientales du pélagianisme', *CRAI* (1968), 459–72

'Autour de la bibliothèque du pape Agapit', *MAH* 48 (1937), 124–69

Mousikos aner: Etude sur les scènes de la vie intellectuelle figurant sur les monuments funéraires romains (Bibliothèque de l'Institut Français de Naples, I/4. Grenoble, 1938; repr. Rome, 1964)

'La place du Haut Moyen Age dans l'histoire du christianisme', *Settimane* 9 (1962), 595–630

The Resurrection and Saint Augustine's theology of human values (The Saint Augustine Lecture, 1964. Villanova, 1966); = 'Le dogme de la résurrection des corps et la théologie des valeurs humaines selon l'enseignement de saint Augustin', *REAug* 12 (1966), 111–36

Marsili, S., *Giovanni Cassiano ed Evagrio Pontico* (Studia Anselmiana, 5. Rome, 1936)

Meredith, A., 'Asceticism – Christian and Greek', *JThS* n.s. 27 (1976), 313–32.

Meslin, M., *La fête des kalendes de janvier dans l'empire romain* (Collection Latomus, 115. Brussels, 1970)

Momigliano, A. D., 'Popular religious beliefs and the Roman historians', *SCH* 8 (1972), 1–18

'Time in ancient historiography', *History and Theory*, Beiheft 6 (1966), 1–23

Moorhead, J. A., 'Adam and Eve and the discovery of sex', *Parergon* n.s. 1 (1983), 1–12

Morard, F.-E., 'Monachos, moine: histoire du terme grec jusqu'au 4ᵉ siècle', *Freiburger Zeitschrift für Philosophie und Theologie* 20 (1973), 329–425

Morin, G. 'Arnobe le Jeune', in his *Etudes, textes, découvertes* (Maredsous and Paris, 1913), 309–439

Murray, A., 'Peter Brown and the shadow of Constantine', *JRS* 73 (1983), 191–203

Musurillo, H., 'The problem of ascetical fasting in the Greek patristic writers', *Traditio* 12 (1956), 1–64

Mutzenbecher, A., 'Der Festinhalt von Weihnachten und Epiphanie in den echten Serm. des Maximus von Turin', *StPatr* 5 (TU 80. Berlin, 1962), 109–16

Natali, A., 'Tradition ludique et sociabilité dans la pratique religieuse à Antioche', *StPatr* 16 (TU 129. Berlin, 1958), 463–70

Nautin, P., 'Felix III', *DHGE* 16 (1967), 889–95

Niebuhr, H. R., *Christ and culture* (London, 1952)

Nock, A. D., *Conversion: the old and the new in religion from Alexander the Great to Augustine of Hippo* (Oxford, 1933)

Nuvolone, F. G., 'Pélage et Pélagianisme', *DSp* 12 (1986), 2889–942.

O'Daly, G. J. P., and L. Verheijen, '*Actio – contemplatio*', *Augustinus-Lexikon*, vol. I (Basle and Stuttgart, 1986), 58–63

O'Donnell, J. J., *Cassiodorus* (Berkeley, Calif., 1979)

'The demise of paganism', *Traditio* 35 (1979), 45–88

Olphe-Galliard, M., 'Vie contemplative et vie active d'après Cassien', *RAM* 16 (1935), 252–88

Parente, F., 'L'idea di conversione da Nock ad oggi', *Augustinianum* 27 (1987), 7–25

Patlagean, E., *Pauvreté économique et pauvreté sociale* (Paris, 1977)

Perler, O., *Les voyages de Saint Augustin* (Paris, 1969)

Peterson, E., *Das Buch von den Engeln*, 2nd edn (Munich, 1955)

Pietri, C., 'Aristocratie et société cléricale dans l'Italie chrétienne au temps d'Odoacre et de Théodoric', *MAH* 93 (1981), 417–67

'Concordia apostolorum et renovatio urbis', *MAH* 73 (1961), 275–322

Roma christiana. Recherches sur l'Eglise de Rome, son organisation, sa politique, son idéologie de Miltiade à Sixte III (311–440), 2 vols (BEFAR 224. Rome and Paris, 1976)

'Le temps de la semaine à Rome et dans l'Italie chrétienne, (IV–VIe s.)', in *Le temps chrétien*, 64–97

Pietri, L., *La ville de Tours du IVe au VIe siècle: naissance d'une cité chrétienne* (CEFR 69. Rome, 1983)

Plinval, G. de, *Pélage: ses écrits, sa vie, sa réforme* (Paris, 1943)

Plumpe, J. C., 'Pomeriana', *VC* 1 (1947), 227–39

Pomarès, G., *Gélase Ier: Lettre contre les Lupercales et dix-huit messes du Sacramentaire Léonien* (SC 65. Paris, 1959)

Prendiville, J. G., 'The development of the idea of habit in the thought of Saint Augustine', *Traditio* 28 (1972), 29–99

Secondary literature

Pricoco, S., *L'isola dei santi. Il cenobio di Lerino e le origini del monachesimo Gallico* (Rome, 1978)

Prinz, F., *Askese und Kultur* (Munich, 1980)

Frühes Mönchtum im Frankenreich (Munich and Vienna, 1965)

Rambo, L. R., 'Current research on religious conversion', *Religious Studies Review* 8 (1982), 146–59

Ranger, T., 'Taking hold of the land: holy places and pilgrimages in twentieth century Zimbabwe', *Past and Present* 117 (1987), 158–94

Rief, J., *Der Ordobegriff des jungen Augustinus* (Abhandlungen zur Moraltheologie. Paderborn, 1962)

Riggi, C., 'Il cristianesimo di Ausonio', *Salesianum* 30 (1968), 642–95

Rondet, H., 'Essais sur la chronologie des "Enarrationes in Psalmos" de saint Augustin', *Bulletin de littérature ecclésiastique* 61 (1960), 117–217; 258–68; 65 (1964), 11–136; 68 (1967), 180–202; 71 (1970), 174–200; 75 (1974), 161–8; 77 (1976), 99–118

Rordorf, W., 'Aux origines du culte des martyrs chrétiens', in *Forma futuri. Studi in onore del Cardinale Michele Pellegrino* (Turin, 1975), 445–61; repr. in his *Liturgie, foi et vie*, 363–79.

Liturgie, foi et vie des premiers chrétiens. Etudes patristiques (Théologie historique, 75. Paris, 1986)

Der Sonntag. Geschichte des Ruhe- und Gottesdiensttages im ältesten Christentum (Zürich, 1962)

Rousseau, P., *Ascetics, authority and the Church in the age of Jerome and Cassian* (Oxford, 1978)

'Cassian, contemplation and the coenobitic life', *JEH* 26 (1975), 113–26

'In search of Sidonius the bishop', *Historia* 25 (1976), 356–77

'The spiritual authority of the "monk–bishop": Eastern elements in some Western hagiography of the fourth and fifth centuries', *JThS* n.s. 22 (1971), 380–419

Rousselle, A., *Porneia: de la maîtrise du corps à la déprivation sensorielle, IIe–IVe siècles de l'ère chrétienne* (Paris, 1983)

Sage, A., *La vie religieuse selon saint Augustin* (Paris, 1972) (Ch. IV 'La contemplation dans les communautés de vie fraternelle', *RechAug* 7 (1971), 245–302)

Salomonson, J. W., *Voluptatem spectandi non perdat sed mutat: observations sur l'iconographie du martyre en Afrique romaine* (Koninklijke Nederlandse Akademie van Wetenschappen. Verhandelingen Afdeling Letterkunde, N.R. 98. Amsterdam, 1979)

Sanders, E. P., ed., *Jewish and Christian self-definition*, vol. I (London, 1980)

Saxer, V., *Morts, martyrs, reliques en Afrique chrétienne aux premiers siècles* (Théologie historique, 55. Paris, 1980)

Schindler, A., 'Sur l'attitude des Donatistes envers le temps', in *Le temps chrétien*, 143–7

Secondary literature

Schmitt, E., *Le mariage chrétien dans l'oeuvre de Saint Augustin. Une théologie de la vie conjugale* (Paris, 1983)

Schmitt, J.-C., '"Religion populaire" et culture folklorique', *Annales économies, sociétés, cultures* 31 (1976), 941–53

Schöllgen, G., *Ecclesia sordida?: zur Frage der sozialen Schichtung frühchristlicher Gemeinden am Beispiel Karthagos zur Zeit Tertullians* (*JAC* Erg. Bd. 12 (1984))

Séguy, J., 'Une sociologie des sociétés imaginées: monachisme et utopie', *Annales économies, sociétés, cultures* 26 (1971), 328–54

Settimane di studio del Centro di Studi sull'Alto Medioevo, Spoleto

Shaw, B. C., 'The family in Late Antiquity: the experience of Augustine', *Past and Present* 115 (1987), 3–51

Shils, E., *The centre and the periphery* (Chicago, 1972)

Sicard, D., *La liturgie de la mort dans l'Eglise latine des origines à la réforme carolingienne* (Liturgiewissenschaftliche Quellen und Forschungen, 63. Münster, 1978)

Smith, J. Z., *Map is not territory: studies in the history of religion* (Leiden, 1978)

Snow, D. A., and R. Machalek, 'The sociology of conversion', *Annual Review of Sociology* 10 (1984), 167–90

Solignac, A., 'Julien Pomère', *DSp* 8 (1974), 1594–600

Solin, H., and H. Brandenburg, 'Paganer Fruchtbarkeitsritus oder Martyriumsdarstellung? Zum Grabrelief der Elia Afanacia im Museum der Prätextat-Katakombe zu Rom', *Archäologischer Anzeiger* (1980), 271–84

Sottocornola, F., *L'Anno liturgico nei sermoni di Pietro Crisologo. Ricerca storico-critica sulla liturgia di Ravenna antica* (Cesena, 1973)

Stancliffe, C., *St. Martin and his hagiographer* (Oxford, 1983)

Stern, H., *Le Calendrier de 354* (Institut Français d'Archéologie de Beyrouth., Bibliothèque archéologique et historique, 55. Paris, 1953)

Strathmann, H. and P. Keseling, 'Askese', *RAC* 1 (1950), 749–95

Tedlock, B., *Time and the highland Maya* (Albuquerque, N. Mex., 1982)

Le temps chrétien de la fin de l'Antiquité au Moyen Age (Colloques Internationales du Centre National de Recherche Scientifique, 604. Paris, 1981)

Thébert, Y., 'Vie privée et architecture domestique en Afrique romaine', in *Histoire de la vie privée*, ed. P. Veyne, vol. I (Paris, 1985), 301–97

Thonnard, F. J., 'La notion de concupiscence chez saint Augustin', *RechAug* 3 (1965), 59–105

Tibiletti, C., 'La teologia della grazia in Giuliano Pomerio: alle origini dell'agostinismo provenzale', *Augustinianum* 25 (1985), 489–506

'Teologia pelagiana su celibato/matrimonio', *Augustinianum* 27 (1987), 487–507

Secondary literature

Tsafrir, Y., 'The maps used by Theodosius: on the pilgrim maps of the Holy Land and Jerusalem in the sixth century CE', *DOP* 40 (1986), 129–45

Turner, V., 'Variations on a theme of liminality', in *Secular ritual*, ed. S. F. Moore and B. G. Myerhoff (Assen and Amsterdam, 1977), 36–52

Valli, F. *Gioviniano* (Urbino, 1953)

Van Dam, R., *Leadership and community in late antique Gaul* (Berkeley, Calif., 1985)

Van der Meer, F. *Augustine the bishop* (English trans. London, 1961)

Van Enghen, J., 'The Christian Middle Ages as an historiographical problem', *AHR* 91 (1986), 519–52

Verheijen, L., 'Saint Augustin', in *Théologie de la vie monastique* (Théologie, 49. Lyon, 1961), 201–12

'Spiritualité et vie monastique chez saint Augustin. L'utilisation monastique des Actes des Apôtres 4, 31, 32–35 dans son oeuvre', in *Jean Chrysostome et Augustin*, ed. C. Kannengiesser (Paris, 1975), 83–123

Vessey, J. M., 'Ideas of Christian writing in Late Roman Gaul', unpublished Oxford D.Phil. thesis, 1988)

Veyne, P., *Le pain et le cirque* (Paris, 1976)

Violante, C. and C. D. Fonseca, 'Ubicazione e dedicazione delle cattedrali dalle origini al periodo romanico nelle città dell'Italia centro-settentrionale', in *Il romanico pistoiese nei suoi rapporti con l'arte romanica dell'Oriente* (Atti del I Convegno internazionale di studi medioevali di storia e d'arte. Pistoia, 1966), 303–52, and plans

Vogüé, A. de, 'Monachisme et église dans la pensée de Cassien', in *Théologie de la vie monastique* (Théologie, 49. Lyon, 1961), 213–40

La Règle de saint Benoît, vol. VII (Paris, 1977)

Les Règles des Saints Pères (Paris, 1982)

Waddell, H. *The wandering scholars* (Pelican edn, Harmondsworth, 1954)

Wallace-Hadrill, J. M., *The Frankish Church* (Oxford, 1983)

Walsh, P. G., 'Paulinus of Nola and the conflict of ideologies in the fourth century', in *Kyriakon: Festschrift für Johannes Quasten*, ed. P. Granfield and J. A. Jungmann, vol. II (Münster, 1970), 565–71

Ward-Perkins, B., *From classical antiquity to the Middle Ages. Urban public building in Northern and Central Italy, AD 300–800* (Oxford, 1984)

Weismann, W., *Kirche und Schauspiele. Die Schauspiele im Urteil der lateinischen Kirchenväter unter besonderer Berücksichtigung von Augustin* (Würzburg, 1972)

Weitzmann, K., '*Loca sancta* and the representational arts of Palestine', *DOP* 28 (1974), 31–55

Wilken, R. L., 'Heiliges Land', *TRE* 14 (1985), 684–94

John Chrysostom and the Jews (Berkeley, Calif., 1983)

Williams, R. D., *Arius: heresy and tradition* (London, 1987)

Secondary literature

Workman, H. B., *The evolution of the monastic ideal from the earliest times down to the coming of the friars* (London, 1913)

Zerubavel, E., 'Easter and Passover: on calendars and group identity', *American Sociological Review* 47 (1982), 284–9

Zumkeller, A. *Das Mönchtum des heiligen Augustinus* (Würzburg, 1950; 2nd edn 1968; English trans. New York, 1986)

Index

Abraham, abbot, 192–3
active life, *see* contemplation
Ad Diognetum, 100
Adam, 51, 58, 59, 61
    see also Fall, the
Africa, -n, 41, 51, 58–9, 63, 73, 92, 117,
    125, 142, 148, 149, 169, 171, 173, 213,
    214–16, 218, 222, 223
Agapetus I, pope, 217
ages of the world, 88
Agrigentum, 154
Alexandria, 27, 69, 166
alms, 127–9
altar, 145, 147–8
Ambrose, St, 19, 34, 35, 36, 40, 47, 48, 49,
    60, 62, 71, 76, 82, 104, 130, 143–5,
    149, 204
'Ambrosiaster', 32, 59, 83
anchorites, *see* monasticism
Andresen, C., 110
angels, 21, 22, 97, 99
Angenendt, A., 6
Anglo-Saxons, 155
animals, cruelty to, 120
Antioch, 118, 119, 120, 210, 227–8
Antiochene exegesis, 59
Antony, St, 47, 69, 74
Apollinarian games, 128, 129, 217
Apostles, -olic, 98, 125–7, 144, 165–7
    see also Peter and Paul, SS,
Aquitaine, 171
architecture: of churches, 125–6
Arian, -s, 214
aristocrat, -s, -ic, 28–31, 41–2, 126, 132–3,
    171, 199–201, 214, 216–17, 223
Aristotle, 73, 216
Arles, 160, 172, 177–9, 194, 202, 204, 208
Armstrong, A. H., 49
Arnobius, the Younger, 71, 82

ascetic, -s, -ism, 34–43, 49, 63–83, 157–79,
    181–5, 191, 197, 199–208, 213–14,
    222, 226
Athanasius, St, 69, 74
Athens, 27, 140
Attila, 126
Augustine, St, of Hippo, 8, 19, 29–30, 32,
    33, 34, 40, 42–3, 45–62, 76–83, 85, 89,
    102, 108, 132, 134, 139–40, 157–8,
    164, 171, 172, 173–7, 177–8, 204–5,
    208, 214, 215, 221, 222, 223, 225, 226,
    227
conversion of, 47–8, 73
on active and contemplative life, 186–7,
    189–90
on City of God, heavenly City, two Cities,
    79, 97, 174–6
on cult of martyrs, 93–4, 97–9
on Genesis, 51, 57–8
on grace, 63–5, 77
on institutions, 112, 121
on Manicheism, 62, 159
on marriage, 45–6, 50–62, 159
on martyrdom, 71
on monasticism, 63–6, 76–83, 158–62,
    164, 167–8, 182, 195–6, 202
on music, 111
on names of week-days, 131
on nature and miracles, 149
on obedience, 162–4
on order, 48–51, 62
on Pelagianism, 51–2
on pride, 51, 78
on property, 78
on prophecy, 87–8
on relics, 93–4, 148
on sexuality, 57–62, 76, 159
on shows, 110–23, 173–4
on sin, 50–1

Index

on the Church, 22, 52–5, 79–80, 97, 175–7
on virginity, 50, 57
spiritual development of, 46–52, 55–62, 149
Augustus, emperor, 87
Ausonius, 33–6
autarkeia, 73
Auxerre, Council of, 209
Avitus, bishop of Vienne, 150
Babcock, W. S., 5
Badewien, J., 173
Badot, P., 171
Banniard, M., 210
banquets, 112–15, 119
  see also shows
baptism, 53–4, 172, 205
Barnes, T. D., 25, 70, 91
Barnish, S. J. B., 150, 217, 220
Basil, St, of Caesarea, -ian, 66, 75, 158, 182
  see also Cappadocian Fathers
Basil of Ancyra, 82
Baus, K., 110
Baynes, N., 40
Beatrice, P. F., 59
Beck, H. G. J., 70, 143, 202
Bedouins, 4–5
Benedict, St, *Rule* of, 22, 71, 78, 164, 196–7
Berrouard, M. F., 61
Bible, reading of, 187–8, 190, 195, 203, 221–5
Bieler, L., 74
bishop(s), 91, 189, 190, 191, 194–7, 199–202, 207–9, 211, 214
body, the, 48–9, 62, 75, 81–2, 127
Boethius, 129, 216, 218, 219, 220, 221, 225
Bohlin, T., 56
Boniface, St, 208, 210, 211
Bonner, G., 33, 41, 52, 56, 61
Bowersock, G. W., 34
Brandenburg, H., 131
Brown, P. R. L., 12, 23, 25–6, 27, 40, 41, 53, 54, 57, 61, 81, 94, 108, 119, 131, 146, 151, 206, 228
Brown, T. S., 129, 218
Bulgars, 5
Bulla Regia, 115
Bullough, D. A., 146, 150
burials, 144–6, 147–8, 150, 152
  see also dead, cult of
Caesarius, St, of Arles, 70, 104, 140, 194, 195–6, 199, 202–8, 209, 210, 211, 213, 222
Calama, 115, 119, 223
calendars, 98–100, 102–3, 110, 131

Cameron, Alan, 33, 120, 121
Cameron, Averil, 222
Campenhausen, H. von, 71, 72
Candlemas, 134
Cappadocian Fathers, 49, 60
Cardman, F., 152
Carthage, 101, 110–23, 131, 132–3, 154, 171, 173, 215
  monks of, 159
Cassian, John, 19, 63, 67, 71, 160, 161–8, 177–9, 181–9, 190, 191–3, 196–7, 211, 213, 221–2, 223, 224
Cassiodorus, 216, 217–22
Cayré, F., 187
Celestine, I, pope, 200
celibacy, *see* virginity
Celsus, 100
cemeteries, *see* burials
ceremonies, *see* ritual
Cesa, M., 150
Chadwick, H., 38, 48, 63, 68, 100, 122, 216
Chadwick, O., 177–8, 185, 186
charisma, 25–6, 193, 201
  see also 'holy man'
chastity, *see* virginity
Chéné, J., 63
Chilperic, king, 210
'Christian times', 89–90
'christianisation', 6–9, 14, 16, 31
  of Roman society, 27–34, 89
'Christianity', meaning of, 1, 6–7, 15, 16, 19, 29, 36–43, 53, 55, 65, 108
Christmas, 103–6, 129
chronography, Christian, 141
Chrysologus, Peter, St, 104, 130, 217
Chrysostom, John, St, 19, 33, 69, 89, 104, 135, 227–8
Church, the, 21, 24, 51–5, 79–80, 90, 137, 146, 166–9, 174–7
Church historians, *see* ecclesiastical historians
Cicero, 23, 35, 73
circus, 104, 108, 120, 141, 150, 171–2, 207, 208, 210, 215–16, 217, 228
  see also shows
'civilisation', 13
Clark, E. A., 48, 58, 59, 185
Claudian, 33
Clement, of Alexandria, 71
coenobites, *see* monasticism
'collections', 128–30
  see also alms
'community', -ies, 21–3, 55, 61, 74, 77–81, 97, 137, 140, 146, 147, 157–77, 196–7
  civic and urban, 114–21, 125–35, 174, 200–4

252

monastic, 158–64, 182–3, 193–7
concupiscentia carnis, 60–1
Constantine, I, emperor, Constantinian, pre-, post-Constantinian, 16, 24–5, 27, 32, 69, 70, 81, 85, 89, 98, 102, 108, 137
Constantinople, 33, 134, 219, 223
  Council of, II (553), 218
contemplation, contemplative life, 68, 73–4, 182–92, 193–6
  see also theoria
conversion, 3, 4, 5–8, 9, 28, 29, 35–7
  see also 'christianisation'
Corycus, 139
Councils, Gallic, 208–9
  see also Auxerre, Mâcon, Tours
Courcelle, P., 29, 47, 164, 173
Cranz, F. E., 50
Crispinianus, 37
crusading, 72
Csányi, D. A., 187
Cullmann, O., 88
'culture', 2, 3, 6, 8, 13–16, 216–18
  aristocratic, 34–6
  literary, 30, 34, 203, 217
  secular, 27, 30, 31, 217–35
Cyprian, St, 99
Dagron, G., 141, 150
Damasus I, pope, 126
Dassmann, E., 144
Daut, W., 33
De Vogüé, *see* Vogüé, A. de
De Waal, E., 197
dead, cult of, 21–2, 24, 34, 99, 145–7
  see also burials
Deichmann, F. W., 147, 148, 154
Delehaye, H., 71, 99, 146
Demetrias, 41–2, 157–8
'de-secularisation', 16, 226
'Desert', 68, 157–79, 181–4, 194, 196–7, 199, 213
Devil, 62, 159, 160, 186, 197, 204, 207, 215, 228
diathesis, 164
  see also friendship
Didache, 100
Didascalia Apostolorum, 100
Dihle, A., 100
Diocletian, emperor, 91
Diospolis, Synod of, 51, 54
discourse, 16, 203, 222–6
Doblehoeffer, E. R., 33
Dodds, E. R., 81–2
Dölger, F. J., 103, 129
Donatist, -s, -ism, 51–3, 79, 85, 92–3, 148
Dupront, A., 151

Durán, Diego, 1-3
Duval, Y. M., 35, 40, 110, 131, 132, 134
East, turning to, 129
Easter, 98, 100
ecclesiastical historians, 91–2
Eck, W., 222
education, 15, 194–5, 217, 220–1
Egeria, 153
Egypt, -ian, 69, 75, 152, 159–60, 162, 165, 185, 188, 193, 205
Elia Afanasia, sarcophagus of, 131
Eligius, St, 210
Eliot, T. S. (quoted), 146
Elvira, Council of, 92, 107
Emery, P. Y., 21
emperors, Christian, 108–9, 110, 117
  see also Constantine, Theodosius, Valentinian III
encratite, 58
'enculturation', 3
Ennodius, 218, 220, 221
Epiphany, 130
'epistemological crisis', 50, 224
epitaphs, of bishops, 201
Erdt, W., 36
eschatology, eschaton, the end, 79–81, 87–90, 168, 175–6, 215
eucharist, -ic, 21–2, 98, 141, 145
Eucherius, St, 143, 160–2, 164, 177, 194, 213, 214
Eugendus, St, 196
Euladius, 177
Eusebius, of Caesarea, 32, 38, 40, 72, 74, 89–92, 166
'Eusebius Gallicanus', 143, 162, 164, 194
Evagrius of Pontus, 185
Evans, R. F., 40, 41, 42, 43, 51
Eve, *see* Adam
evil, 47
Facundus of Hermianae, 217
Fall, the, 51, 57, 61
  see also Adam
fasting, 68, 127–8, 167
Faustus of Riez, 67, 162, 194, 195, 200
Faustus the Manichee, 102
Felix St, 35
Felix III, pope, 131, 133
Ferrandus, 67
Ferreolus, 201
festivals, 2, 93, 97–106, 107–35,
Février, P. A., 21, 150
flesh, 60–2, 160, 176, 197, 204
  see also Devil
'folklorique', 11, 12, 14
Fonseca, C. D., 150
Fontaine, J., 35, 36, 71

Index

Foucault, M., 74
Fowden, G., 74, 113, 140
Fox, R. Lane, 139
Frank, S., 167
Franks, -ish, 208–11
Fredriksen, P., 50, 53, 57, 215
freedom, *see* grace
Frend, W. H. C., 35
Freud, 82
Freund, W., 219
Friday, 98
friendship, 80, 164
Fulgentius of Ruspe, 202, 214
Galicia, 104
games, *see* shows
Gaudentius, 92
Gaul, Gallic, 41, 63, 70, 94, 104, 143, 148,
    171–4, 177–9, 181, 192, 194–7, 199–
    211, 212, 213–14
Gaza, 22, 114, 146, 154
Geertz, C., 13
Geffcken, J., 14, 110
Geiseric, 126
Gelasius I, pope, 131, 133
'generation gap', 90–1
Gennadius of Marseille, 195
Germans, -ic, 3, 5, 8, 9, 208
Germanus, St, 202
Gervasius St, 143, 144
Gnostic, -s, 49, 82
Gospel, Fourth, 48
Goths, -ic, 171, 219, 220
grace, 54–7, 63–5
Graecus, 195
grapes, sour (spiritual), 190
Gregoria, 157
Gregory I, the Great, pope, 21, 71–2, 155,
    223–8
Gregory XIII, pope, 109
Gregory Nazianzen, St, 38, 85
    see also Cappadocian Fathers
Gregory of Nyssa, St, 60, 62, 154
    see also Cappadocian Fathers
Gregory of Tours, 22, 210
Gregory, T. E., 8, 154
Greshake, G., 53, 56
Gross, J., 61
Guignebert, C., 8, 33
Guillaumont, A., and C. Guillaumont, 165,
    185
habit, Augustine and Pelagius on, 54
Hadot, P., 28
Hadrumetum, 63–4
Haight, R., 56
'half-Christians', 8, 33, 109
Haller, W., 76

Halporn, J. W., 110, 111, 122
Harl, M., 135
Harnack, A. von, 7, 68, 69, 70, 71
Heinzelmann, M., 201
Helvidius, 39, 40
Hercules, statue of, 115, 116
heresy, 91
hermits, *see* monasticism
Heussi, K., 67, 68, 69
hierarchy: of beings, 48
    see also Neo-Platonism
Hilarion, 153
Hilary, bishop of Arles, 70, 90, 160–2, 177–
    8, 194, 199
Hilary of Poitiers, St, 204
Hilary, Sicilian bishop, 54
Hippo, 116, 119
hippodrome, *see* shows; circus
Hispellum, 32, 108
history, sacred, 87–92, 141
Holy Land, 41, 148, 152–4
'holy man, men', 23, 25–6, 67, 74, 139,
    193, 201, 213
    see also charisma
holy places, 139–55
Honoratus Antoninus, 215
Honoratus, bishop of Arles, 160–1, 164,
    177, 194, 199
Honoré, T., 218
Hopkins, G. M. (quoted), 204
humility, 158
    see also pride
Hunt, E. D., 41
Hunter, D. G., 76, 228
Huskinson, J. M., 125
Incarnation, the, 88
'inculturation', *see* enculturation
Indians, 1–3
innocence, sexual, 58
Innocent I, pope, 98
inspiration, 87
intellect, 48–9
Irenaeus, St, 58
Isidore of Seville, 72, 225
Isidore of Pelusium, 120
Italy, 213, 214, 216–25
Jacob of Seroug, 104
Jerome, St, 19, 30, 35, 36–41, 45–6, 48,
    59, 60, 62, 68, 71, 75, 76, 104, 145,
    148, 153, 157, 159, 163, 166
Jerusalem, 1, 27, 89, 152, 153
    see also Holy Land
Jews, -ish, Judaism, 1, 73, 92, 97, 100–1,
    103, 116, 140, 185
John of Ephesus, 210
John, abbot, 163, 182–4

Index

Jovinian, 39–42, 45–8, 59, 75–6, 159
Jovius, 36–7
Judaism, *see* Jews
Judge, E. A., 67
Julian, emperor, 30, 31, 89, 114
Julian of Eclanum, 55, 57, 62
Julianus Pomerius, 189–91, 205, 221
Jura, monasteries of: fathers of, 196, 213–14
Jürgens, H., 110
Justinian, emperor, 218, 219
Kahl, H.-D., 8
Kalends, of January, New Year, 14, 103–6, 129, 209, 211
Kantorowicz, E. H., 125
Kelly, J. N. D., 39, 41
Kennedy, H., 150
Keseling, P., 68
Klauser, T., 98, 99
König, D., 196, 214
Kötting, B., 21, 146, 148
koinobioi, 74
   see also monasticism; community
Krautheimer, R., 126, 143, 150
Kuhn, H., 9
La Bonnardière, A.-M., 118, 122, 123, 187
Lamirande, E., 53
Landes, R., 215
'last times', 88–90
Lawless, G., 78, 163, 167
Le Goff, J., 13
Leipoldt, J., 72
Leo I, pope, 71, 105, 118, 125–30, 133, 135, 162, 172, 217
Leonardi, C., 168
Leontius, 154
Lepelley, C., 119, 127, 222
Lerins, 160–2, 164, 168, 181, 194–6, 200, 202, 211, 213, 222
Leyser, C., 160
Libanius, 113
Licentius, 37
Liebeschuetz, J. H. W. G., 43
Lienhard, J. T., 36, 37, 39, 76
Lieu, S. N. C., 47, 48
literacy, 15, 203, 219–20
   see also education
Lods, M., 71
Lombards, 219
Lorenz, R., 63, 77, 78, 80, 83
Lupercalia, 131–5
Lupicinus, 213
lust, 61–2
   see also concupiscentia carnis
Lyon, 213
McCabe, H., 163

MacCormack, S. G., 154
McCulloch, J. M., 149
Machalek, R., 4
MacIntyre, A., 50, 197, 224
MacMullen, R., 5, 6, 7, 8, 28, 110
Mâcon, Council of, 8
McShane, P. A., 125
Madauros, 119, 223
Madec, G., 47
Maiouma, 109
Malone, E. A., 70
Mandouze, A., 8
Manichee, -s, -aean, 47, 49, 112, 127, 129, 159
Mark the Deacon, 22, 146, 154
Markus, R. A., 15, 27, 28, 47, 49, 50, 53, 54, 57, 62, 79, 88, 89, 91, 117, 121, 134, 149, 155, 175, 179, 208, 218, 222
marriage, 38, 46, 48, 82
Marrou, H.-I., 16, 42, 50, 74, 104, 217
Marseille, 162, 192
Marsili, S., 185
Martin, St, of Tours, 38, 71, 75, 187–8
Martin of Braga, 104, 209, 210
martyrs, 14, 24–5, 69–73, 75, 85, 90–5, 118
   cult of, 92, 94, 97–9, 118, 131, 142–50
   memoriae, 144–8, 149–51
Mary and Martha, 184, 186–7
   see also contemplation
material world, 49, 82
Maximus, bishop of Riez, 194
Maximus, bishop of Turin, 103, 104, 128, 130, 143
Maximus, of Madaura, 299
medicine, 207
Melania, the elder, 42
Melito, of Sardis, 58
Meredith, A., 75
Meslin, M., 103, 104, 110
Metz, 210
Milan, 29, 34, 48, 67, 143–5
militia, 70–1, 160, 193
Minucius Felix, 140
'modern', 219, 224
Momigliano, A. D., 13, 88
monachos, 67
monastic, -ism, monks, monasteries, 39–40, 63–83, 157–79, 181–3, 188, 192–3, 195–6, 214, 219–20, 223
Monica, 33–4
Montalambert, C. R. F., 69
Moorhead, J. A., 59
Morard, F.-E., 67
Morin, G., 82
Moses, 161
Moses, abbot, 183

255

Index

Murray, A., 12
Muses, man of, 74
Musurillo, H., 68
Mutzenbecher, A., 130
Narbonne, 172
Narcissus, 74
Natali, A., 118
Nautin, P., 131
Nectarius, 223
Neo-Platonic, -ism, 29, 48–50
New Year, see Kalends
Nicaea, Council of, 38, 90
Nicholas I, pope, 5, 7
Nicomachus Flavianus, 31
Niebuhr, H. R., 13
Nock, A. D., 4, 5
Nola, 35
Noricum, 173
Novatian, 101–2, 118
Nuvolone, F. G., 41
obedience, 162–4
O'Daly, G. J. P., 187
O'Donnell, J. J., 33, 219, 221
Olphe-Galliard, M., 184
Origen, 71, 100–1, 140, 185, 205
original sin, 56–7
   see also Fall, the
Orosius, 66, 68
Ostrogoths, 217
pagan, -s, -ism, 2, 16, 27–33, 102, 110,
   112–19, 134, 210
Pagan revival, 28, 30–2
'pagan survivals', 9, 14, 17, 103, 108–10,
   206–11
Palestine, 152
   see also Holy Land
Pammachius, 35
Pamphilus, 74
Paphnutius, confessor, 38
Paphnutius, abbot, 183, 186
Parente, F., 4
Paris, 210
Parousia, the, 88–90
   see also eschatology
'passionlessness', 186
Passover, 100
past, the, 24, 85, 90–5, 137, 141, 142, 147
   Roman, pagan, 32, 108
Patlagean, E., 118, 127
patronage, 170
Paul, St, 5, 48–51, 55, 64, 140
Paula, 153
Paulinus of Nola, 35–9, 75, 82, 153, 169
Pelagius, -ian, -ians, 19, 40–3, 45–6, 51–8,
   62, 63–5, 157, 158, 178
Peregrinatio Egeriae, 153

perfection, 41–3
Perler, O., 123
persecution, -s, 24, 70–2, 91
Peter and Paul, SS, 126, 154
   see also Apostles
Peterson, E., 21
Philo, 140, 166
philosopher, -s, -y, 73–5, 140
Pietri, C., 130, 133
Pietri, L., 154
pilgrim(s), -age, 151–4
Plato, -nic, -nism, 48, 49
   see also Neo–Platonism
Plinval, G. de, 27
Plotinus, 49
   see also Neo-Platonism
Plumpe, J. C., 189
Polybius, 107
Polycarp, 71
Pomarès, G., 133
Pomponius Mela, 139
Porphyry, bishop of Gaza, 154
Possidius, 77, 202
praktike, see theoria
Prendiville, J. C., 54
Pricoco S., 162, 165, 203, 213
Primuliacum, 39
Prinz, F., 67, 181
Priscillian, -ism, 38
'privacy', 'private', 51, 78–9
Proba, Faltonia Betitia, 59
Procopius, 208, 220
Proculus, bishop of Marseille, 192
'profane', 134, 207
   see also 'secular'
prophets, 87
Prosper, 63, 126, 177–8
Protasius, St, 143, 144
Provence, 177–9, 192, 210
Prudentius, 118
Pythagoras, 74
Quodvultdeus, bishop of Carthage, 118,
   120, 154, 173, 214, 215–16
Rambo, L. R., 4
Ranger, T., 142
Ravenna, 126, 130, 173, 217
Reformation, 23, 154
Regula Magistri, 22, 71
relics, cult of, 24, 93–4, 142–50, 153
'religion', 2, 3, 7, 8, 12–15, 206
   popular, 13, 28
   Roman, 107
renewal, 105–6
renunciation, see asceticism
Resurrection, 98
Revelations, Book of, 215

256

Index

riches, *see* wealth
Rief, J., 49
Riez, 194
Riggi, C., 34
ritual(s), 2, 11, 107, 111, 118–19, 141, 206
Rome, 38, 40, 67, 101, 125–35, 145, 152, 173, 211, 217, 223, 228
Rondet, H., 123
Rordorf, W., 72, 97, 103
Rouen, 37, 95, 146
Rousseau, P., 114, 167, 181, 185, 194, 201
Rousselle, A., 82
Ruricius, 67, 195
Rutilius Namatianus, 33, 141
sacraments, 52
'sacred' and 'secular', 3, 6–8, 10, 13–17, 107–21, 131, 133–5, 174–7, 225–8
Sage, A., 78
saints, communion of, 23, 97–9, 146
see also community
saints, cult of, 23–4, 25
see also martyrs, cult of
Salomonson, J. W., 93, 118
Salvian, 36, 70, 71, 108, 118, 168–75, 205, 207, 208, 211, 215, 216
Saul, 5
see also Paul
Saxer, F., 34, 99, 149
Schindler, A., 93
Schmitt, E., 10
Schöllgen, G., 101
scripture, -al, *see* Bible
'secular', *see* 'sacred'
Séguy, J., 166
self, 47, 51, 54, 56, 61–2, 78
'semi-Christians', *see* 'half-Christians'
'semi-Pelagian, -s, -ism', 177–9
Seneca, 140
Septimania, *see* Aquitaine
Severinus, St, of Noricum, 173
Severus, bishop of Antioch, 120, 135
sexuality, 57–62, 76, 81–3
Shaw, B., 82
Shils, E., 25–6, 119
shows, 32, 101, 104, 108–23, 170–4, 207–8, 210–11, 215–16, 217
Sicard, D., 97
Sicily, 41, 129, 158, 217
Sidonius Apollinaris, 172, 181, 200, 201, 208
Simittu, 116, 119, 125
Simplicianus, 28, 55
sin, 54–6, 59
Sinai, 153
Siricius, pope, 76
Sixtus III, pope, 63, 133

Smith, J. Z., 26, 139
Snow, D. A., 4
Socrates, 38
Soissons, 210
Solignac, A., 189
Solin, H., 131
Sottocornola, F., 130
Sozomen, 92, 114
Spain, 41, 109, 148, 173, 209, 210
spectacles, *see* shows
Stancliffe, C., 38, 41, 148
Stephen, St, martyr, 71, 93–4, 148, 149
Stern, H., 108, 110
Stoic, -s, 80
Strathmann, H., 68
Sufes, 115, 119
Sulpicius Severus, 36, 38, 39, 69, 71, 75, 188, 200
Sunday, the Sun, 101, 103, 105, 109, 129
symbols, 13
Symeon, St, the Stylite, 4–5
Symmachus, Q. Aurelius, 31, 32
Symmachus, Q. Aurelius Memmius, iunior, 218
Syria, 152
Tedlock, B., 100
'temple of the Holy Spirit', 82
temples, 32, 108, 140–1, 145, 147, 150, 154–5
tepor, lukewarmness, coolness, 159–60, 166–7, 183, 195
Tertullian, 27, 72, 101, 102, 103, 107, 108, 112, 120, 140, 141, 215
theatre, -s, 93, 118, 172–3
see also shows
Theban legion, 213
Thébert, Y., 150
Theodore of Mopsuestia, 59
Theodoret of Cyrrhus, 5, 114
Theodoric, king, 129, 216
Theodorus, Mallius, 29–30
'Theodosian renaissance', 30
Theodosius I, emperor, Theodosian, 27, 89, 117, 159
theoria, theoretike, 184–6, 187
see also contemplation
Thonnard, F. J., 61
Tiberius, emperor, 87
Tibiletti, C., 42, 189
topography, sacred, 141–2, 151–5
see also towns
Tours, 200, 209
towns, 141, 146–9, 151, 172–4, 199–200, 222–3
traditio, 52
Trajan, emperor, 91

257

Index

Trier, 173
trousers, wearing of, by Bulgarian women, 6
Tsafrir, Y., 152
Turin, 130, 143
Turner, V., 3, 119
Tyconius, 52–3, 215
Tylor, E. B., 13
Valentinian III, emperor, 126, 201
Valli, F., 76
Van Dam, R., 36, 48, 203
Van der Meer, F., 117, 122
Van Enghen, J., 11
Vandals, 171, 214–16, 219
Varro, 107
Venus, 111
Vercelli, 76
Verheijen, L., 78, 167, 187
Vessey, M., 194, 195, 203
Veyne, P., 127
Victor of Vita, 215
Victorinus, Marius, 28–30
Victricius of Rouen, 37, 94–5, 146
Vigilantius, 39–40, 148–9

Vincent of Lerins, 161
Violante, C., 150
Virgil, 35
virgin(s), -ity, 38–42, 45–6, 62, 71–2, 75, 81–2, 158–9
virtue, 49
Vivarium, 220
Vogüé, A. de, 71, 164, 165, 166, 196
Waddell, H., 33, 36
Wallace-Hadrill, J. M., 209
Ward-Perkins, B., 129, 150, 173, 217
wealth, 158, 169–70
Weber, M., 25–6
Weismann, W., 110, 111, 122
Weitzmann, K., 152
wilderness, *see* 'Desert'
Wilken, R. L., 89, 152
will, 64–5
Williams, R. D., 90
women, *see* trousers
Workman, H. B., 70
Zerubavel, E., 100
Zumkeller, A., 65–78